James Baldwin Brown

The Higher Life

Its Reality, Experiences and Destiny

James Baldwin Brown

The Higher Life
Its Reality, Experiences and Destiny

ISBN/EAN: 9783744774741

Printed in Europe, USA, Canada, Australia, Japan

Cover: Foto ©Lupo / pixelio.de

More available books at **www.hansebooks.com**

THE HIGHER LIFE

ITS REALITY, EXPERIENCE, AND DESTINY

BY

JAMES BALDWIN BROWN, B.A.

MINISTER OF BRIXTON INDEPENDENT CHURCH
AUTHOR OF 'THE HOME LIFE' 'FIRST PRINCIPLES OF ECCLESIASTICAL TRUTH'
ETC.

'Nor must we, as some advise us, being but men, think only of the things of men, being transient, of transient things; but as far as in us lies we must live the immortal life'—ARISTOTLE

'For our citizenship is in the heavens'—PAUL

SECOND EDITION

HENRY S. KING & CO.
65 CORNHILL & 12 PATERNOSTER ROW, LONDON
1874

TO

MY DEAR DAUGHTER

MY LOVING AND DEVOTED HELPER

IN MY MINISTRY

I INSCRIBE THIS BOOK

ON

THE HIGHER LIFE

J. B. B.

PREFACE.

I SEND FORTH this book on The Higher Life, in the hope that it may help some, especially among the young, to hold fast their faith in the great facts and truths, which alone seem to me to make this life of ours worth living at all. The elder Mill, as we learn from the autobiography of his distinguished son, rejected "all that is called religious belief." It does not surprise one to learn further, that "he thought human life a poor thing at best, after the freshness of youth and of unsatisfied curiosity had gone by." I fear that there is a large class of cultivated men and women among us who are falling into the same unbelief, and into the sadness which is its inevitable fruit. If what I have written should afford any help to such against this pressure of the times, the labour which it has cost will be amply repaid.

The sermons, as will be seen, do not form anything like a consecutive argument. Each has a completeness of its own, and a definite theme ; yet they form a course of connected thought on the subject of The Higher Life, its reality, its experience, and its destiny.

In the earlier chapters I have glanced at some of the recent speculations of science, in which solutions have been offered of the mysterious problems of Creation, which theologians, as a rule, have fiercely assailed. It seems to me that if we consider them patiently, and let development "have its perfect work," they may open to us a larger vision of the way of God in the creation and the government of His world. The chapters which follow deal mainly with the higher Christian experience, and the spirit which Christianity seeks to quicken and to nourish in men. God forbid that the Church should ever be unmindful of the large blessing which intellectual culture and political activity bring in their train. There are periods in which this side of human development needs to be vigorously pushed forward. But in these days it seems well able to care for itself; while the side of man's nature and activity to which the Cross appeals, is in danger of being slighted, and thrust out of the field. But none the less is it the salt of the world's life in all ages, and .will be, while the world endures. In treating of this portion of my subject, I have dropped for the most part, all reference to current controversies; while in the closing chapters I have brought back the thread of my thoughts, to the questions which are in such eager debate among us, once more.

Each sermon, as I have said, has a certain completeness of its own; and, as a book like this is mostly read in sections, I have not been over studious to avoid the presentation of central ideas again and again, from different points of view, and often with the same illustrations from Scripture. I have used in quotation the authorized version, except where my argument rendered a more accurate translation needful; and throughout the book I have kept steadily in view, the difficulties, burdens, and needs of those who are hardly pressed by the battle, or sharply exercised by the discipline, of life.

J. BALDWIN BROWN.

KENT VILLA, BRIXTON HILL:
March, 1874.

CONTENTS.

		PAGE
I.	WHAT IS MAN?	1

"*What is Man?*" Ps. viii. 4.

II. THE UNIVERSAL TRAVAIL 25

"*We know that the whole Creation groaneth and travaileth in pain together until now.*" Rom. viii. 22.

III. THE ATHEISTIC LIFE 49

"*Having no hope, and without God in the world.*" Eph. ii. 12.

IV. THE MEANING OF REDEMPTION 70

"*I have called you friends.*" John xv. 15.

V. THE PAIN OF PROGRESS 92

"*Thy heart shall fear and be enlarged.*" Is. lx. 5.

VI. THE LORD IS MY LIGHT AND MY SALVATION . 114

"*The Lord is my light and my salvation, whom shall I fear? The Lord is the strength of my life, of whom shall I be afraid?*" Ps. xxvii. 1.

VII. GOD'S GREAT WORLD 131

"*He brought me forth also into a large place.*" 2. Sam. xxii. 20.

		PAGE
VIII.	THE PILGRIMS	150

"*For they that say such things, declare plainly that they seek a country.*" Heb. xi. 14.

| IX. | THE NOBLE ARMY OF MARTYRS | 169 |

"*And ye became followers of us, and of the Lord, having received the word in much affliction, with joy of the Holy Ghost.*" 1. Thes. i. 6.

| X. | THE TWO SORROWS | 185 |

"*For it is better, if the will of God be so, that ye suffer for well doing than for evil doing.*" 1. Pet. iii. 17.

| XI. | THE SACRED DARKNESS | 205 |

"*Who is among you that feareth the Lord, that obeyeth the voice of His servant, that walketh in darkness, and hath no light? Let him trust in the name of the Lord, and stay upon his God.*" Is. l. 10.

| XII. | THE SACRED JOY | 227 |

"*As the sufferings of Christ abound in us, so our consolation also aboundeth by Christ.*" 2. Cor. i. 5.

| XIII. | THE GARDEN BY THE CROSS | 248 |

"*Now in the place where He was crucified there was a garden.*" John xix. 41.

| XIV. | OH, THAT I HAD WINGS LIKE A DOVE! | 266 |

"*Oh, that I had wings like a dove! for then would I fly away and be at rest.*" Ps. lv. 6.

| XV. | FAINT, YET PURSUING | 288 |

"*Faint, yet pursuing them.*" Judg. viii. 4.

Contents.

		PAGE
XVI.	THE VICTORY OF LIFE	305

"*I am He that liveth and was dead; and, behold, I am alive for evermore.*" Rev. i. 18.

XVII. THE KEYS OF HELL AND OF DEATH . . 321

"*Amen: and have the keys of hell and of death.*" Rev. i. 18.

XVIII. THE RESURRECTION OF MAN 338

"*But now is Christ risen from the dead, and become the first-fruits of them that slept. For since by man came death, by man came also the resurrection of the dead.*" 1. Cor. xv. 20, 21.

XIX. THE DESTINY OF THE CREATURE . . 364

"*The creature itself also shall be delivered from the bondage of corruption into the glorious liberty of the children of God.*" Rom. viii. 21.

XX. THE DESTINY OF MAN 387

"*What is man that Thou art mindful of him? and the son of man that Thou visitest him?*" Ps. viii. 4.

THE HIGHER LIFE.

I.

WHAT IS MAN?

THE SCRIPTURE sets man before us as a being whom his Maker cares to redeem at quite infinite cost. This affords to us the one true measure of the quality of our nature, and assigns its place in the scale of the Creation : it is Heaven's own answer to the fundamental question of philosophy, What is man? The Bible, happily for us, is not a book of definitions. It offers little that can be regarded as a scientific elucidation of the dark problems of Being, human or Divine. Its concern is supremely with man "in relation;" as bound in duty to the Creation around him, to his fellow men and to God. The chief part of it is history, and it is the history of Redemption. From the first act of the Divine drama in the hour of man's transgression, to the vision of the purified and perfected Creation which is unveiled in the Apocalypse, it treats of the world as the theatre of Redemption, and of man as a being born to be redeemed.

Whatever man may be in his interior structure and constitution, by whatever stages of development he may have attained to his present goodly stature and power, thus much is clear about him to the loving students of Scripture; he is a being whose redemption, whose salvation from the pit into which moral evil steadily settles and buries itself from the light, is held on high to be worth the agony and bloody sweat, the cross and passion, the precious death and burial, the glorious resurrection and ascension, of his Redeemer, Christ.

This is the central thought of this series of discourses on the higher life, and the travail through which it is born. Some of them are more speculative; some of them are directly practical in tone; but I seek to develope through the whole of them the ground of my belief, that the redemption which is by Christ Jesus is the one key to all that man is and to all that man endures. I hold that the existence of such a world as this, and such a creature as man has come to be through sin, would be a burning stain on the government of the righteous Ruler of the universe, but for the end to which it is working through Redemption; while in the light which the gospel of God's love and mercy casts upon the world, life, with all its pain, becomes a holy and blessed culture, binding man to God in a fellowship of interest and spirit, which is destined to furnish the highest developments of being through eternity.

I can see no light about man, about his capacities, his experiences, and the possibilities of his life, except

when I regard him as a being born to be redeemed.
I can see no light about life, its broken promises, its
poor fulfilments, its frustrated hopes, its ideal always
far up in the height, except when I regard it as a
redeeming process, which earth commences in pain
and travail, but which heaven will complete in glorious
joy. This is why I believe the Bible. It is a light
shining for me in a dark place; it lights up man, it
lights up life, it lights up God. And the light seems
to be of heaven. All things within and all things
around, when I look at them in the light of the love
of God which is in Christ Jesus our Lord, resolve
themselves into an order, which, obscure as is much
of its method, and sad as is much of its aspect, I
joyfully recognise as Divine. It commends itself as
"of God" to the purest and justest judgment which
I can frame of Divine things; while it lays the basis
of an intelligent hope for myself and for the world
which justifies patience and sanctifies pain. Therefore, I believe.

Rob me of this faith, give me such a world to live
in as some of our wise ones are doing their best to
make for us, and the only question of supreme
interest would be, which is the quickest and the
easiest way out of it into the everlasting night?

There are certain views as to the nature of man,
as to his place in the Creation, and the way in which
it becomes him to look at his life, which are kept
very prominently before the eye of the intellectual
world in our day by able thinkers, who state them
with great force, and with an earnestness of con-

viction and contention, for which there seems to be little room in the pale of their narrow and cold philosophy.

The grounds on which we base our view of man, of his relations and his destiny, are to them simply non-existent, or at least non-apparent, and not capable of being made to appear. God, Revelation, Redemption, to them belong to the world of dreams. Man is to their apprehension the last and completest product of that organising principle or force which somehow—that is all that they can say about it at present—has introduced itself into the inorganic matter of the world, and behold it lives! it becomes plastic at once to the inward pressure of the vital principle, and reveals a capacity for the assumption of an inconceivable variety of organic forms. These shape themselves, we are instructed, under the stress of constant pressure, collision, and struggle for existence; in which the strongest, or rather the fittest, the best adapted to the external conditions prevailing around, survives and perpetuates itself. Thus there rises in the Creation an ascending series of specific forms, order rising out of and resting upon order, each more complex in structure and manifold in function than that on which it rests, until passing through countless stages of evolution, the series emerges and completes itself in man.

Man, according to this view of Nature, is simply the most complex, the most capable, and the most largely developed of the creatures. But all the human faculties and qualities, judgments, emotions, passions and volitions, are held to be but the highest functions of kindred qualities and capacities which are found in the lower stages of Creation. This school can find no sufficient evidence of a breach of continuity in the chain of evolution, from the lowest organism which manifests vital functions—some are bolder yet, and include the inorganic—to the genius that created Hamlet, or read the secret order of the stars.

Reason and will, the distinctive human endowments in the popular judgment of all ages, are, in this scheme, but the highest function of that finest form of matter which enters into the composition of the human structure; "*ohne Phosphor, kein Gedanke,*" without phosphorus, no thought: volition being equally the evolution of that battery of material elements in man's bodily organisation, on which the unseen currents are ever playing; motion having its key in the chemical constituents of his nature; all that he is, all that he does, all that he can become, being as surely settled by the arrangements of the particles of his frame and their relation to the currents of force around him, as are settled, on the same basis and with the same certainty, the track of a storm or the path of a star.

For such a being, if this be the true account of man's nature, Redemption can have no meaning, for there is absolutely nothing to redeem. His every act and every state is under the calm resistless rule of that law which maintains all the "sequences" of the Creation; to make man other than he is and must be, would be to break up the whole order of the world.

I am very far from connecting what is called the theory of evolution as a means of accounting for the infinite variety and yet the perfect order of the developments of life, with a materialistic or atheistic philosophy. The two have unhappily been closely associated, and mainly, I think, from two causes. The first is the eagerness with which thinkers of the atheistic school have seized upon it, and sought to claim it as their own; the second, and I think the main cause of this evil association, has been the improvident and, indeed, insane dread of the theologians. They have to thank themselves if this attractive theory is supposed popularly to favour their opponents. How much of the atheism of this age, and of every age, is generated by the antagonism and denunciation of the Church, is a question which, while it fills one with shame, is not unsuggestive of hope. When the Church grows less fearful, more faithful and more far-sighted, we may believe that atheism will disappear from the world.

But there is no necessary, or even I venture to think, natural antipathy between evolution and a sound Christian philosophy. Conservative thinkers are beginning to acknowledge that this law of evolution plays a very distinguished part in the ordering of the majestic procession of life. At the same time, the gap between man and the lower animals is, in the judgment of accomplished students of nature, yet unbridged, and is not even in process of being bridged.

What is Man? 7

Nothing is established which destroys the belief that man's body reveals the direct, original touch of a creative hand. I do not presume to offer a decisive judgment on a point which it needs very deep and accurate scientific knowledge even to appreciate. Whether the views which have been stated with such learning and force by Mr. Wallace are right, or those which follow the direction of Mr. Darwin's book on the "Descent of Man," I do not attempt to decide. I can only say, that, as far as I am able to judge, Mr. Darwin's case seems very far from proved.

But it can hardly be denied that the course of modern scientific thought and discovery seems to be in the main following the track which Mr. Darwin has opened. It may find its limit speedily, and science may uphold the received theological ideas. But it is, at any rate, quite possible that we may have to accept it as a settled truth, that the human form has been developed, by a process of natural evolution (not natural selection, that could only have been one of the principles at work), out of the highest types of form in the animal creation, and that man began his career in this world in a condition but a very little raised above the brutes. It is not proved; I have no idea that it can be proved; but if it should be proved, it may open to us a new and very wonderful vision of the way of God in the creation and the ruling of the world.

There is a stage in which the human embryo cannot be distinguished from the embryos of the lower orders of the Creation; there is a stage at which, by some process which utterly evades us, it becomes distinctively human; and there is a further stage in the development of the infant, in which the higher qualities of our nature unfold themselves in their full spiritual form, and are dealt with as the ruling powers in the house of life. It is possible that this may prove to be an image on a small scale of the travail of the Creation; there may be a working through all the stages of creature development up to the human, and a point—it has never been discovered as yet, nor has anything near to it—at which this creature which has shaped itself through the inward and outward pressure to the likeness of the human, becomes distinctly Man.

There is really nothing to startle or to frighten us in this doctrine of a law of evolution, of which natural selection will be one of the factors, and but one, which are at work. The doctrine will accord with an intelligent Christian theory of life. It is evolution by chance medley, as it were, which seems so absolutely incredible, things chancing to settle themselves by internecine struggle into this wonderful cosmos. An intelligible theory of evolution seems to demand a forecasting intelligence behind it. We seem to be brought face to face with a far-seeing mind and a far-reaching will, when we catch the first sign of an outward and upward pressure in the primal matter of the Creation, which, through innumerable ascending stages, was to issue forth at last in the human race.

There can be no doubt that the idea, were we

bound to accept it, would give a grievous shock to our popular theological notions. We should have to re-read the third, as we have had to re-read the first chapter of the book of Genesis. We have come to find in the one an ideal picture of the Creation, the essential truth of the matter to the eye of a spirit, seeking a principle of order, of cosmos, and seeking the means of connecting that order with God. The first chapter of Genesis means more and not less to us than it meant a generation ago, before the light of science was brought fairly to bear upon it. Just so, if this new idea can be established, shall we find in the third chapter an ideal portrait of man in his spiritual and Divine relations, a revelation of the meaning of life and of the principle of moral development, to the full understanding of which he is meant to grow; a picture painted by God's own hand to light the path of man's pilgrimage, to sustain his soul in that higher region of spiritual freedom to which he has found entrance, and to explain to him, as his Maker only could explain to him, the profoundest mysteries of his life. But there is nothing inconsistent with the fundamental truths of Christianity in this or in any intelligent theory of the way in which man's physical system was developed out of the dust, and made capable of the reception and manifestation of that reasonable soul which relates him with a loftier sphere. Being found in form as a man, he belongs to the world of spiritual intelligence and activity; the qualities which foreshadow reason and will, which he shares with the animal creation, become absorbed in the superior powers; and the spiritual facts which find a continually clearer forecast through the ascending types of the Creation, as the organs are growingly perfected of which a spirit alone can make full use, Reason, Will, and Moral responsibility, rule thenceforth supreme over his life.

There is a kindred theory of moral development, which might fairly be called the theory of moral evolution, which resolves into an inheritance of the accumulated experience of the race as regards the utility of actions, those moral judgments and habits which we are wont to regard as the signs of the presence in man of a spiritual nature, having knowledge of good and evil; by the possession of which he is distinguished absolutely from the lower spheres of the Creation, and related to the spheres above him and to God. Just as we are assured by physiologists of this school, and they have evidently much truth on their side, that the instinct of animals is but accumulated and transmitted experience, which has shaped itself into a habit of action, useful to the creature for its protection, or for the fulfilment of the functions of its life; so we are told that in the matter of man's moral judgments and emotions, "the experiences of utility, organised and consolidated through all past generations of the human race, have been producing corresponding nervous modifications, which by continued transmissions of accumulation, have become in us certain faculties of moral intuition, active emotions responding to right and wrong conduct, which have no apparent basis in the individual experiences of utility." These moral intuitions an intelligent and conscious being comes to regard as having a sanction in the constitution of things outside him, and in the nature and will of an Almighty Being above him; their only real sanction being their utility, their adaptation to the preservation and the welfare of society. But it is acknowledged that at length man comes, and ought to come, to lose sight of this relation of utility, that is, of that which is regarded as the ultimate test to which the conceptions of "ought" and "ought not" must be referred; and to regard duty, even when its higher sanction is denied, as having the right to claim from him the sacrifice of pleasure, utility, and even life, at need.[1]

Among the gravest of the objections to this system is the breach of continuity which arises when a conception so large, reaching to such heights and depths as duty, first appears; just as in the theory of physical evolution, there is a break in the line somewhere, when the creature first steps upon the stage of life who is endowed with the distinguishing attributes of man. A morality like this of the utilitarian, which has constantly to forget its origin, which has studiously to refrain from reference to that utility by

[1] This is not stating the matter at all too strongly. Mr. Mill, in a noble passage, declares that if he must go to hell for refusing to worship a being whom he cannot call good, "to hell he will go." It is very difficult to extract from Mr. Mill's works any clear statement of his view of the ultimate basis of morals. It is probable that no small part of his influence on his generation is due to the fact that he seemed to claim ever and anon a higher sanction for the right than his system appeared to allow. In other words, his belief was greater than his creed.

which during all its earlier stages it grew; which has to train itself to substitute for it some higher conception, more in accord with what we regard as the spiritual nature of man, had better, one would think, be referred at once to that spiritual nature whose movements it simulates so admirably, and to that God to whom it strives by natural effort to lift its ideas.

But again I say, suppose that this could be the right theory; suppose that brutes and men through an almost endless series of stages of development, could have gradually formed those instinctive habits of action, rising at length into what looks like moral choice, which secure on the whole a course favourable to the best interests of the race or the community, regarded on a large and, we should say, a provident scale—what then? It is clear that the whole course of things in this world, its constitution and the currents of force which act upon it, must have been so ordered as to press the action of animated beings, with great limitation of their own private pleasure, into a mould which secures in a large form, such as we might imagine only a most wise and provident Ruler could forecast, the greatest good of the whole.

Thus we find a being who inherits all this accumulated experience in the form of emotions and propulsions, in whom there is present too a faculty which can reflect upon it, can examine it, can see how and why certain actions secure this general good, and certain others hinder it. In this being, further, a consciousness has somehow dawned that there is a yet higher sanction for this action than utility, that the utility is of so very high and subtile a kind, that it demands a Divine foresight to forecast it; that he is under the law as a being with the endowment of freedom to the God who made and who rules both him and the world ; a God who demands the exercise of this wise judgment which is so good for all as matter of duty to Himself, while He continually educates and purifies that judgment, and draws it forth to larger and nobler ministries to the general good.

What shall we say to these things, even on the poor and thin hypothesis of the evolutionists ? What, but that the creature thus trained and shaped by the obscure influences of the material sphere, was born at last, when his development so far was complete, into a world in which his developed nature found a response to its new-born cravings, support for its new-found convictions, the explanation and the justification of those loftier and more unselfish modes of action, to which some inward pressure had compelled it, and a home wherein its longings for the good, the true, and the unchanging might be at rest. It seems to me that on this theory of the physical and moral development of man, as clearly as on ours, the whole process presupposes, demands the existence of a world of spirit, of moral freedom, of responsibility, of knowledge of and relation to God ; a world which is ready to receive as its citizen the creature thus developed up to the pitch of its life; unless, indeed, this marvellous vital instinct, to put it no higher, which guided development with such grand success through its myriad stages, ends it at last in illusion, with bitter fruit of misery and despair.

As matter of fact, we find beings, who have gradually, whether as the result of pure evolution or otherwise, left their proneness, their front towards the dust, and who lift their heads on high, and seem to be looking beyond the world. In accord with this physical habit and gesture, we find that the idea has not only dawned upon them, but possessed them, that there is a world invisible to sense around and beyond this visible sphere, with which, rather than with the creature, their true relations and destinies are intertwined. It is a world which lays heavy demands of duty upon them, while it stimulates them to noble and fertile activity. It has inspired all the brightest, most glorious, most blessed passages in the history of the race; it has made, as we shall see, the grandest and most heroic human spirits its pilgrims, and has sent martyrs by myriads to the rack and to the stake, that they might keep unsullied their loyalty to its King. Are we to be told as we rise to meet the messengers of this spiritual world with joy, and to listen to its Gospel, Ah! here you are entering into a world of dreams?

Dreams! Why the whole system of the universe, according to these theorists, has been so shaped, or has so shaped itself, as to press development up to the type of the human. And man is moved by the same pressure—for if the supernatural be denied, the reason of it all must lie within the physical organisation—to entertain and to cherish those views of his obligations to his fellow men around him, and as he thinks to God, which led Christ to Calvary to die for humanity in unutterable anguish and shame. The same idea made Paul a debtor to men of every clime and grade, to spend his life in preaching to them the Gospel, and has inspired all the movements in heathendom and Christendom which have given shape and impulse to the progress of the world. And it is this, just this, which has demanded and constrained the toil and the travail of the very noblest human spirits, which, you say, belongs to an unreal world, and is but the projection of man's own shadow, and the shadow of his life, on the curtain of the unknown around him, forming there some dim lines which he thinks are the track of duty, and an awful image which he mistakes for God. Is then the very saddest school of Oriental philosophy right after all? Is the end of all creature development Maya, illusion? Does the creature at his very highest point of elevation find himself lifted into a world of mocking and misleading dreams?

Would to God, we should be tempted in that case to cry passionately, that this wonderful development had been ended by some shattering stroke, before it touched the edge of this world of illusions, from whose dread region the Creator has mercifully withheld the brutes! If this were the truth, then the whole system of things which has pressed on to this issue from the first, an issue the germ of which must have been hidden in the first monad that became quick with life, this universal system, I say, would be a horrible abortion; and Creation, if there be a God, must be, as the Orientals teach us, the disease or the sick-dream of the Supreme.

No! to me it is supremely wonderful, and most manifestly of God, that just when a being appears in the procession of life whose port and gesture manifestly difference' him from the brutes—who is conscious of the awfulness of that " I " which describes the personality of a spirit—who finds himself laden with a burden which no one can share with him, of a duty which no one can fulfil for him, and a destiny which he must create and face for himself—to whom the word " I ought" has sacred meaning, seems to represent the thought of a mind above him, and to appeal to him with the authority of God—who is awake to the realities of a life which demands from him constant self-control, and no small measure of self-denial and self-sacrifice, binding him to his fellow men by obligations which may demand from him, not through blind instinct, but with that full intelligence which looks before and after, the gift of his very life—I say it is very wonderful and very beautiful, that just in this crisis in the history of Creation, there is unveiled the existence of an unseen spiritual world. In that world the thoughts that haunt man find realities on which they can rest, and to which they can cling; out of that world a revelation comes to him which explains and justifies his ideas of duty, which purifies and elevates his moral judgments, and strengthens his resolution in the direction in which he is conscious that the true path of his progress lies, while it opens to him the vision of an eternal state, where all the pain to which it subjects him shall bear blessed harvest, and where all the sacrifice which it demands of him shall draw him close to the bosom of his God for ever.

I seem to see here, in this order of the world—man raised up, no matter how, in the dignity and responsibility of a free spiritual being, on the one hand, and a revelation meeting him on the other, which deals with him as a free spiritual agent, and trains him for a life of immortal liberty and joy—a sign, a wonderful and glorious sign, of the presence of the Father of spirits among the children whom He has formed to know and to delight in Him ; and I am full sure that the book which thus takes up and carries on man's culture for eternity, is the Word of God.

It is hard to speak without bitterness of the shallow and vain philosophy, which asks us to believe that all the phenomena which appear in the procession of life, up to the point where man comes forth, dowered with an irresistible yearning for immortality, and with an irrepressible sense of the reality of the world of spiritual being, are solid realities, standing all the tests which the scientific intellect has the right to propose ; while everything which seems to satisfy these cravings, every promise which seems to nourish these beliefs and hopes, is a false light, hung out to lure him to everlasting wreck. For me it would be " the last thing but one," could I believe that the only being in the universe, who is systematically bewildered, befooled, and bemocked, is its masterpiece—Man.

On the contrary, our whole observation of life, of man's nature, constitution, obligations, and possible destinies, presses on us the idea which the Scripture presents to us, that man is a being born into this world to be redeemed; and who, weak and poor as he is without God, is yet, because of what he can grow to in God, worth redeeming at infinite cost. Man is found here with a nature, which, if it has free course as a nature, if no quickening come to it from on high, if no new heart—for which in some shape or other, all peoples in all ages are sighing—be given to it, must inevitably be a curse to him. How the nature comes to be what it is, is not the question. The evolutionists have their theory, the orthodox theologians have theirs. But if Adam be invoked to account for man's moral condition, it is manifest that the Author of life, and the Ruler of the world, accepts the responsibility of the perpetuation of the present fallen estate of our race. Man, by no act of his own, by the action of laws which God ordained and which God upholds, is born into this world with a nature which, unless it be renewed by Him who first created it, must bury itself in the darkness of death for ever. This is the doctrine of Christian theology; it is also the doctrine of universal experience. Dark and sad as it is if you close your ear to the gospel of Redemption, it is terribly evidenced by the fact, that all heathen thought tends in the long run, inevitably

What is Man? 19

to nihilism; or at best regards the utter loss of all consciousness of personal existence as the only exodus from the ills and the burdens of life : while it is sustained by the parallel fact, that among cultivated peoples, when the sense of the reality of the spiritual world has been weakened by wanton prosperity or vicious indulgence, and all hope concerning the soul and God has died down in human hearts, suicide has been the refuge to which man has fled most eagerly, life has been the burden which he has most joyfully cast away.

Nor can we fail to note that, even on the theory of those who hold that a bestial savage condition is the earliest estate of our race,[1] as man emerges

---

[1] There is no subject, perhaps, on which there is more unsound dogmatism (always excepting theology) than on the original estate of our race. It would be idle to deny that an immense body of evidence of great seeming weight has been put forth by those who hold that we can trace man back to a condition but a little higher than a brute. But nothing is more easily misunderstood and misinterpreted than the signs of the savage condition. As with childhood, it needs a special and large experience to comprehend all its bearings; and looked at simply from the scientific point of view, there is a very strong body of evidence on the other side. Mr. St. George Mivart in his " Genesis of Species " has some very interesting and able remarks on the subject. Readers of Mr. Wallace's book on the Malay Archipelago will remember his testimony as to the morale of some savage peoples among whom he dwelt so long. But the following passage from Sir H. Maine's " Village Communities " is worthy of special attention, inasmuch as his opportunities of observation were peculiarly ample, and his insight is indisputable:—" It has been strongly contended of late, that by investigation of the practices and ideas of existing savage races, at least two earlier stages of human society disclose themselves through which it passes before organising itself in family groups. In two separate volumes, each of them remarkably ingenious and interesting, Sir J. Lubbock and Mr. McLennan conceive themselves to have shown

from the life of the savage, he acquires ideas, habits, emotions and propensities to action, which seek increasingly to sustain themselves by clasping the objects of the spiritual world. The savage in his lowest condition sends his wife into the field while he takes his ease until hunger or passion moves him to the excitement of the chase or of war. As man becomes developed, that is, as we see in him with growing clearness what is meant by man, not only does he feel after a world of spiritual being around him and above him, and a Father of his spirit to whom he can commit the destinies of his life, but he becomes conscious of burdens, of obligations, of

that the first steps of mankind towards civilisation were taken from a condition in which assemblages of men followed practices which are not found to occur universally even in animal nature. Many of the phenomena of barbarism adverted to by these writers are found in India. The usages appealed to are the usages of certain tribes or races, sometimes called aboriginal, which have been driven into the inaccessible recesses of the widely-extending mountain country in the North-east of India by the double pressure of Indian or Chinese civilisation, or which took refuge in the hilly regions of Central and Southern India from the conquest of Brahminical invaders, whether or not of Indian descent. Many of these wild tribes have now for many years been under English observation, and have, indeed, been administered by British officers. The evidence, therefore, of their usages and ideas which may be forthcoming, is very superior to the slippery testimony concerning savages which is gathered from travellers' tales. . . . . Much which I have personally heard in India bears out the caution which I gave as to the reserve with which all speculations on the antiquity of human usage should be received. Practices represented as of universal antiquity, and universally characteristic of the origin of mankind, have been described to me as having been for the first time resorted to in our own days through the mere pressure of external circumstances or of novel temptations." P. 16.

duties, which strain every nerve and fibre of his nature, and which he can bear joyfully only on condition of full citizenship of that spiritual and eternal world.

To take a strong but decisive instance, whatever we may be disposed to think of Christ and Christianity, one thing is patent, that the life of Christ is not only the most pathetic, but the purest, the noblest, the most fruitful chapter of human history. It had been simply impossible for Christ to have lived the life that He lived, and to have died the death that He died, unless from His inmost soul He could have said, "Alone, yet not alone, for the Father is with Me." The enthusiasm of humanity will carry a man far; but the Cross and Passion can only explain themselves by the word, "*My meat is to do the will of Him that sent me, and to finish His work.*"

Redemption means the presence of the Father with the world. "*God is in Christ, reconciling the world unto Himself,*" is the marrow of the Gospel. Man, in his creature nature, has to do with the Creator and the Ruler of the world system around him; as he realises the possession of that spiritual nature which has been embreathed into the physical, and which makes him, on the summit of the mere creature development, the first born of a new and higher order of life, Redemption takes him out of the sphere of the natural—which is no longer strong enough, rich enough, deep enough, to nourish him, which must become a grave to the spirit which seeks to live by it—and plants him in the sphere of the

Divine love. "*Howbeit that was not first which is spiritual, but that which is natural, and afterward that which is spiritual.*" "*The first man, Adam, was made a living soul, the last Adam was made a quickening spirit.*" "*As in Adam all die, even so in Christ shall all be made alive.*"

This life of man, when he is conscious of the full burden of his obligation, and is drawn forth in devotion to the higher aims and objects, is so solemn a thing, it costs so much, and it carries in its bosom such tremendous issues—as all will understand who know the full meaning of "I"—that it seems to appeal importunately to God for His living sympathy and fellowship, and for the help of His strengthening and quickening hand. As men rise higher in culture and moral nobility they become more painfully and sometimes miserably conscious of this burden. It was Paul of Tarsus who called himself the "*chief of sinners,*" and who cried, "*O miserable man that I am, who shall deliver me from the body of this death?*" So heavy is the responsibility of moral judgment and action, with the issues which grow out of it, that we may well believe that God would not have laid the burden on any human spirit, but for the purpose and the promise that He Himself would take part in our nature, and would make all its solemn and profound experiences the means of drawing His child through Redemption into perfect fellowship with Himself. A world like this, a life like ours, if nothing is to grow out of them when the burden is laid down and the groaning is stilled,

What is Man? 23

would be a weltering chaos of wrong and wretchedness. But if there is a Hand above us which has hold of us and is lifting us, unveiling to us the vision of a boundless future, then we can understand how all life's strain and agony may be the noblest culture of our freedom; enlarging us, enriching us, and preparing us for the unknown, unknowable developments of eternity.

At the root of the whole, of the whole higher life of man, in which, however he may have come to it, we at any rate find him established, and which lays such heavy burdens on his spirit, lies the gospel of Redemption, the gospel of "*the love of God which is in Christ Jesus our Lord.*" You, my readers, live in and move about the world as men and women who were born into the world to be redeemed. The Cross of Redemption is signed upon your brow; the blood of Redemption is on the lintel of your house of life. And yet, how many of you are drawling and slouching through the world, trying to make life a pastime, dreary enough in any case; to empty it of all its deeper meanings; or it may be to turn it into a hotbed of corruption, spreading the taint of a pestilence around you wherever you move. And there is the Lord who died for you, on high, watching it all; marking the waste and wreck of the being whom He redeemed unto Himself at such awful cost; saddening at the sight of the woe and the wrong, with which you are helping to fill the world which He gave His soul to save. Oh, men, men! why *will* you reject the counsel of your Saviour to your ruin?

Why *will* you count yourselves unworthy of the place in His eternal kingdom, which His boundless love and mercy have prepared? Why *will* you shut your hard, cold hearts against this blessed message of the Gospel, "*Unto you first,*" and now, "*God, having raised up His Son Jesus, hath sent Him to bless you, in turning away every one of you from His iniquities*"?

II.
THE UNIVERSAL TRAVAIL.

"For we know that the whole creation groaneth and travaileth in pain together until now."—Rom. viii. 22.

WE know! Else what mean our tragedies? What mean those ancient shadows of the Fates? Nature is truly, not what is, but what is becoming, what is coming to be, what is about being born. And all birth is by travail. The creation groans as it gives birth to its heir; to-day groans as it gives birth to tomorrow; the old generation groans as it gives birth to the new; earth groans as it gives birth to the kingdom of heaven.

Man shares the groaning. His "state of nature" is a state of travail. He too is here that he may be born to something greater. To abide in a state of nature, is to refuse the benign and fruitful anguish which issues in Redemption; it is to become willingly the abortion of this terrestrial sphere. And this is to judge oneself unworthy of everlasting life, and to choose the death which is eternal.

Paul seizes firmly, and utters in one large sentence, the meaning of this tragedy, which, if the end of it be here, is played out under the eye of Heaven. The tears that have channelled, through all these ages, the worn cheek of humanity, the groans that have burdened the air, the blood that has stained every great pathway that man has trod, are the human form of this universal groaning. From man it comes laden with a deeper sadness than can burden the voice of the Creation; for man knows what he was born for, and what he has missed, when he is dull to the voice that calls him to be redeemed. Surely it is one of the most fundamental truths of a sound philosophy of life which is uttered in these profound and pregnant words.

To all seers, among all peoples, in all ages, this truth has unveiled itself. They seemed to catch the voice of a groaning, and they give it utterance in their tragedies, their sad epics, their litanies and psalms of life. The deep sadness of the Homeric poems is plain to every thoughtful student; it has been indicated eloquently by a master of Homeric lore. Tragedies, or comedies sadder than tragedies, are the masterpieces of the golden age of Athenian literary art. The interest of Greek philosophy centres round a prison cell, where an old man lies numb and cold; cheering his friends with the hope of the welcome which awaits him "in some happy state of the blessed," while the poison steals up to his heart. The wisest seer of Nature in Republican Rome, fairly weary of Jupiter and Juno and all the rout of Olympus, as the groundwork of the order of Creation, thought that a wild concourse and shock of atoms, by some dull chance shaping themselves into an order, might be the key to the mystery of life.

He uttered his thought on the development of Nature in a poem of wonderful power and splendour; but he left life sadder than he found it; to him there was little to live for in such a world.

The next era of human development was founded on the Cross, which has since guided the destinies of Christendom; and must guide them still, through new depths of pain, to the issue in which the travail of man and of Nature shall ultimately fruit.

In the sagas of Northern Europe, the bright god of life dies at last under the stroke of a cruel and inexorable destiny, and the twilight of the gods settles over all. To Goethe, in our modern world, Nature seemed "like a dumb captive, sighing to be delivered." Art with him was the minister of her redemption. Art in all ages, did she understand her mission, has, like her loftier sister, a message to the captive, and should be the eager handmaid of our higher life. And is not the struggle for existence the one key to the order and progress of life, in the judgment of the keenest student of the living creation who has prophesied to our times? The struggle for existence! Are there not times when man asks himself madly— Is there anything else, anything higher, at the root of such order or disorder as reigns in the human world?

The struggle begins very low down indeed in the scale of the Creation. The very molecules of matter are in ceaseless clash and conflict, dashing against each other with swift flight and fierce momentum, in the air around us and in the blood within us. Everywhere there is storm and stress, pressure, conflict, defeat and victory; while everywhere an order, a progress, slowly evolve themselves out of it all. Professor Maxwell, of Cambridge, read at the Bradford meeting of the British Association, a discourse on molecules, in which he gives us a startling vision of the storm of motion which is raging round us in the world.

"If we wish to form a mental representation of what is going on among the molecules in calm air, we cannot do better than observe a swarm of bees, where every individual bee is flying furiously, first in one direction and then in another, while the swarm, as a whole, either remains at rest, or sails slowly through the air."

He tells us that invisible molecules in countless throngs are in rapid motion all round us, jostling with each other, fighting hard to keep their course, but hindered by kindred molecules that are fighting too; the whole resulting in a certain balance and equilibrium, in the midst of which, as in the centre of a cyclone of whirling atoms, we can move and work.

"We have now to conceive the molecules of the air in this hall flying about in all directions, at a rate of about seventeen miles in a minute. If all these molecules were flying in the same direction, they would constitute a wind blowing at the rate of seventeen miles a minute, and the only wind which approaches this velocity is that which proceeds from the mouth of a cannon. How, then, are you and I able to stand here? Only because the molecules happen to be flying in different directions, so that those which strike against our backs enable us to support the storm which is beating against our faces. Indeed, if this molecular bombardment were to cease, even for an instant, our veins would swell, our breath would leave us, and we should, literally, expire.

"But it is not only against us or against the walls of the hall that the molecules are striking. Consider the immense numbers of them, and the fact that they are flying in every possible direction, and you will see that they cannot avoid striking each other. Every time that two molecules come into collision the paths of both are changed, and they go off in new directions. Thus each molecule is continually getting its course altered, so that in spite of its great velocity it may be a long time before it reaches any great distance from the point at which it set out."
.... "I have calculated the number of collisions which each (molecule) must undergo in a second. They are given in the table, and are reckoned by thousands of millions. No wonder that the travelling power of the swiftest molecule is but small, when its course is completely changed thousands of millions of times in a second."[1]

Thus the struggle begins very low down in the scale of the creation;[2] it seems to be a necessity

---

[1] Discourse on Molecules, pp. 5, 6, 7.
[2] It is wonderful, too, how low down in the scale we find the first rudiments of love. In a passage on Electrolysis, Professor Maxwell says, "Here is an electric current passing through acidulated water, and causing oxygen to appear at one electrode, and hydrogen to the other. In the space between, the water is perfectly calm, and yet two

imbedded in the very constitution of the world. As we pass up through the successive stages of the organisation, the struggle becomes more intense, the waste and wreck more dire. Each particle of rock has as hard a fight for its place as the molecules of air or water. It too is pressed and crushed by its fellows; by its strength and toughness it shoulders its way to the place which it is bound to occupy in the scheme of "the all."

See how the great mountains have writhed in their agony; solid sheets of rock are there crumpled like paper, and masses of stone that have been tossed like leaves before the drift. Enter the gates of the hills and pass up to their wilder altitudes; trees are there, lonely, scattered, fighting sternly with rock and avalanche this battle of existence; great pine forests torn and maimed and splintered, shrouded with the wasting lichen as with grave clothes, but still holding on grimly to life. A flower

opposite currents of oxygen and of hydrogen must be passing through it. The physical theory of this process has been studied by Clausius, who has given reasons for asserting that in ordinary water the molecules are not only moving, but every now and then striking each other with such violence that the oxygen and hydrogen of the molecules part company, and dance about through the crowd, seeking partners which have become dissociated in the same way. In ordinary water these exchanges produce, on the whole, no observable effect, but no sooner does the electromotive force begin to act, than it exerts its guiding influence on the unattached molecules, and bends the course of each towards its proper electrode, till the moment when, meeting with an unappropriated molecule of the opposite kind, it enters again into a more or less permanent union with it, till it is again dissociated by another shock. Electrolysis, therefore, is a kind of diffusion assisted by electromotive force."—Maxwell, "On Molecules," p. 8.

The Universal Travail. 31

is there lifting its pendulous delicate bell, pallid with its struggle, through a gap in a ghastly snowdrift; the fairest forms, the rarest hues gleam out on heights and edges, where every moment is a battle with death. Nature grows more stern and savage daily, unless she is fought by man's intelligent strength, and mastered. The seeds of lovely and goodly things in all her regions perish by myriads, for one that blooms and fruits. It is the molecule struggle repeated under higher and more visible conditions. How rare is a crystal developed in freedom, its figure perfect, its substance pure! Few work themselves out to fair completeness, unmaimed by the assaults and shocks which they endure. As rare is a perfect frond or flower. And yet the gleam of beauty lies bright upon it all, prophetic of the glory in which all the groaning shall issue at last.

As we ascend into the higher region of the animate creation, the struggle becomes apparently more dire and destructive still. In one sense it is a terrible picture which the author of "The Origin of Species" paints of the development of Nature. The race is to the swift and the spoil to the strong everywhere; weakness crushed out of existence, strength standing on the wrecks of shattered organisms, pluming its crest and passing on to new conflicts, until in turn it too meets with the stronger, and goes down with all its pride and beauty to the dust. To those who have an ear only for the groaning, there is enough to fill it, and to feed that horror of Nature with all its pain and waste, into which heathen peoples settle at last. They see that for one living thing that survives and brings forth a progeny, myriads perish, the prey of the stronger creatures that hunt them with eager persistence, and live upon their life. They see that each organism has its parasite that preys on it inwardly, and its natural foe that is born to pursue it. They think that were the veil lifted and the vision of life in all its ranks and orders laid bare, we should see through this whole world-system, perhaps through other worlds, clouds of living creatures of delicate workmanship and exquisite hue flying in quivering terror before fierce pursuers, who in turn have a fiercer in their tracks to seize them when their prey is gorged. They point to whole species which Nature seems to protect by clever artifice from extinction. There are fish whose markings simulate the sand in which they hide themselves from their pursuers. There are insects which put on the forms of rare and delicate flowers; and some that take a loathsome or fetid likeness, and are hardly saved. Everywhere terror, struggle and destruction; the animate molecules clashing with deadlier purpose and direr ruin than the inanimate, the lower strata of Creation furnishing the grandest hecatombs, while the upward procession of life treads on their dust.

There is strife enough and pain enough all round us in the Creation to justify this picture, but that the terror is wanting. This ceaseless clash and struggle is the method by which the Creator wills that stronger, purer, nobler forms of things shall constantly

The Universal Travail. 33

be brought forth. But the terror and anguish are largely in our imagination. There plays everywhere through the Creation, the light of a glad and victorious life. Even the prey of the "young lions, which seek their meat from God," seems emancipated from the terror;[1] the pain is of the moment, while life on the whole is good to them and glad. Still, the groaning and travailing is carried up through the animal creation, with an energy which would be terrible, but for the order and progress which visibly spring from it, and the fairer forms that emerge from what otherwise we might sigh over as wreck.

But the groaning becomes articulate, and is burdened with anguish, when we rise into the human world. How long, O Lord, how long? is the cry which generation by generation is wrung out of the pain of the noblest and most faithful hearts. Sad as may seem the aspect of the struggle which everywhere attends the evolution of nobler forms in the lower Creation, we must use a darker word to describe the cost of human development; the stains that redden the track of civilisation, the masses of victims who lie crushed to bloody clay under the chariot wheels of progress, the holocaust which is offered on the shrine of every improvement, the anguish that writes its record on the faces of the myriads, who, too weak for life's struggle, fall out of the ranks of the advancing army, stagger awhile painfully in the rear, and then drop in heart-broken despair. There is something in the

[1] The carnivorous animals, as Dr. Livingstone found, seem to exercise a kind of fascination on their prey.

D

"vision of the human" which explains the groan, "Eh man, it's a sair sight!" which broke from the lips of him who, of all our teachers, has the keenest eye for the sad side of life and of Nature, when he was bidden to look up at the bright stars and rejoice.

When we read of the heroic achievements of the past, our eye flashes and our blood fires. We have no thought for the hearts that were aching and breaking for the heroes; the homes left desolate, the schemes of life on which much precious treasure had been spent, broken up, and wrecked. We mark with profound interest the great steps of human progress, Nebuchadnezzar's golden empire, Medo-Persian dominion, Alexander's splendid conquests, and the revolution of revolutions which seated the Cæsars on the world's imperial throne. Millions of human lives were spilt like water in working out each of these schemes of dominion. Cities burnt, provinces wasted, wide fertile regions made over to lasting desolation, plague and famine, and unutterable horrors of human cruelty, make in all ages the march of humanity sadder than a battle-field strewn with slaughter. Our eye follows the jubilant host to its triumph; but it is well sometimes to look round and survey the wreck. Caius Julius Cæsar brought that country which has been one of the morning stars of progress for ages, within the field of civilisation and ultimately of the Gospel. It cost the lives of at least a million of men, and the heart-broken anguish of how many millions more! Read the history of the tremendous wars

The Universal Travail. 35

by which the Reformation finally upheld itself against Rome. Legions of cruel fiends in human form went storming and burning through the fairest fields of Europe, and wasted what the toil and the thrift of two centuries have not been able to repair. There are tales to be told of those wars, the storm of Magdeburg, and the like, which make the blood run cold, and the very marrow shiver in the bones.

And now, in this nineteenth century of Christian culture, with the full sunlight of the Gospel shining, as we please ourselves by dreaming, on the world, the greatest step of human development which marks our era, has cost, perhaps, the bloodiest and most tremendous battles which are recorded in history. The largest hosts which Cæsar or Charlemagne could have put into the field, would have been swept like straws before the armies whose "blood and iron" have built up and cemented the edifice of German unity before our eyes. It is a terrible sign of the measure in which the struggle for life rules still in the domain of human history. Kings, statesmen, parliaments, poets, had tried to build the edifice peacefully, in vain. The wisest words, the most ardent aspirations, the most strenuous endeavours of peaceful thinkers and workers, had been spent fruitlessly on the enterprise. The man of "blood and of iron" took it in hand, and it was done at once. But who has summed up the cost? And there seemed to be some dire necessity for it. Neither men nor things would wait till nobler agencies could build up a fairer structure than can be built by war. This thing, for which millions of earnest hearts were pining, seems to have been possible only at this crisis, through all this agony and blood.

I will not speak of the triumphs of civilisation on its distant borders; the withering of whole tribes and nations before the vices of the leaders of the culture and progress of mankind. Nor will we boast of the glories of peaceful industry; so gentle, they tell us, so holy, so benign. We might come across ranks and classes whose bread fails, who are set face to face with starvation, as every step is gained in the art of manufacture. There are millions in Europe and America whose eyes are dim, whose cheek is sunk, whose fingers are worn to the bone, whose heart is strained to breaking, that our magnificent commerce may spread its benign ministries over the world.

And is it all to be like this, and for ever? Struggle, struggle, struggle, everywhere; men, animals, molecules of matter, hustling in perpetual shock; moans filling the air; maimed, crushed, shattered things and creatures laid everywhere as the foundation on which the survivors build the edifice—if this be all, we dare not call it the temple—of life. Great God! the soul sickens, shudders at the vision; the heart stays its beat under such burdens of pain and death.

And yet, one of the very cleverest books which has been written recently, and by one of the ablest men of our time, seems to take it for granted that things will be in the future very much as they have been in the past; that selfishness, on the whole, will remain the mainspring of human action, and that religion will be found necessary mainly as a police system, to drive men by the terrors of judgment to keep their selfishness within moderately decent bounds. The book means that this is a hard world, with a hard God to rule it. Things are so arranged by the Creator that the strong ones shoulder their way on in the world, while weak ones are shouldered to the wall or trampled to the dust. The struggle for life meets us everywhere, and is always likely to meet us. The race is to the swift and the spoil to the strong, in the human as in the lower spheres of the Creation. Liberty is a snare, equality is a lie, fraternity is a dream, in this scheme of life. The only sensible plan of a society will be organised on the basis of this selfish struggle for existence; and, as the writer holds that Christianity is largely based on the doctrine of hell, no hope can be gathered from it for the future of Creation, or the reign of more blessed relations in fairer worlds than this.

To me, I confess, this book[1] presents about the dreariest view of life which I have ever looked upon. I turn with relief from this Christian writer to the sentence of Comte which he holds up to scorn. He at any rate has a vision of a fairer scheme of human relationships, and says, "The great problem is, to raise social feeling by artificial effort to the position which in the natural condition is held by selfish feeling." If the Comtists would give up their "artificial effort" as in its very nature unfruitful, and have faith

[1] "Liberty, Equality, Fraternity." By James Fitz James Stephen, Q.C. Smith, Elder & Co.

in the profoundly natural effort of the Creator and Redeemer of the world to bind and to hold men together in love, I should be with them on this point entirely. As also with Mr. Frederic Harrison, who, with his usual eloquence and force, pourtrays what, but for the disavowal of Christianity, might be a Christian prophecy of the future : " A religion of action, a religion of social duty, devotion to an intelligible and sensible head, a real sense of incorporation with a living and controlling force, the deliberate effort to serve an immortal humanity,—this, and this alone, can absorb the musings and the cravings of the spiritual man." [1]

But to return to this groaning and travail of Creation. It is essential that we should understand that the groans are groans of travail. They are birth-pangs, these throes of the Creation ; and this truth, if we can look forward as well as backward, if we can grasp what is being born out of the travail of the human, casts a glorious lustre over it all. The groaning is distinctly in travail. Out of all the struggle and visible wreck which we have glanced at, purer, nobler, more beautiful things and beings are continually being born. We have but to compare the huge saurian monsters which once wallowed in the marshes of nascent Europe, with the finer, compacter creatures which now roam its forests and crop its pastures, to measure the enormous advance which has been gained. Out of this tremendous and destructive struggle for existence, man

[1] " Fortnightly Review," Nov. 1872, p. 529.

somehow, somewhere emerges; and with man a host of nobler forms of flowers, fruits, and creatures; while the grosser flora and fauna of the earlier eras rot into coal, or petrify into rock, to bear up the structure, and to minister to the life of the human world.

Here, then, is distinctly travail. Things struggle on and struggle up into finer and compacter forms. As Creation grows towards man, prophetic images of human intelligence and will appear. Images only, but prophetic. They are the form which the spirit in man will quicken with life. At last, when man emerges and stands at the head of the creatures, we might well believe that the groaning is ended; that the being in birth of whom the whole mundane system of things had been travailing, has at length come forth into the living world. " Man is in little all the sphere ;" the whole structure of the Creation finds its key in the human organisation. Rudiments of things which struggle dimly into shape and use through all the lower stages of development, take their perfect form and fulfil their complete function in man; while, as if to connect man by the closest links with the whole chain of organic forms, organs and lineaments which find their use in the lower spheres through which the creature has slowly struggled, but which superior organs supersede for the uses of the human, shrink back to rudimental proportions; they are mere hints of what has been, but they are still found in the physical structure of our race.

And this is certainly one of the very strongest points in the argument of the evolutionists; unless we are to believe the Creator made of set purpose in the human organisation these traces of the inferior types; as it has been gravely contended that when the world was created, fossil carnivora were created in it with the prey between their teeth, evidently with the purpose of bewildering the philosophers. Here, then, in the human form, we might be tempted to believe that the struggle terminates; the series of organic forms is at length complete. Travailing Nature may surely sing over the Adam of the Creation, " Unto us a child is born, unto us a son is given," and settle herself to her well-earned rest.

Alas! when man appears upon the scene a sadder groaning is heard, a sharper travailing is seen. The struggle prolongs itself with fiercer passion. But there is an onward and upward pressure through the ages. Man developes continually new ideas and aspirations. The effort is always to rise. We watch man in travail, like Nature, through all his generations; there is something still struggling to the birth, something which, through all the pain and strain of life, is about being born.

As man, where he becomes visible through the mists of the past, commences his career of development, we find in him a vision of a serene and holy order of life, in which the dire confusion of the struggle shall be ended, and heart shall be knit to heart, and hand to hand in fellowship and love. Man dreams this dream; he passionately clings to it. Far from accepting the struggle as the ultimate condition of his existence, all which seems highest within him, the fruit of the noblest effort and the completest culture of his being, earnestly protests against it. A faculty is born within him which can survey the strife of the Creation. He considers it, reflects upon it, judges it, and the idea shapes itself within him that he is born to end it; that he has been lifted to the edge of a higher order, that there is that within him which is in relation with that higher order; and that in him and in that which is to grow out of him, the travailing Creation is to see "the beginning of peace."

He sees the strife within him and around him; he knows that the selfish struggle for existence prolongs itself into his world. But he has a vision which haunts him in all countries and in all ages; it possesses his wisest and holiest seers, it floats before the mind even of his godless philosophers; it is the vision of an order in which a holier principle, fertile in peace and benediction, shall assume the supremacy in his house of life, and shall organise his relations on a basis of sympathy, ministry and love. He looks to it to tame that spirit of strife which, in the human sphere, assumes the aspect of a demon; while it gathers up all the fruits of the travail, and makes that liberty, equality, and fraternity, in the heavenly sense of them—lies or dreams as, we are justly told, they must be, so long as the law of struggle is reigning—the blessed realities of that state up to which humanity is pressing, where bonds of law are replaced by bands of love.

This is distinctly the human vision and aspiration. There is nothing so universal, nothing so deep-seated in humanity as this. Men have prayed for it, fought for it, suffered for it, died for it, age after age. And the progress of society is literally measured by its realisation. We say that humanity advances just as it works up to this condition; and the fact that the progress is so dim and slow, that the struggle prolongs itself through the ages, and that selfishness reigns and riots in the world, is the chronic agony of human society. Not over the first Adam, who was born for the struggle, but over the second Adam, the child of the travail, who was born for the peace, the music of the heavenly anthem floats: "*Unto us a Child is born, unto us a Son is given, and the government shall be upon His shoulder. And His name shall be called Wonderful, Counsellor, the Mighty God, the Everlasting Father, the Prince of Peace. Of the increase of His government and of peace there shall be no end, upon the throne of His father David, and upon His kingdom, to order it and establish it, with judgment and with justice, from henceforth and even for ever.*"

Here then is, not the groaning, but the travail of the human. The creature form touches its highest in man. Something enters into that form which comes from and looks to a higher than the creature region. A new order of ideas, aims, hopes possesses man the creature, of which all that he shares with the Creation is not continent, which it groans and strives to bring forth into a higher sphere.

What is it that stands next in the order of development? To what shall man, standing on the summit of the creature level, strive and aspire? What has to be born out of this more grievous travail of the intellectual and spiritual part in the human? What but Christ's " Kingdom of Heaven"?

The intellectual and spiritual part! What is this? To those who look at the struggle only, there is something sad, profoundly sad, in the aspect of Creation. But there is gladness beside the sadness. As Creation approaches the human type, as creatures grow more sensitive, we see something dawning in the animal nature which in man puts on the perfect form of pity, sympathy, and love. Mothers of wild cubs will deny themselves, suffer, and even die for their offspring; animals will help and soothe each other in pain; mates will cleave to each other with fond fidelity, and in some rare instances pity for weakness begins to appear.

Now all which looks towards sympathy and tenderness would seem to be a weak point in the Creation, on the materialistic theory. All that helps a weak thing to hold its life against a strong thing, would really, on this scheme, be marring the order of the universe and prolonging a useless conflict, adding a fresh note of sadness thereby to the universal moan. But in man these sentiments of pity, tenderness, cherishing ministry, yearning, redeeming love, pass to the front rank, and come to be counted the best things, the most helpful things, to the true development of the human world. And everywhere these sentiments and principles seek to root themselves in the world of spirit, in the sphere of moral freedom, of duty, immortality, and God. They are strong and victorious in man just as they connect themselves with the world which we call spiritual, with God, with the ministering angels, and with the recompenses of eternity.

And these are the blessed things, the healing things, the saving things of society. This weltering chaos of struggle, as it sometimes seems, is very terrible to contemplate; but while it is development in the mere creature sphere, it is destruction in the human, unless it be tamed and ruled by the higher law. Awful is the struggle of selfish passion, and the waste and wreck which everywhere attend it. But heaven sees too, white troops of helping, healing, saving ministers, mingling in the conflict, repairing the waste, and restoring the wreck. Agony there is enough everywhere, but love with its benign touch is moving amid the anguish, and life looks up and smiles and hopes. Where mere strength is let loose on earth to work its imperious will, where the strong hand, knowing no law but its own pleasure, is master in society, man languishes and perishes, and all the gathered treasures of the ages are scattered in the dust. Where the healing, helping, saving ministries are strong, where the weak have a stay, where the poor have a shield, where the gentle have honour, and the good have power, all that man thinks most precious in society, grows and flourishes; life blooms with beauty, or glows with rich and golden fruit.

And everywhere and always the spring of all that heals and saves has been fed from heaven. It is true of heathendom as well as of Christendom. Marco Polo was filled with amazement at the vast and admirably organised system of poor-relief which he found in the Chinese cities. He learnt at Cambulu, that "the Tartars before they were converted to the religion of the idolaters (that is of Buddha), never practised almsgiving. Indeed, when any poor man begged of them, they would say to him, Go, with God's curse, for if He loves you as He loves me, He would have provided for you. But the sages of the idolaters told the great Kaan, that it was a good work to provide for the poor, and that his idols would be greatly pleased if he did so. And since then he has taken to do for the poor as much as you have heard."[1]

That was a grand answer, too, which Demonax suggested to the Athenians, when there was a question of their establishing gladiatorial games, "You must throw down the altar to pity first." But it was an *altar* to pity, an acknowledgment of a power which belonged to a celestial sphere; and it was a spiritual teacher who taught Cublay Kaan the lessons of charity. It is spiritual influence which has quickened and upheld the graces by which society lives and grows, from the days of Adam until now.

The Jewish nation was a compact and strong society, after the model which our liberal philosophers chiefly honour. It was a nation of freemen, of free-

[1] See Colonel Yule's edition of Marco Polo's travels. Vol I. 398.

holders, in which the tyranny of the strong was restrained, and the rights of the weak were upheld by admirable institutions; where the poor and broken, instead of being crushed, by wise helps were lifted and restored. The law of that people was God's commandment, and the example which He set them to imitate was Himself. And thence, out of the heart of the nation which was nursed on Revelation, have come those holy and blessed visions which have lit the path of toiling and suffering generations with the lustre of heaven. All that man holds best and happiest, all that most works for the healing and saving of mankind, finds utterance in the words of Hebrew Prophets and Psalmists; who promise, who prophesy, the reign of a King of righteousness and peace over a regenerate restored Creation; a new heaven and a new earth, wherein dwelleth righteousness for evermore.

Development! Yes, we believe in development. We only ask our philosophers to help us to complete it. First the natural, then the spiritual, is the Divine order. Here is the fruit of the groaning and travailing of Nature. The creature at its highest, by a last and crowning effort, brings forth the human form; man at his highest, by the supreme act of travail, in God and through God, brings forth the new man, who is destined to reign with God in heaven and through eternity. Yes! we believe in development, we rest in it, for we believe in the intelligence that originated and that guides it, and assures and will secure its fruits. We dare not stay on this creature level. We dare not say, here the Creation ends its travail, in the sighing and groaning of man the captive, bound and barred in his prison house for ever. We catch the voice, we grasp the hand that seems to seek us from a higher sphere. We yield ourselves joyfully to the force that draws us upward, and we gain new and larger thoughts of the future developments of Being as we rise. We trace the outlines of that Redemptive plan which is transmuting tears into joys, pangs into glories, the din of battle into the victor's triumph, this groaning and travailing into a redeemed and restored Creation, this vile body into the transfigured body of the resurrection, and the wilderness of earth into the kingdom of heaven. "*This corruptible shall put on incorruption, and this mortal shall put on immortality.*"

I could far rather believe that this solid earth is but vanishing vapour, the procession of creature-forms a shifting illusion, and man with all his achievements and attainments a puppet shadow on the wall, than I could imagine for an instant that the world of spirit to the edge of which the development of the creature presses, and into which in man it seems to rise, the world in which humanity seeks with passionate eagerness to root itself, and from which it draws the vital nourishment of its life, is the one unreality of our experience. It is the sphere into which all the noblest human thinkers and workers have constantly lifted themselves, and from which all the inspiration which has made our seers and prophets has flowed down; it has furnished age after age the forces by which man has fought the battle against selfishness, violence and lust; in it all the springs are found which have purified, healed, and saved society; and I say again, I could more easily believe that all things that I look upon, and myself among them, are ghastly spectres, whirling in a mad dance of death, than that this only, of all the things that seem to be, belongs to your "world of dreams."

III.

THE ATHEISTIC LIFE.

"Having no hope, and without God in the world."—Eph. ii. 12.

THE value of human life in any generation may be measured, on the whole, by its faith in God. Life grows cheap as sense grows masterful, and as faith, and the hope that is born from faith, expire. It may help us to understand the sphere of being to which man truly belongs, and in which alone he can complete his life, to note that a sensual age, instead of clinging to life more fondly for the sake of its pleasures, comes to curse it as a dire endowment, and to escape from it joyfully even into the everlasting night. Life had become next to worthless in the estimation of the ablest men in the Roman Empire, in the age in which the apostles relaid the foundations of human society in man's spiritual relations to his fellow man, to the unseen world, and to God. So long as man was regarded as the centre of his sphere, man's life became impoverished generation by generation, until in the age of the Advent human life seems to have touched its nadir, its minimum of value to the man and to mankind.

E

The Emperor Tiberius was probably one of the ablest men who has ever occupied a throne. His state papers, if we may use the term, some of which are preserved to us, are singularly luminous and masterly. Yet it was the Emperor Tiberius, the world's undisputed master, who wrote to the Senate these terrible words: " May all the gods and goddesses, if there be any, damn me worse than I am damned already, if I know what to write to you." Seneca, whose intuitions of spiritual truth have suggested to theologians the baseless idea that he must have become acquainted with the teaching of the Apostle Paul, if ever he grows enthusiastic, grows enthusiastic upon suicide. Epictetus, individually a far nobler man, utters, in the most intense passage of his writings, a bitter wail over the impossibility of finding a man who was trying, with even a decent measure of success, to live after the pattern which, in his judgment, could alone make life worth the living at all.

In an earlier generation Lucretius, quite the deepest thinker and the loftiest genius among all the Roman poets, wrote a poem of marvellous beauty and power, in which he proved that the whole mythology of Rome lay about as near as old wives' fables to the heart of the mystery of the Creation. He did much, perhaps more than any other man, to shatter the ancient belief about the origin and the government of the world, which still stood between many a sad heathen heart and the hopeless exclamation, " What is truth?" He developed the idea that a fortuitous

The Atheistic Life. 51

concourse of atoms was the key to the order of the Creation.

> Namque ita multimodis multis primordia rerum
> Ex infinito jam tempore percita plagis,
> Ponderibusque suis consuêrunt concita ferri,
> Omnimodisque coire, atque omnia pertentare,
> Quæcunque inter se possint congressa creare,
> Ut non sit mirum si in taleis dispositura
> Deciderunt quoque, et in taleis venere meatus
> Qualibus hæc rerum genitur nunc summa novando.—B. v. 188.

He gave a picture of the inner order of the Creation which left no room for man as a moral and immortal being, which made responsibility a superstition, and immortality a dream; and then with all his splendid faculty and promise, in the very prime of his manhood, at the age of forty-four, he killed himself out of such a world!

"*Gallio cared for none of these things.*" Gallio was one of the most perfectly accomplished, admirable, loveable men, if Seneca may be trusted, in the whole Roman Empire. A complete and graceful scholar, a masterly administrator, a friend whom his friends held in the highest honour and love, he *was* everything and he *had* everything which could dignify and embellish life, except that which Paul was and had. But for this he had no care. The deep thoughts about God, about life, about man's nature and destiny, with which Paul was charged, he would regard as a poor and base superstition. The mission which was burning in Paul's great heart, and which made him a debtor to the whole world to preach to it the Gospel, was a thing quite outside the sphere of his thoughts. He cared to cultivate his faculties, to enjoy philosophical discussion with his friends, to repress wrong and wicked lewdness in the region over which he ruled with a touch of lofty Roman scorn; but for the truth, the power, the life, with which that Jew was charged whom he drave with the rest from before his judgment-seat, he had no recognition; he was blind to it all as was Pilate to Christ; and Gallio too finished his brilliant career by suicide.

Now these men whom I have mentioned were among the very foremost men in the world in their times. They were the ablest, the wisest, the most distinguished; the men in whom we might most fairly hope to see the spirit of the times reflected, and by whose way of living and thinking about life, we might gain the best insight into the thoughts of the undistinguished mass who leave no definite record of themselves in history. And their witness is a profoundly sad one, and true as it is sad; for every when and every where the student of history notes that life grows sad in itself and worthless to men, just in the measure in which it seems to them that they have only this world to live for, and nothing to do in it but to speculate and to enjoy. An atheistic age inevitably comes in the end to make light of life.

And I note a very clear tendency to cheapen life, to make light of it, and of the sanction by which its sacred treasure is guarded, in the atheistic literature of our times. There are hints, and something more than hints, that suicide may be regarded as an open question, and that life may be mercifully shortened to avoid inevitable pain, in periodicals conducted and written by some of the ablest intellectual men of the day. Now, one of the most marked of the earlier fruits which Christianity bore to the world, was the bound that it set to the age of suicide and infanticide. The age of the first Cæsars was emphatically *the* age of the suicides. Tacitus tells us of a man who simply killed himself in indignation that he had been born ! Even the easy, complacent Horace, the pet poet of the Augustan Court, could only say of his times :—

> Damnosa quid non imminuit dies ?
> Ætas parentum, pejor avis, tulit
> Nos nequiores, mox daturos
> Progeniem vitiosiorem.

It was a time when a favourite topic of discussion was the easiest means of escaping into the valley of the shadow of death, whatever that might be, as better in any case for a man, than such a world as this. To this propensity, I may almost say, passion for suicide, Christianity set a bound at once. I do not mean to say that it had not a hard battle with it ; but it shewed at once, within the wide circle of its converts, its victorious power. There was evidently ample power there, the power of faith and hope, to master it.[1] And the glow of the hope which Christianity had kindled, spread far beyond its pale,

---

[1] It is curious enough that Christianity had before long to deal with a tendency to suicide within the Church, in the form of voluntary martyrdom ; which was suicide through excess of hope.

and infected with a loftier and more trustful spirit the tone of heathen thinking and living in the great world around. It was not very perceptible at first; but I think that no careful student of the history of those times can fail to note a certain set of the current of heathen thought and aspiration, in the direction in which Christianity was destined to guide mankind, dating from the close of the age which heard the preaching of the Apostles, and witnessed the foundation of the Christian Church.

Indeed, it seems as if the minds of the wisest and most far-sighted men in heathendom were led on to utter just that cry which Christianity was destined to answer, and to formulate the desire which it was sent into the world to meet. When Seneca says in utter hopelessness of his own age, " There is no one strong enough of himself to lift himself up, some one must stretch out a hand to him," does it not seem to say, that the world was waiting for the word, " *The Lord hath visited his people;*" " *The Son of man is come to save that which was lost;*" " *Look unto Him and be ye saved, all ye ends of the earth*" ?

When Epictetus cried with such passionate earnestness, " Shew me some one person formed according to the principles he professes. Shew me one who is sick, and happy; in danger, and happy; dying, and happy; exiled, and happy; disgraced, and happy. Shew him to me, for by heaven I long to see a Stoic . . . . . . Let any of you shew me a human soul desiring to be in unity with God; not to accuse either

God or man ; not to be angry; not to be envious; not to be jealous ; in a word, desiring from a man to become God," is it not as though there had been born within him, an intense unconscious longing to stand face to face with such a man as the Apostle, who could write these words, and live them, and teach others to live them too ?—*But in all things approving ourselves as the ministers of God, in much patience, in afflictions, in necessities, in distresses, in stripes, in imprisonments, in tumults, in labours, in watchings, in fastings ; by pureness, by knowledge, by long-suffering, by kindness, by the Holy Ghost, by love unfeigned, by the word of truth, by the power of God, by the armour of righteousness on the right hand and on the left, by honour and dishonour, by evil report and good report ; as deceivers, and yet true ; as unknown, and yet well-known ; as dying, and behold we live ; as chastened, and not killed ; as sorrowful, yet alway rejoicing ; as poor, yet making many rich ; as having nothing, and yet possessing all things . . . . . . And what agreement hath the temple of God with idols ? For ye are the temple of the living God ; as God hath said, I will dwell in them, and walk in them ; and I will be their God, and they shall be my people. Wherefore come out from among them, and be ye separate, saith the Lord, and touch not the unclean thing; and I will receive you, and will be a Father unto you, and ye shall be my sons and daughters, saith the Lord Almighty."*— II. Cor. vi. 4—10, 16—18.

What would Epictetus have given to commune with the man, who, advancing to scenes of struggle and anguish, at the vision of which even the pure and noble Stoic might have stood appalled, could ring out a joyful welcome to it all : "*None of these things move me, neither count I my life dear unto myself, if I might finish my course with joy, and the ministry which I have received of the Lord Jesus, to testify the gospel of the grace of God*"!

To me there seems to be nothing so wonderful in the apostolic age, as the way in which the ablest thinkers and the noblest men in heathendom, were led to pine for the very deliverance which Christianity was already beginning to accomplish. It is as though the confession were wrung from them, by their earnest but vain endeavours, "We would aim at the ends which these Christians are aiming at, we would do the things which these Christians do, but the very root of the power to do them seems to be dead in us, and in the world."[1]

Christianity saved human society by lending new worth and sacredness to life. Life became inexpressibly precious to men who believed, and who knew that they had a right to believe, that out of the pain and travail of the present, a future of glorious liberty, power and joy was being born. And when I speak of life, I use the word in its larger sense, and not of this mortal life only ; *that* they were only too ready to lay down because of the far more exceeding and

---

[1] A very full and able discussion of this great subject will be found in "The Light of the World," by Professor Wilkins, of Owen's College, Manchester (Macmillan), to whom I feel indebted for many valuable suggestions.

eternal weight of glory which this light and momentary affliction would bear as its fruit. Their existence, instead of becoming a bitter curse to them, as it was to Tiberius on the world's imperial throne, was a possession of priceless worth. Christ laid a consecrating hand upon it; He claimed it as His own, and it became a sacred thing from that hour; sacred for its uses of service to this world, to which the example of Christ irresistibly drew them; and sacred as a sacrifice to be freely, joyfully offered, when claimed for the service of a higher world.

I shall have more to say of this in the next discourse. I simply note now, as matter of history, that Christianity at once made life an inestimably precious endowment, branding suicide as a shameful treason, as well as a wanton waste; while, on the other hand, it called forth martyrs by myriads, men not ready only, but eager to pour out life like water, if they might bear witness to that which alone made it worth while to live. This new sense of the sacredness of life, arose from the idea which Christianity implanted, that it was a trust from the Highest; to be used bravely, nobly, at His commandment, and at His commandment at any moment to be bravely, joyfully laid down.

I have dwelt thus largely on the state of thought and of life in the heathen world at the time of the Advent, because I believe that it affords us a valuable clue to some of the deeper tendencies and experiences of our own times. We are endeavouring to look at life in the light of modern Atheistic ideas. And I use the word modern in this connection advisedly.

It is not the Atheism of the end of the last century which I am asking you to consider; but that which meets us in the literature and in the life of our own generation. It has a special character of its own, and a special affinity, I think, with that of the age of the Advent of which I have spoken already somewhat at large. The Atheism of our day differs in many very important features from that of a hundred years ago, which culminated in the wildest excesses of the French Revolution. In that there was a bitter, malignant hatred of Christianity, a fierce fury against it, from which we are now happily delivered. Why? What was its spring? I do not hesitate to express my belief that this bitter, furious hate was due almost, if not quite, entirely to the practical Atheism of the Christian Church. Just as through the vices, the self-seeking, and the spiritual pride of the chosen race, " the name of God was blasphemed among the Gentiles," so in the dark days of which we are speaking, a Christless Church caused the name of Christ to be blasphemed in the world which it was set to teach and to save.

Picture to yourself the state of the French Church about the middle of the eighteenth century, read any chapter out of its history, and add a chapter out of the history of the "most Christian" Government which it supported, sanctioned and applauded, and then wonder if you can that men betook themselves in despair to the old Paganism, and thought that " Demoiselle Candeille " might be better worth worshipping, as goddess of Reason, than the God who

The Atheistic Life. 59

was pourtrayed to them by the idols, and the harpy prelates and priesthood of the Gallican Church.

Read, too, any honest pourtrayal of the character and habits of the average Anglican parson of that same period, study the temper and morals of our Episcopate, at which Gibbon delighted, not without justice, to sneer; see the shameless traffic, political and mercenary, in the care of souls, which was understood on all hands to be a mainspring of action in a Church which was set to teach that covetousness is idolatry; consider, too, the kind of Government in England with which the Church was inextricably associated, and to which the toast "Church and King" gave a kind of bibulous consecration; estimate its relation to freedom of thought, freedom of worship, and to the wrongs and the miseries of the poor; remember, too, how Church and Government stood together in defence of bigotry, worldliness, cruel oppression, shameful wrong, and all that works impoverishment and misery among a people; and again wonder, if you can, that some of the most passionate and aspiring idealists of the day were driven into wild atheistic ravings against a Gospel, whose quality seemed to be certified to them by such an organ as this.

A man like Shelley, driven half mad by the wrong, the falsehood, the hate, the misery, which he saw around him, was goaded into glorying in the name of Atheist; while his soul was full of profound homage for the ideas of truth, liberty, and charity, which the Gospel came to establish and to magnify, but which all around him that called itself Christian seemed to him to deny. But these men had their Bibles, it may be said, and should have judged Christianity more justly. So too, Marcus Aurelius had the lives of the Christians before him, and ought to have found out that a power from God was at work in his Roman world. But, practically, it is hard for men to take a fair view of that which lies out of the track of their current beliefs, experiences, and sympathies; and whenever the visible life of the Church seems to dishonour the truths on which it is founded, it is very hard for the Book which would teach men nobler Christian lessons, to establish and to maintain a hold on their hearts.

There was the stir and the glow of a true Christian life in the sects outside the pale of the Establishment in that generation, but they were about as far removed from the observation and sympathy of the unbelieving school of which I am speaking, as was that obscure Jewish sect, said to be "hostile to the human race," from the intelligent, sympathetic contemplation of the philosophic master of the Roman world. We shall never understand the Atheism of a century ago, nor its Deism, until we can measure how far the writings of a man like Rousseau, for instance, restored to the common world of his time some precious elements of that truth with which Christianity had dowered it, but which had been turned into base merchandise, and been thereby made hateful to men, by a lying, tyrannous, and grasping Church.

The Atheism of these days and the Deism

The Atheistic Life. 61

—you will wonder at my grouping them together, but there is no pure Atheism long possible for man; the Atheist is but the Deist searching for his god—differ from that which I have been describing by a whole earth, if not by a whole heaven. They are morally at the opposite pole. The one was strong in hate and defiance, the other is serene and suave in ignorance. " I hate such a God as you present to me," was the cry of old. " I really know nothing about it, and can find out nothing," is the bland utterance now. The old infidel stormed and screamed; the modern one shrugs his shoulders and goes on with his work. He has no quarrel with the Christians if they will let him alone; he simply tells them that their ideas are incapable of the kind of verification which alone satisfies him of the reality of phenomena, and enables him to deal with them as matters with which his life has practically to do. The Christian facts may be true, he says, or they may not be true, he has no means of settling the question; nor, he evidently thinks, would it make much difference in the sphere of thought and interest to which he cares to confine himself, if he had. There is a great deal of unbelief in our times which is just of this complexion; I think that it is altogether the most formidable phase of unbelief with which we have to deal. It is something like the " caring for none of these things "[1] to which I have already

---

[1] I have, of course, given a wider reference to this phrase than applies to the actual matter then in hand. As concerns the riot, Gallio

adverted, and whose influence on society I have already traced. Society has become very weary of our dry, hard, theological gospel; as in the days before the French Revolution it had become very weary of the venal gospel of the priests.

Men see plainly enough that the order of the universe is a thing much too complex and profound, to be covered by the narrow dogmatic schemes which we think that we draw from the Scriptures of Truth. They say that the discovery of the secret of the Creation is a thing entirely of observation and inference; and they regard our Scriptural cosmogonies and views of Creation generally, as so many idols of the mind which must be cleared out of the track of truth. There is a hardness, a narrowness, a selfishness, they think, nor are they far wrong, in the popular theology of our day, which runs counter to all the best ideas and tendencies of society; and so they cast us out of their synagogues of science, and treat that world from which we say that our inspiration comes to us, as a world of dreams.

Will, moral freedom, responsibility, immortality, heaven, and God, find no room in their philosophy. No room, I say, for its domain is rigidly restrained to the temporal and the expedient; while man, if he is to find freedom of action and development for the spiritual part of him, must 'come forth into a larger

---

was probably quite right in having nothing to do with it, especially as he saw, with that keen eye of his, that the beating had fallen on quite the right man. Had Paul been beaten, perhaps he might have stirred himself to care.

The Atheistic Life. 63

world. But as for them, they believe in no "spiritual part." Thought is but the product of phosphorus in certain combinations; and choice—the free play of the will by which we elect blessing or cursing, life or death, the service of God or the service of the devil—is but the shock of that battery of material force which we carry about in our physical organisation; it is but one of the inevitable sequences of Creation, and carries with it no more burden of responsibility than the path of a bullet or the bolt of a storm. We are but atoms, we are told, among kindred atoms; we dance our day like the motes in the sunbeam, giving out hues and influences according to our nature; then, like all other atoms, we enter into fresh combinations, and renew, in other forms which look like persons, what looks like the play of a free individual life. But there is nothing in it but seeming; and nothing can grow out of it but the repetition of the ceaseless inevitable round. Verily a Dance of Death!

And then the question arises—it will soon become the question of questions with this generation—what is the worth of such a life? We are assured that there is no moral personality, no moral responsibility. But this sense of moral responsibility, the responsibility of man as a person to the Ruler and the Judge of the personal beings whom He made to serve Him and to fulfil His will, is the root of the chronic agony of mankind. From the most ignorant heathen to the most instructed Christian, from Judas Iscariot to Saul of Tarsus, it haunts, it distracts, it maddens men, until Christ has laid the spectre. There is no explaining it away; there is no getting rid of it. It is at the root of all the religions; it is the subject matter of all the philosophies; it sits as a spectre at all our banquets; it looks out on us through the sad eyes of death.

But you say, it *is* a spectre; it has no substance out of man's imagination. Be it so. But what is the worth of a spectre-haunted, spectre-hunted life? Can one conceive anything more wretched than a life which is the sport of shadows; in which creatures of a day cannot enjoy the day, because they are kept in terror by evil and frightful dreams. But let them philosophise, you say: let them steadily look at these shadows, and see how vaporous they are. Let them dismiss these haunting thoughts, and give themselves to noble, unselfish endeavours to help and to bless mankind. Why? The work of the teacher and the saviour is hard work, and for the most part very thankless. Who, what, is to sustain men under the strain of self-sacrifice, and to teach them to find the end of their being in the universal good? A man like Saul of Tarsus may find such a life come natural to him; it may be as much a matter of course to such an one to care for others, as it is to most men to care for themselves. But then what made Saul of Tarsus such a man; what sustained him in the lofty region to which he climbed? What called him, what strengthened him, to live the life of an apostle? What but the sense of the reality of this invisible world, and its supreme claims? What but the knowledge that his destiny and the destiny of the race which he served "entered into that which is within the veil" and had to do with God and the spiritual world through eternity?

Philosophy does not travail in birth of apostles. "Philosophy," says Voltaire, "was never made for the people; the *canaille* of to-day resembles in everything the *canaille* of the last four thousand years. We have never cared to enlighten cobblers and maid-servants. That is the work of apostles." And this is the secret mind of Philosophy in all ages, as it would not, I think, be difficult to prove. I find something in the same key, in the Autobiography of Mr. Mill, the model intellectualist, rather than philosopher, of our times. He says, in his Autobiography, "A person of high intellect should never go into unintellectual society, unless he can enter it as an apostle, yet he is the only person with high objects who can ever enter it at all." No; the power to originate and to sustain a life of lofty and noble self-devotion to the ignorant and the wretched, flows down from higher springs. And if that fails, what remains? I need not tell you that it is the fashion of our modern atheistic philosophy to smile at this self-devotion. "Altruism" is the barbarous name which they have invented for it; with some subtilty, I think, for if you can get a noble principle or power labelled as an "ism," it is the first step towards laying it on a shelf for the study of the antiquarian philosopher. It is hinted now that in our efforts to help the weak and to save the lost, we are interfering with the operation of a benign natural law which dooms them to speedy extinction, and are trying in vain to mend the hard, inexorable order of the world.

And who has not noted the vein of deep sadness which runs through the literature of the school, and finds fullest expression in the masterpieces of art with which our most accomplished and powerful novelist from time to time adorns and enriches our literature? Their philosophical writings, too, are very clever, very thoughtful, very learned, very just, after a fashion, but very cold, very hopeless, very lifeless. There is no glow about them, no fire. There is nothing to kindle a spark of enthusiasm, nothing that can stir itself to praise. Life must be lived, and the best must be made of it for ourselves and for others, is the loftiest thought to which the teachers of this school seem to be able to climb. And there is a dark tendency already very manifest, to make light of the sanctions by which the sacredness of life is guarded. The putting of the old and the sick whose case seems hopeless quietly out of the way, is already, as I have pointed out, openly advocated as a duty. I referred, too, to significant indications that it will not be long before we find suicide justified as a refuge from suffering, or magnified as it was of old as man's ultimate and victorious argument against a tyrannous Fate. "This is as a rule the course of man's life," says Schopenhauer, "that befooled by hope, he dances into the arms of death."

Schopenhauer is one of the leading prophets of the school, perhaps the ablest, and his influence is very powerful and wide-spread on the cultivated youth of Europe; and this is his view of life. It is but a step from this to argue that the sooner we dance into the arms of death the better. Nor does the philosopher at all shrink from the conclusion. What else does this terrible passage mean?—" The history of every life is but a history of suffering; the course of life is generally but a series of greater or of less misfortunes. The true sense of the monologue in Hamlet may be thus summed up. Our condition is so wretched that utter annihilation would be decidedly preferable." .... " The oft lamented shortness of life may perhaps be its best attribute." .... " Life may be represented as a constant deceiver in things both great and small. If it makes promises, it never keeps them, except to show how undesirable is that which was desired. First the hope, then the thing hoped for disappoints us. Life gives only to take away. The charm of distance shows us a paradise, which vanishes like an optical delusion, if we allow ourselves to approach it." .... " The general structure of life would rather produce the conviction that nothing is worth our efforts, our energies, and our struggles; that all possessions are vanity, the world a bankrupt in all quarters, and life a business which does not pay its expenses." .... " The existence of the world is a matter not of rejoicing, but of grief; its annihilation would be preferable to its existence; it is fundamentally something which ought not to exist. Human life, far from wearing the aspect of a gift, has every appearance of an incurred debt, the payment of which is exacted in the form of the urgent necessities, the tormenting desires, the unceasing want which life involves. The whole period of life is generally consumed in the liquidation of this debt, and yet it is only the interest which can be thus paid off. The payment of the capital is effected by death."[1] It would be hard to uphold the sin of suicide against such a "vision of life."

This is the ultimate estimate of life as weighed in the Atheist's balances. This is life in the light of modern Atheistic ideas. Is it noble? Is it beautiful? Is it joyful? Is it not terrible, horrible, maddening, to think that the blind force of things, which there is absolutely nothing in or above the universe to arrest or to guide, should be able to make and keep alive such a world as is pictured here? To me, if all that I see around me, and all that I feel within me, were the all of my life; were I compelled to regard Redemption as a mere mirage in life's desert, God as a shadow, and the blessed and glorious future, to which His book has taught me that all things tend, the delirious dream of a fevered heart; I would curse the day on which I was born as bitterly as Job did, and maintain as strenuously as Seneca—after the fashion of that brilliant Frenchman who repeated, at Washington, the traditions of imperial Rome—man's indefeasible right to kill himself out of such a world.

And some of you say sometimes, often I dare say,

[1] Quoted by Canon Liddon, in his very able and interesting work, "Some Elements of Religion" (Rivingtons), p. 132.

The Atheistic Life. 69

"I am tired of life, I am sick and weary of it all; would God I were at rest!" Why? When has this heart-sickness overtaken you? When has life seemed so poor and worthless? When has your soul thus preyed upon itself, filled your face with restless sadness, and sapped your health in its very springs? Was it in the seasons when faith was strong, when the vision of the unseen realities was keen, when the light of God was on your tabernacle of life? Was it when your soul was armed and paraded for duty in God's service, and your noblest powers were drawn forth and strained in work for Christ and for mankind? Nay! I see your form then, it is erect and eager; I see your eye, it flashes with ardour; I hear your voice, it rings with exultation; I catch the heart-beats, they are full and musical, and they throb with the energy of victorious life. No; no faintness then, no heart-sickness, no life weariness then; but abounding strength, abounding joy, abounding hope. There is but one thing, friends, which makes life worth having, worth living, and that makes it simply of priceless worth; it was expressed in one brief phrase by the lips of the dying Wesley: "The best of all is, God is with us."

IV.

THE MEANING OF REDEMPTION.

" Henceforth I call you not servants; . . . . but I have called you friends."—John xv. 15.

MAN the friend of God—acquainted with His mind, sympathetic with His purposes, devoted with the passionate ardour which love inspires to the fulfilment of His will, and destined to dwell in His home and to share in all the unfolding joy and glory of His kingdom through eternity—is the idea of humanity which the Bible unveils. I cling to it because it alone seems to me to explain the scale of man's nature, it alone gives the clue to the meaning of his deepest experiences, and it alone justifies the tremendous discipline which he is called to endure.

Against this, set the image of man according to the Agnostics; the school whose lofty tone assures us that they regard themselves as the intellectual tutors of our times. Man, the highest evolution as yet of that blind force which has wrought, has pressed out from within, the successive orders of the inanimate and the animate creation; a mere product of the Creation, as absolutely as the crystal in the rock or the lichen on the wall; sharing with the creatures beneath him, though in a more developed form, all the organs and faculties with which he is fearfully and wonderfully endowed ; born, like them, of the dust, and destined, when he has fretted his little day, to settle, like them, into the dust again.

He is on safe ground, they say, and within the true compass of his powers, when he deals with the visible things around him, and the impression which they make on the nerve substance within what he thinks is himself—though what "he" means, or what right or power that which is conscious, not of the moment's impression even, but of the impression of the past moment, has to call itself a man, is a problem to which this philosophy apparently offers no satisfactory solution—but when he conceives of himself as having freedom of choice, and as being under moral obligation to the God who made him to choose the good and to hate the evil ; when he talks about an immortal spirit, sin, redemption, judgment, and eternal life, he loses himself in a world of dreams.

Choose ye the picture of your nature, the vision of your destiny which seems to you most consonant with the experiences of which you are conscious, and the struggles and sufferings which you have to endure. But as for me, let me hear the voice out of the unseen and eternal world meeting my spirit in its lonely toil and battle: "*Henceforth I call you not servants; for the servant knoweth not what his lord doeth; but I have called you friends, for all things which I have heard of the Father I have made known unto you.*"

If we are shadows and pursue shadows when we

aim at the fulfilment of a Father's will, or yield to the constraints of a Saviour's love; if all that lifts us above the brutes in origin and destiny be an iridescent bubble of the imagination; then I say with the common-sense philosopher who has last undertaken to enlighten us, "It is a hard God, a hard life, and a hard world." The strong coarse natures may be able to live in it with decent composure and even comfort; but Heaven pity, it does not pretend to help, the weak, the tender, the gentle, the souls that are touched to the finest issues; life for them must be one long sharp agony, and death their best, their only friend.

I have spoken of man as a being born to be redeemed. This seems to me to be the testimony of Scripture concerning him when traced to its central idea. How he came to be what he is as a creature, is one question; what God means by him as he is, and what God intends to do with him, is another. He is here as a spiritual being consciously under a law. The Scripture tells us that he has suffered a fall, that he has lost an estate of purity and blessedness in which he was created. The school of thought which is now to the front tells us that he has suffered a rise; that he has probably grown out of an animal into a man. I say suffered a rise, for the suffering is in any case indisputable. Whether he has risen or whether he has fallen, it is as clear that he is born to sorrow as that the sparks fly upward.

This fact, with his ceaseless moaning over a lost

estate, and his utter dissatisfaction with his present condition, can be comprehended perfectly on the Scriptural theory of his nature and destiny; but it seems utterly incomprehensible on any scheme of philosophy which connects his whole nature with the dust. Being, as he is, a man, he is meant for Redemption. The whole system of things contemplates this higher evolution of humanity; the fall enters into the fundamental scheme of the Divine government; earth is made to be the theatre of the discipline whereby the fallen is to be restored. The whole Creation travails in birth of redeemed humanity, and this groaning and travailing of all things is but the beginning of that deeper and more mysterious pain, by which man the sinner is to be redeemed from the bondage of corruption, to abide with God as a friend, a son, in fairer homes than this, eternally.

Man is, as we have seen, a being born to be redeemed. We may well believe, nay, I may even say that we are bound to believe, that a merciful and righteous God would long ere this have terminated this dread experiment of freedom, and would have swept by another and yet more merciful deluge man's sin and misery together from the world, but for the Redemption in which it is the Divine purpose that all this sin and wretchedness shall fruit. Mr. Stephen says that if he were asked "if God were good," that is, "disposed to promote the happiness of mankind absolutely," he should answer, "No."[1] And if this

[1] "Liberty, Equality, and Fraternity," p. 310.

world be all that he can take account of, I entirely agree with him. It is in Redemption that we learn that God is Love. The continued existence of the world, to those who believe in the loving and merciful Ruler, means that it is being redeemed.

What is it to be redeemed? This question must be fully considered before the purpose which I have in view in writing the present book can be in any measure fulfilled. The Scripture is, in the main, the history of a Redemption. The life, the death, and the resurrection of the Lord Jesus, are the core of the whole book. To this all the lines in the Old Testament converge; from this all the lines radiate in the New Testament and in human history. The history of Christendom is but the Apocalypse "writ large." Of the purpose of that Redemptive work it is written,—"*But when the fulness of the time was come, God sent forth His Son, made of a woman, made under the law, to redeem them that were under the law, that they might receive the adoption of sons.*" The Lord means precisely the same when He calls His disciples friends. Till then servants; through the fulness of Redemption, friends. "*Now the heir,*" says the apostle, speaking of the estate of a servant, "*so long as he is a child, differeth nothing from a servant, though he be Lord of all.*" He differeth in nothing but in the fact that he is the heir, and is being trained to reign. This makes the difference, as the apostle elsewhere fully recognises, at root essential. There is no breach of continuity in the dispensations. It is all Redemption, the giving to men power to become the sons of God.

Sons, friends, the words are equally expressive. Moral sympathy, moral likeness, identity of interest and hope with God, are implied in either term. To rise to this is to be redeemed. This world is either the scene and the instrument of this resurrection, or it is the Valley of Hinnom of the universe, foul with all its wreck. Life must be regarded in the light of all that is to grow out of it. Seeds of things are planted here, foundations are laid, perhaps only ground is cleared. There is eternity to work out the results. If we look simply to what we can see and measure, we should say that Redemption seems to be a greater failure even than the experiment of freedom, so far from anything which we may dare to call "salvation," is the condition of the great mass of mankind. But "blessed are they who see not, and yet believe;" who believe that the travail of the Redeemer's spirit is precious in the sight of the Father, and that He shall see of the fruit of that travail, and be satisfied in the Redemption of a world.

But who is this Being to whose fellowship we are called ; what is that Nature, that Mind, that Will, conformity with which is Redemption ? Miss Nightingale complains that so few of our theologians tell us what God is, what His character is like. " Is it not the most important and at the same time the most neglected point in theology, to determine *what* God is—what His character is like ? " " Reams of sermons are written on every point but this. And yet this is the foundation of all . . . . . . How can man give his best unless he knows, unless you will try and find out for yourselves and for him, what is God's plan for him in this world, and in the next, why there are such sufferings in this world, who is this God who has put him here, and put him here to suffer so much ?"—*Fraser's Magazine*, May 1873.

The complaint is most just. To know God, to whom the Redemption which is by Christ Jesus seeks to conform us, is eternal life. And yet how little we endeavour to search out the secret of God, to know what it is in God, to be in communion with which is Redemption ; what is that mind with which we are to be in sympathy, what is that plan of life which we are to adopt as our course of duty, what is that purpose which we are to devote ourselves to fulfil.

The Scripture tells us in one pregnant sentence, " God is love." And it unveils to us the nature, the meaning and the measure of love. "*Herein is love, not that we loved God, but that He loved us, and sent His Son the propitiation for our sins.*" "*And hereby we have knowledge of love, that He laid down His life for us.*" " *He spared not His own Son, but freely delivered Him up for us all ;* " and those who know the nature of love, will understand that in delivering up the Son He delivered up Himself. The nature of God is love. The love manifests itself by sacrifice. It is by a sacrifice of awful, of infinite pain and effort, that the nature of God is manifested to the world. To grow like that nature is to be redeemed. Because of the awful pain of that sacrifice which was accomplished on Calvary, the symbols of which are still worn on high—which means that it abides still as the power by which the world is being ruled to its redemption—Christianity has been called " The worship of sorrow." But that is a partial view of it. It is really the worship of love, of life. To the life of spirits, to the life of that world to which we are being born, for which we are being redeemed, sacrifice is bliss. The pain of it is the thing of time, and of the accident of transgression. It is because we are so weak, and poor, and sick, that we feel this life which is like God's a pain and a strain. As we grow under this discipline, as we become redeemed, we shall find it the natural habit of our spirits; we can gather from what, in rare moments, we now find in it of joy, and even of rapture, that one day it will be our bliss.

We shall learn then how the most blessed One, in manifesting the life of God in a world so jangled and discordant as this, became of necessity the Man of Sorrows; and how there was a joy in the heart of that pain which was borne for others, was borne for man, which mounted to rapture when He realised all the fruit of blessing which the travail of His soul would bear in eternity. The sorrow is not the essential thing in Christianity; that is the accident of time. The essential thing is the Love; that abides a fountain of blessing for ever.[1]

---

[1] This subject is treated with great fulness, and with singular beauty and power, in the " Mystery of Pain," by Mr. Hinton.

And this seems to be the point where the ascetics go so drearily astray. They think that the sorrow is the essential matter, the germ of the glory, and they afflict themselves wilfully with new measures of pain. It is the life of love, which cannot but manifest itself by sorrow here, which is the Christian life; the sorrow is only beautiful, healing, redeeming, when it comes through and grows out of the manifestation of love in a world eaten up by the selfishness of sin. Those who seek sorrow as being in itself in a Christian sense a good, are seeking what is really an evil thing. They miss all elevating and purifying influences, and bury themselves in confusion and ultimately in despair. But the life of God, to the fellowship of which man is to be redeemed, is the life of a Saviour; One who lives only to help, to heal, to save; One whose joy is in giving, whose bliss is in drawing the world through His great sacrifice to Himself. The men who have lived most fully in the light of God's countenance, the men after His own heart, the men on whom the world has set its mark as its Psalmists, Prophets, and Apostles, and whose memory it will never let die, were, as I hope to make plain in succeeding discourses, the men who in their time lived most purely this life of sacrifice, and who found the joy and glory of their being in service to mankind.

Self-sacrifice is now but a cheap virtue, in the judgment of some of the most influential thinkers of our day. The worldly wise laugh at it; the keen politicians, with their ruthless common-sense and

The Meaning of Redemption. 79

common-place, leave it quite out of the account. But it is wonderful to consider how we are all standing, and working, and denying the divine beauty and grandeur of sacrifice, on ground which has been cleared and levelled for us by men and women who wrought entirely in the spirit of sacrifice ; who had caught the infection of the great Example, and who believed, in their heart of hearts, and lived out their belief, that " it is more blessed to give than to receive." Ah! it had been a dreary world—nay, would it by this time have been a world at all ?—but for such self-denying, self-sacrificing, Christ-like work.

It is easy to say, as is said constantly now, that " self-love is the fountain from which the wider forms of human affection flow, and on which philanthropy itself is based ;" that if men deny themselves, or sacrifice themselves for mankind, it is because it pleases them to do it, and therefore it is but self-love which moves their action, after all. Be it so. The problem of society on which its salvation hangs, is how to discover or to create the men and the women whose self-love will take this benign and holy form, who please *themselves* by serving and saving their fellow men. There are two selves ; the lower which isolates a man, and makes him, if he obeys its mandate, a centre to himself ; and this is the self-love, or rather it is the love of this self, which distracts, disrupts, and destroys society. And there are those who find "themselves" in the higher part, which is born of God and which obeys His attractions ; it becomes their second and higher nature to fulfil the mandate and to enter into the joy of Him who gave Himself for mankind. They learn to love to do it in their measure; it fills them with such peace and such joy as the self-centred can never dream of, far less taste. You may say, if you will, that they please themselves in doing it; but you dare not call it selfishness; you feel instinctively that it belongs to an altogether higher sphere, to the sphere in which, as Epictetus says, man is "seeking to enter into fellowship with God."

And this is the key to what is said in Scripture about God making His own glory the end of His action. His glory is His love. To give His love full play in radiating blessing around, in cherishing the weak, in comforting the sad, in saving the lost, is His glory. It is His nature, He cannot but do it; but it is the joy, the life of the universe that it is His nature, and that He is ever seeking through Redemption to plant that nature in mankind. I say that the problem of society is how to multiply such natures, if a holy and benign order is ever to rise out of this chaos, if ever the world is to be saved. And where shall we seek them? What can create and multiply such friends of God? I answer, Christ, and Christ alone. This is the Redemption which is by Christ Jesus; not an arrangement which simply assures a personal salvation, which is mostly conceived of in these days as an immunity from penalty and pain, but that quickening of the life of love which makes men seek their joy in serving, in blessing, in saving, through eternity.

And it is through sorrow that this Redemption is carried on and perfected. It lies at the root of all the most grievous pain that torments mankind. What may be called the pangs of nature are but slight and fugitive, compared with that anguish of man's spirit which grows out of his spiritual impulses and sympathies, which is connected with his duties and relationships, and involves, in some shape or other, sacrifice of himself. He may obey the impulses, and pain will attend and consecrate the sacrifice, but he will win the blessing; he will find a joy in the duty done, the gift given, the sacrifice offered, such as springs from no other fountain, and in which he is truly tasting the joy of God. He may refuse the duty or the sacrifice, as we are refusing them every day, and pain of another order, the pain which hath torment, will grow out of and punish the refusal. A man may live studiously to himself, in his home, in his business, in his kingdom, and may have the art and the power to make others minister to him. He is simply sowing the dragon's teeth which will spring up as armed men to smite him. But this ordinance of pain also is healing, not destroying; it is unto life and not unto death. Though there is intense bitterness in it, it is a bitterness which is doctrinal; it is God's warning to, God's compulsion on, men to choose the nobler life of duty and self-denial, in which, though there *may* be pain, though there *must* be pain in a world out of tune with the Divine idea, the pain is a fountain of pure and everlasting joy. We fear, like the disciples, entering into the cloud ; in the heart of the cloud was Christ in His glory. We shrink from the pain in which, in our present condition of sickness and disorder, all holy and godly effort must involve us ; in the heart of the pain, if we have courage and faith to face it, there is the very joy of God.

We need only to look faithfully, with open face, now that the sunlight is shining upon them, at the dark, sad passages of our lives, to see how God was busy about us, by them and in them, developing the nobler part of our nature, that which draws us to the life of love ; and rebuking, chastising, and perhaps crushing the baser part which draws us to the life of self, and to the sorrow which hath torment in which it issues at last. And in the very suffering a thousand tender and beautiful efforts and ministries were drawn forth around us, opening a new spring of the purer joy in the hearts that offered them ; tending to the rebuke, the humbling of the pride and self-seeking which distracts and weakens, and to the increase of the love which heals and saves.

We are not always conscious of the redemption which pain is working ; nor know we the ways in which it is preparing the soul to listen to the word which will surely reach it, " Rise up and live." And this unfolds to us the difference, which is profound and vital, between the Stoic and the Christian philosophy of life. Both agree that man is born to trouble, and that life must be a long, stern battle with pain. The Stoic tries to isolate himself, to detach himself inwardly even from the body, and from its surroundings, and to inure himself to believe that the pain which touches these does not truly touch the man. Epictetus puts this view with singular sharpness; "If a raven happens to croak unluckily, let not the appearance hurry you away with it, but immediately make this distinction to yourself, and say, 'None of these things is portended to me, but either to my paltry body, or property, or children, or wife, but to me all portents are lucky if I will.'"

The Christian, on the other hand, is taught not to detach but to relate himself. The whole genius of the Bible, and of the teaching and influence of Christ, is distinctly against the ascetics, who reproduce in Christendom, with other and deeper principles of action than the Stoics dreamed of, the ideas of the Stoic School. Many motives conspired to draw men to the "religious life" in the "ages of faith." Some were attracted to it as to a quiet nook of peace and of silence, in the midst of a world full of cursing and bitterness, of violence and blood. Some were tempted to what they took for a closer imitation of Christ — imitating the outward conditions of his life. Some by a passion for pain as a means of purification; and some by the Stoic idea that it is the part of a wise man to curtail to the utmost the surroundings and the external necessities of his life. But Christianity seeks distinctly to multiply and to strengthen the bonds of association, to develope man's dependence on his fellows, and thereby to feed, a Stoic would say, the sources of human pain.

Christ teaches us to cultivate the tenderest human affections, and to widen to the very utmost the circle of our sympathies and loves. "*Who is weak and I am not weak? Who is offended and I burn not?*" said the man who held himself forth as an example whereby men might the more closely follow their Lord. Christianity, far from corrugating us, far from hardening and reducing our surface, expands it immensely, and makes us sensitive to pain at every pore. Christ was actually touched to tears by the sight of a sorrow which He knew that He could turn, and which He meant to turn, to exulting joy. And why is this? It is *from* pain that the Stoic seeks to save himself; it is *through* pain that Christ seeks to guide His friends to the springs of joy that lie within and beyond. Was not Marcus Aurelius on the track of this deep truth when he wrote the words, "Accept every thing that happens, even if it seem disagreeable, because it tends to this —the health of the universe"?

The more intensely we feel, the more this redeeming force finds in our nature to work upon, the more the God who is Love can breathe by His spirit through the whole organ of that nature, and draw forth from it music in tune with the songs of Heaven. God would not have us harden ourselves to any affection, deny ourselves to any claim, or hide ourselves from any sorrow. He has no will that we should suffer; His will is that we should be blessed. And therefore He will have us "deny ourselves" and "bear our brother's burdens," and "look upon the things of others" with the same tender consideration that we bestow upon our own. And all the pain which comes to us through the service which we render, the sacrifice which we offer, the loves which we cherish, He knows will be a true fountain of benediction; which, troubled and turbid as it must be through life's confusions for the moment, will flow bright and clear through eternity.

·And what is meant by the redemption of the world? Simply the spreading through it of this life of love; love to God, love to man for the dear love of God. The worldly wise, the economists, the believers in that which they can see and measure, and in that alone, smile at this notion or laugh it to scorn. Mr. Stephen, from whom I have already quoted passages from which I utterly dissent, says plainly—indeed there is no sort of want of the most utter plain-speaking in his book—" The great mass of mankind are and always will be; to a greater or less extent, the avowed enemies of considerable sections of their fellow-creatures; at all events for certain purposes and up to a certain point . . . The question is this : Are the interests of all mankind identical ? Are we all brothers ? Are we even fiftieth cousins ?" p. 286.

Now I do not simply say that a passionate yearning for brotherly relations between men and nations has been developed by Christianity, though the fact is unquestionable. Brotherhood was near to the heart of all the great movements of human society during the formative ages of Christendom. It was the idea which sustained the Holy Roman Empire; it possessed and animated the Monastic Orders; it was steadfastly witnessed to by the strongest institution which has ever established itself on earth—the Holy Roman Church. But I do not insist here on this aspect of the subject. I say that it is the dominant idea of our era, and it furnishes the one hope that some great step towards the social salvation of humanity is about to be gained. When I speak of it as the dominant idea, I mean not so much that it is the idea which has visibly mastered, and is visibly reigning in the popular sphere, as that it is the idea which has the strongest hold upon the master-minds of our era, is behind all its most powerful and progressive movements, and is winning its way to recognition as the power which will one day make a holy and benign order in our chaotic and distracted society.

The passionate ardour with which the Christian lover of his fellow men asserts it, on the one hand; the enthusiasm with which men like Mr. Mill and Mr. Harrison, and those from whom they differ as widely as from us,—the ranting democratic leaders,—preach it on the other, is profoundly significant and full of promise. All round society there is a ring of influence which draws it to the recognition of the life of love, that love which "seeketh not her own," as the one power which can heal the breaches and repair the waste in the shattered social order of our world. And it is the conservator of human society at this moment. There are passions every-

The Meaning of Redemption. 87

where in full force which are straining and rending the fabric, and would speedily shatter it to fragments, but that it is bound together by stronger loves. We talk much, and most justly, of the terrible selfishness, the brutal doggedness and fierceness with which men are fighting for their own interests, and carrying up the dread struggle for life, which rules through the Creation, into the human sphere. But we forget the myriad charities—I mean by that, the words, the looks, the deeds of which love is the inspiration —which underneath all this outward and visible struggle are weaving the bonds which hold homes and States together, and which constitute families, tribes, and nations, instead of mere herds of men.

There is a man, for instance, who is cold, stern, pitiless, in business, prompt to seize every advantage, and to act out to the full the maxim "every man for himself." But he has a sick wife, let us say, at home, or a family of orphans which his dead brother left to his care, or children of his own, on whom he lavishes the tenderest solicitude, and for whose culture and welfare he is content to toil, and would be content to die. And thus he is building on the one hand by love, while on the other, by hard selfishness, he destroys. There is a poor woman who earns her bread hardly, and has to fight and wrestle for her beggarly share. She has a sharp tongue, a wild temper, and seeks solace now and then in a drop of drink, or in ugly words. But there is a poorer next door, sick and helpless. And she will take her last loaf, her last pinch of tea, and share it with the poor sufferer; she will watch by her sick-bed night long, and then will go off, more cheerfully than you from your soft couches, to her round of toil. There is a rude, rough lot of reckless fellows, a curse to their neighbours, a curse to themselves. Their country gets hold of them, dresses them, drills them, and sends them off to fight her battles. It is poor pay that she gives them, and hard fare. But there they will stand, cool and confident, the long day through, to be shot at; and when shot down,—bleeding, shattered, tortured—they will shout "Hurrah for old England!" with dying lips, and feel a glow about their hearts, as they drop and die for the dear country that bred them and nursed them to manhood, which Dives there might envy, wallowing in his purple and gold.

Ah! the world is full of noble heroisms and gentle charities, which already hold it together by their bands of strength and tenderness, with a force of cohesion which, blessed be God, all the pressure of selfish greed and passion is powerless to destroy. And what is wanted for the salvation of society but that this life of love shall spread its healing, purifying, compacting ministry through all its spheres? As men rise higher they find growing joy in these ministries; the pain of such effort and sacrifice is to them sweeter than the most vivid self-seeking pleasure. When the great world is lifted to the same level to which God from heaven has drawn, and is ever drawing, His friends; when men, the wide world through,

The Meaning of Redemption. 89

live as brethren in one Father's home, the world of human society will be saved.

This is the power which has abolished slavery in Christendom. It is often said that the Old Testament sanctioned slavery. It tolerated it for the time, carefully mitigating its harshness, while it was planting the principle which would strike it to the heart. Thou shalt not enslave thy brother, was the stern command. As the idea of brotherhood widened its scope, slavery narrowed its area. When men came to understand that all men are brethren in Christ Jesus, slavery was doomed. It was by the sword of that old Jewish commandment, wielded by men who believed in the brotherhood, that slavery was killed.

This, then, is the power which is to heal and to save man in his societies and in his world. Is it not transcendently wonderful and beautiful, that it is to this life of love that God is redeeming mankind by the sacrifice of Himself? It is this life of holy, self-denying ministry which He came down to live among us, to reveal to us as the Eternal Life, wherein is the perfect and perennial bliss. The philosophers see in all ages that love is the power which helps and heals, and God has kindled by the breath of His own great love the fire of this holy life on all the sacred altars of the world. His redemptive work brought it down from the sphere of ideas to be a living, practical power. Through Christ it entered the congress of the forces which are moulding and moving society, and at once by divine right it took the command of the whole. "*Hereby know we love, because He hath laid down His life for us, and we ought to lay down our lives for the brethren.*" The heart of the whole mystery is here. We have but to lift our lives, and to help to lift mankind, to the level of this sympathy, and the problem of society is in process of solution; the world as a world is being saved.

The struggle for life which rules in the lower spheres of the Creation becomes transformed, transfigured, when it enters the human; it is thenceforth through God's redeeming touch a struggle to comfort, to cherish, and to bless. Man, lifting up his head as he emerges from the material order of Creation, and becomes consciously a spirit, with a spirit's burden of duties and destinies, is met by God with a Gospel which unveils to him the deepest mystery of spiritual being, which teaches him how to grow rich by giving, strong by serving, wise by teaching, blessed by blessing; while it opens for him a field for the expansion of his being, and for the development of his relations with God and with his fellows, which will remain boundless through eternity.

To unfold the mystery of the Divine life, this life of love, Redemption was essential. Therefore I say that man is a being born to be redeemed, and that Redemption is presupposed in the whole structure and constitution of our world. And this vision of humanity at rest at last in the arms of love, they tell me, is a dream, a fable baseless as the legend of

Utopia. Well, I confess that I recognise that Utopia joyfully as "the city which hath foundations," the "fatherland" of my spirit, which has the deepest instincts and the most passionate longings of universal humanity for its witness, the whole development of history for its harbinger, the Bible for its prophet, God for its founder, and Christ for its king.

V.

THE PAIN OF PROGRESS.

" Thy heart shall fear, and be enlarged."—Is. lx. 5.

ENLARGEMENT of heart is the true description of that higher progress to which it is ever the aim of God to lead us; the text pictures the process, and unfolds to us both the pain and the joy. I think that the language of the prophet is intended to present to our mind's eye that nameless dread, that inward shrinking and shuddering, with which the forecast shadows of great crises affect us as we approach them, and through which lies our passage to a larger freedom, a larger power, and a larger joy. Enlargement of heart means truly, the acquisition of a larger faculty for the reception of the thoughts and the plans of God; a new sense of the spiritual breadth and fulness of the world into which we are brought forth by Redemption, and a stirring of the faculty within us to grasp and to wield the powers and prerogatives of this loftier sphere. *" My soul cleaveth unto the dust, quicken thou me according to thy word,"* is really a prayer for enlargement of heart. Let new vital floods permeate and purify the dust-choked channels of my being, and bring a wider breadth of faculty within me to unfold itself to the kindling of the Divine love. The love is always around us; the sunlight of God is always shining; it is just a question of how much we display to it which it may purify and quicken, or how much we shut up within the hard, cold crust of our selfishness, and mix, not with sunlight or sun-warmth, but with dust. It is the self-infolding—the shutting ourselves up in our own little beggarly world, fearing to live at large, and to obey the Divine behests, having a single eye to our own narrowest interests, and no eye for the things not seen and eternal—which makes the dust the congenial field of such dull activity as the self-centred can manifest. And it is the self-unfolding, the throwing wide the gates of the soul that the God of love may enter and claim us as His friends, and use us as His ministers in working out His great plans of blessing, which the text describes as enlargement—an enlargement of life, out of which is to grow a fuller benediction to mankind.

I often think, paradox as it may seem, that it is a sign of the lofty spiritual destiny of our race, that man instinctively cleaves to the past, and shrinks from the future. He is always for returning on the old, well-trodden path to the Paradise of his memory; it is but the loftier and more highly cultured spirits that stretch forward to the heaven of their aspirations and hopes. I have already spoken of this constant back-look of humanity; this bemoaning of a past, which, in the form in which memory cherishes it, can never be restored. It is characteristic of all heathen peoples who have expressed their mind in a literature; always there is the golden past in bright contrast to the dark present and darker future; or if there is some golden gleam in the far distance, it is always the "Saturnian reign restored." It may be said that this is simply the memory of the joy, the carelessness, the vivid delight in beauty, which is the endowment of childhood, recalled by the way-worn pilgrim of the wilderness, and translated into a "Paradise lost" for mankind. If this were a sufficient account of the matter, it would still surely be most significant and prophetic. Is life nothing but disenchantment? Is *désillusionné* the epitaph of our race? The golden glow of the past fondly traced as it lingers on the ridges of the desert, as the way grows sterner, and the pastures barer daily, *must* mean that there will be one day a brighter glow in the future; unless, indeed, a mocking demon has had power to arrange all the order of life and of the world.

It is very wonderful how all the great things which have largely influenced the world, have grown from small, narrow, hard, but intensely vital beginnings, and have grown by enlargement of heart. Indeed, all seeds are small, hard, and dry until the genial moisture touches them, and it is with enlargement that the process of growth begins. Let us look for a moment, from this point of view, at the greatest of all institutions, the Church. To me the Divine Hand is as patent as the sunlight, in the whole order of human development under the in-

The Pain of Progress.

fluence of Revelation. If it be a chance coincidence that the kingdom which the Lord Jesus founded, —which has been the formative influence on the strongest and most cultivated peoples, nursing their infancy, training their youth, arming their manhood, and guiding their steps in the destined path—was prophesied ages before in the literature, and still more notably in the life, of the Jewish people, who believed themselves through eighteen centuries ordained to give birth to such a Deliverer, who sang of the Advent, prayed for it, waited, watched, and suffered for it, with a tenacity of belief which stands entirely by itself in human history; I say, if this be a chance coincidence, reasoning in any high sense seems to become impossible; we can but in that case, after the dreary Positive fashion, watch and register sequences, things that precede and things that follow, resigning all hope of discovering behind or beneath them the reason of their relation, which might give us an understanding of their meanings, and a forecasting of their results. "Looking before and after" would no longer be descriptive of the Godlike faculty within us; it would in that case be altogether a brute-like faculty, seeing only that which is around it in the dust.

There is a clear orderly progress, in the development of a Divine idea, and in the effect of a Divine influence on man, from the day when Abraham "crossed the river" until now. The Church is the depository of this sacred counsel, this redeeming purpose, which, as we have seen, underlies all man's history; and again and again and again the heart of the Church has been enlarged in seasons of sore strain and dread, to take in those wider ideas of its vocation, its mission from God and for God, for which, in the order of Providence, "the fulness of the time" was come. The Church now stands, as she has stood for ages, as the one absolute and authoritative witness for that brotherhood of humanity after which, as the true basis of a perfect human society, the philosophers and the political idealists have long been feeling; as well as for that law of love which alone can bind the bands of human society tightly enough to resist the constant disruptive pressure of man's selfishness and lust. The Church bore witness to these fundamental principles of human development, having revealed their bases in Christ; she clung to them, strove for them, suffered for them, in ages when rivalry and martial frenzy were ruling passions in society, when the sceptre of authority, generation after generation, yielded itself to the grasp of the strongest, and when the rain that fell on the fields of human industry and toil was constantly the red rain of blood.

And yet the Church was cradled and nursed in a narrow nook of the world, and quite out of the visible fellowship of the race which it was set ultimately to save. For ages the community which bore this priceless gift for mankind in its bosom, was distinguished by its isolation, its narrow, secluded field of activity, its shrinking from national intercourse and alliances, and by an attitude towards

The Pain of Progress.

the great world which at last raised against it almost universally the charge of "enmity to the human race." It will not do to say that this was just the natural temperament of the Jewish people; that they cherished a churlish indifference to everything outside their narrow national pale; and that the large expansive ideas which Christianity made current came not at all from Judaism, but from the outside world as the result of the general progress of mankind.

The promise or prophecy which Christianity fulfils was lodged in the heart of the elect nation from the very moment of its birth. When Abraham "crossed the river," and founded in his patriarchal tent a spiritual community which has expanded, without break or pause, during four thousand years, until it now overspreads the world, the announcement of the purpose of his calling was made: "*Now the Lord had said unto Abram, Get thee out of thy country, and from thy kindred, and from thy father's house, unto a land that I will shew thee: and I will make of thee a great nation, and I will bless thee and make thy name great; and thou shalt be a blessing: and I will bless them that bless thee, and curse him that curseth thee; and in thee shall all the families of the earth be blessed.*"—Gen. xii. 1-3.

The leading teachers and rulers of the community, under Jacob's tent curtains, in the wilderness tabernacle, and on David's throne, grasped this promise and purpose, cherished it, and handed it down with new scope and emphasis to their heirs. Nor would it be difficult to shew that it was the tenacity with which they clung to this mission of their nation, which made them, through their narrow and selfish reading of it, a race of jealous, exclusive, and boastful spiritual aristocrats, who earned for themselves, as aristocracies of all sorts rarely fail in the end to earn for themselves, the hatred of mankind. With this great idea and hope concerning the Ruler and Redeemer of men in charge, they thought more of their own dignity as its trustees, than of the world for the sake of which it was entrusted to them; and they held themselves and their gospel jealously aloof from the nations. Their heart had to be enlarged at successive crises of the great world's history, by terrible shattering strokes on that crust of pride in which they had encased themselves. They had to learn, through great pain and fear, to take wider and nobler views of their mission, and to fulfil the very purpose of their calling in benediction to mankind.

I might trace through the whole course of Jewish history how this enlargement of idea and influence always came through shocks, sufferings, and mighty dread; but I will simply indicate two great eras in which the method and the results are very conspicuous, and which will serve as a key to all the rest. The time came when, in the purpose of Providence, these Jews, who had been trained in a narrow school and in almost entire isolation from the nations, were to be scattered abroad through the whole area of civilisation; carrying their knowledge of God, their Revelation, their habit of recognition of the Divine will, and of prayer as to a Father and Friend, among the Gentile peoples; setting up their Sabbath and their synagogue in every chief city of Asia and of Europe, and thus forming a nucleus of spiritual influence in every quarter, in which and by which Christianity might bring its power to bear freely on mankind.

They were to be planted out for the world's good among the nations, fulfilling their appointed task. But how and when did this enlargement begin? Through the terrible pressure, the dismay and dread, of the captivity. They passed through an awful agony as a people, in their long struggle and their final overthrow. Jerusalem was laid in heaps, amid such scenes of misery as hardly find a parallel in history, while "the wind bound them up in her wings" and bore them to a distant land, where they were compelled by the hard yoke of bondage to enter into those relations with surrounding peoples, which marks the opening of a new era in the spiritual history of mankind. How terrible the anguish was, how dark the dread by which and through which they were enlarged, their own oracles full sadly shew. Hear the agonised tones of their lamentation : "*Oh that my head were waters, and mine eyes a fountain of tears, that I might weep day and night for the slain of the daughter of my people!*"—Jer. ix. 1. "*My bowels, my bowels! I am pained at my very heart; my heart maketh a noise in me: I cannot hold my peace, because thou hast heard, oh my soul, the sound of the trumpet, the alarm of war. Destruction upon destruction is cried: for the whole land is spoiled: suddenly are my tents spoiled, and my curtains in a moment. How long shall I see the standard, and hear the sound of the trumpet? For my people is foolish, they have not known me; they are sottish children, and they have none understanding: they are wise to do evil, but to do good they have no knowledge. I beheld the earth, and, lo, it was without form and void; and the heavens, and they had no light. I beheld the mountains, and, lo, they trembled, and all the hills moved lightly. I beheld, and, lo, there was no man, and all the birds of the heavens were fled. I beheld, and, lo, the fruitful place was a wilderness, and all the cities thereof were broken down at the presence of the Lord, and by his fierce anger."*—Jer. iv. 19–26.

It was thus that the work was done; and Judaism from that time forth began to mix itself with humanity, and to help in the direct preparation of the world for the Advent of her Lord.

Ages rolled on, and the fulness of the time came when the great enlargement of the heart of the Church and of the world was to be accomplished. Those who had been trained to believe in the brotherhood of a little national community, and to recognise the duties which sprang from it, were to enlarge their hearts to become witnesses of the brotherhood of humanity, and of the law of love as the one vital bond of souls, of homes, and of States. It was through the strain and the anguish of another more dire, more utter national overthrow, through the crushing of the crust of their self-centred ideas and habits under the iron heel of Rome, through such dread and horror as the Saviour calls unparalleled, and speaks of as the end of the world, that the Jewish was to be enlarged into the Christian Church. Read the twenty-fourth chapter of the Gospel according to St. Matthew if you want to understand what that enlargement cost.

The history of Christendom is precisely in the same key. The tendency of companies and communities entrusted with large gifts for men, is to grow self-enfolded, to limit the field of blessing to the pale which they have fenced round them, and to claim as the property of an election what is the heritage of mankind. And the work of God in all ages is to tear up this " pale," rending its stakes into faggots for the burning, and to stir the nobler and more generous souls among His servants to preach a larger gospel to a larger world. And always it is through fear and anguish that the enlargement progresses ; and it is mostly in the midst of tremendous external shocks and convulsions, and under the pressure of events whose logic is too strong to be gainsaid, that the chosen few find the courage to take the onward step. They tremble as they take it, while the many watch, shuddering, the throes through which a new age of larger liberty, of wider vision, of holier relationship of souls, classes, communities, and nations is being born. It is thus that all great things grow. Even the Son of Man came " not to send peace upon earth, but a sword."

There is just one secular thing, and but one,

which in its world-wide bearings and blessings, offers some faint image in the secular sphere of the benediction with which in every sphere the Church is laden. I refer to the Roman Law, which enters so largely into the code of every State in Christendom, and contains the essential principles of just and righteous law for man in all countries, and under all conditions throughout the world. It began in a very hard, narrow, and separatist doctrine. It enlarged its heart through ages of storm and strife, by throes and with anxious fears such as I may not stay here to dwell upon. Just as the Church was born in Abraham's patriarchal tent, the Roman Law was born of the rule of a stern, hard, patriarchal autocrat in his home. But it expanded through successive shocks, and under the pressure of imperative necessities, until that which was at first a singularly narrow and rigid code, but intensely real, honest, and vital—having its root in the most central of human relations, the *patria potestas*—grew to the largeness of the system which can give righteous judgments to mankind. This golden sentence of Ulpian, for instance, "*Justitia est constans et perpetua voluntas jus suum cuique tribuendo*," contains a catholic doctrine of justice; it is the truth of the matter everywhere round the wide world.

But I am specially anxious that you should see clearly that this growth in the Church itself, and in its relation to society, is strictly an expansion. It is not the putting of new wine into old bottles; it is not the introduction *ab extra* into an old and narrow system of new and universal ideas. All that Christianity has been to the world, and has done for the world, lay latent and germinant within the patriarchal household in Abraham's tents, when he walked with God on the wolds of Canaan, and "became heir of the righteousness which is by faith." He is distinctly, from the spiritual point of view, the father of many nations; he is the father of the whole company of the faithful till the end of time. Nor would it be difficult to show that the legislation of God for the Jewish people, the doctrine of brotherhood which was therein proclaimed, and the duties which were therein enforced, is that which, expanding age by age the circuit of its influence, has grown into the system of human duties which is recognised in Christendom, has abolished slavery, and has maintained against the strong hand and the hard heart "the cause of the afflicted, and the right of the poor."

One hears with a good deal of amazement of the abolition of Judaism. The "ism" of it no doubt died, as it deserved to die, but it died hard, it was so intensely compact and strong. Judaism has been abolished by making its history the sacred literature of every nation in Christendom, which is now being translated into every human language, that it may become the sacred literature of mankind. Abraham, Jacob, Moses, David, Solomon, Isaiah, are at this moment the most familiar names on human lips. The Jewish Psalms, in which is expressed the very spirit of the national life, have furnished the bridal hymns, the battle songs, the pilgrim marches, the penitential prayers, and the public praises of every nation in Christendom, since Christendom was born. It is a sentence from the Jewish Psalm book, which we have written over the portico of the chief temple of the world's industry and commerce, the London Exchange. These Psalms have rolled through the din of every great European battle-field, they have pealed through the scream of the storm in every ocean highway of the earth. Drake's sailors sang them when they clove the virgin waves of the Pacific, Frobisher's when they dashed against the barriers of the Arctic ice and night. They floated over the waters on that day of days when England held her Protestant freedom against Pope and Spaniard, and won the naval supremacy of the world. They crossed the ocean with the "May-Flower" pilgrims; they were sung round Cromwell's camp fires, and his Ironsides charged to their music; while they have filled the peaceful homes of England and of Christendom with the voice of supplication and the breath of praise. . In palace halls, by happy hearths, in squalid rooms, in pauper wards, in prison cells, in crowded sanctuaries, in lonely wildernesses, everywhere these Jews have uttered our moan of contrition and our song of triumph, our tearful complaints and our wrestling, conquering prayer. Yes, Judaism has been abolished, but with a glorious abolition. That which was the precious treasure of a feeble and isolated nation, God has abolished by making it the most cherished and priceless heirloom of our race. It was by enlargement, and not by revolution, that Christianity established its influence in our world.

Very interesting, too, would it be to trace how a kindred, I should rather say a parallel, course of enlargement has gone on in secular society. While God has been enlarging His Church, to comprehend better the meaning and the scope of His Gospel of love on the one hand, He has been enlarging, on the other, man's heart to receive and to rejoice in it. The world was prepared in a wonderful way, and by tremendous shocks and convulsions, for those preachers of the universal Gospel, and those founders of that universal kingdom, which is destined to gather under one sceptre and to bind in one bond of love, the scattered tribes of our race, whom the overthrow of Jerusalem scattered through the earth.

And looking at it only from the secular side, it is most notable, that the periods of man's greatest enlargement, when intellect and spirit have broken out of the old bounds, and have occupied a new world, have been ages of convulsion and revolution, of ceaseless conflict and awful dread. The Homeric poems were the fruit of a great era of struggle, whose special features we but dimly trace, while its broad character is written plainly enough in history. The life of the Greek cities, like the life of the Italian cities throughout the conflict of the Papal and Imperial powers for the mastery and the government of Christendom, was one ceaseless crisis. We may use the same term to describe the life of our own country during her long battle with Catholic Europe, under Elizabeth; and yet out of these eras of constant pressure, intense suffering and dread, the world's masterpieces of art, literature, and heroic achievement were born.

"Yes!" some will be ready to answer, "this is just the struggle for life which lies at the root of the development of the Creation, working up through the human sphere. Conflict and suffering are the conditions of progress. Where the strain is sharpest the faculties are on full stretch, and there the wisest words, the noblest actions, the most perfect works may be expected to appear; there you will find the brightest out-flashings of genius, and the masterpieces of the creative intellect of mankind. But it is only the struggle for life repeating itself under higher forms; it is all battle and blood, always battle and blood, and will be to the end." And there is but one end for those who believe this, but one issue which bounds their sight; the old Stoic vision of the conflagration which shall sweep at last all beings and all things, gods, men, and creatures, into the blackness of an everlasting night!

But I have endeavoured to show how the vision of a fairer order has never been wanting to mankind; an order of which not strength but sacrifice shall be the centre; in which brotherhood shall supplant the unnatural relations of which self is the foundation, and peace shall drive the demon of discord from the earth. Man has never been without such visions to light his sad, dark path. When the path has been darkest, these visions have always been brightest; it is in the seasons of strain and dread that the fairest pictures of this higher order of things have been pourtrayed. There is a vigorous protest in our nature, which will not be silenced, against this confusion, this ceaseless jarring of interests and struggle of forces, as the prime factors of human development. Man knows in his heart of hearts, and he says it in all ages by the lips of his poets and prophets, and in every age with increasing clearness, that while this condition is shared with those lower orders of the Creation with which the material part of him is so closely related, he is to leave it beneath him as he emerges into that higher region for which he was created, and to which he has been redeemed by God.

If life is mainly a mere struggle of force, it is to man's shame, and he knows it. It is his cleaving to the dust that makes it so. God by Redemption has brought a new and holy world of thought and activity within the range of his spiritual powers; a world whose service is ministry, whose life is love. The problem of the life of man as a member of a society, a brother of a race, is how to substitute for the struggle of force which rules the progress of the Creation, that bond and law of love of which Christ's life was the perfect revelation, and which rules, the Scripture tells us, in the kingdom of the blessed ones who are gathered on high. There is travail everywhere through all the spheres of Creation; and man's life, standing as it does on the summit level of mere creature development, travails in birth with a Kingdom of Heaven; a kingdom with a new commandment—Love one another.

We have seen how those who have led the vital development of humanity, and its apostles whose mission is among the masses of its poor, have believed in this Kingdom with unwavering faith, and served it with passionate devotion. Paul when he laid himself on the altar of sacrifice to spend and to be spent for mankind—the most blessed man upon earth, with all his cares and pains, in doing it—had solved for himself life's hardest problem, and indicated the form of its solution to his fellow-men. You may say if you will, that all this is sheer fancy; that "men are to a large extent natural enemies;" that the struggle for life is the one key to the development of man as well as of nature, and will be so while either man or nature endures; and that this is the only "practical" view, and the only solution of the mystery in which "practical" people can rest.

Practical! Tell me, ye who worship the practical, and who see no loftier forms of things beyond it, had you been living in the day when Christ stood to answer before Pilate, and spoke strange words about truth, would you not have been bound to consider it, as Pilate did, the merest dreaming that ever crossed the imagination of an enthusiast? And yet it proved itself practical enough to remake the world. And see you not, that through the whole of society, except in that mid-level region which prosperous common sense and common place have made all their own, there is a deep and passionate dissatisfaction with the selfish basis and constitution of things, which the infidel communist, and the Christian lover and servant

The Pain of Progress. 109

of his race, equally share? The conviction has firm hold on men all round the social sphere, that man alone of all the creatures, is called to live after a loftier pattern, to bear his brother's burdens, and to seek his brother's good, with an earnest sincerity which is caught, little as some may know it, from that God who call us His friends, whose plans and hopes it is the joy and glory of our being to share.

Impossible, you say, men are selfish, they are born selfish, and will be selfish to the close. I believe, on the contrary, that a fire of zeal and of love is kindling in the great heart of Christian society, which will burn up your "impossibles" as grass shrinks before flame when it roars through the forest. I believe that the long groaning and travail of man's life is ending, and that the heart of Christendom is being enlarged, through pain and fear and pressure, as of old, to take in a wider thought and a more blessed hope of God's kingdom; though the perfect fulfilment of the hope may still be far, far away.

I said, that it seems to me a sign of the lofty destiny of our race, that man unconsciously, or half consciously, clings to the past and shrinks from the future. The statement may seem like a paradox, and the fact, if it be a fact, may appear to tell quite the other way. I will explain what I mean. I think, too, that it will explain much of the strife and pain which attend the development of the life of society. What man shrinks from is just the strain. It is the greatness of his destiny which oppresses him, and sometimes appals. The child is careless of the future as of the present. The experienced know the meaning of the burden of life. It was his vision of the magnitude of his work, and of the load which it would lay upon him, which made Moses tremble as he touched it; not otherwise was it with Peter and with Paul. And further, all the great stages of growth are through sickness, in all the levels of the creation. The eagle moulting is sad and puling as the dove.

There is always an inward disturbance and sickness as the great crises of life approach us. Who is sufficient for these things? is the cry of the weak, sad heart, as it measures the greatness of its vocation and feels the trembling and fluttering within. I believe that this has more to do with the offence of the Cross than many of us dream. It is not vanity, or indifference, or sensuality, which hinders in so many the welcome of the heart to the Gospel of the Kingdom; but the dread of the lofty life to which it calls them, the heavy burden, the cross which it means to lay upon them, the sharp pain through which all its joy and glory are to be won. You know now your bearings, as it were; how much life demands of you, and how much you are willing, and think you are able to pay. "But," you say to yourself, "if I launch out from my quiet cove, into this vast unknown sea of being, whose only shore is God, who can tell what experience may await me, what dangers may assail me, through what storms I may have to urge my way?" Thy heart shall fear and be enlarged, if thou hast faith to hold on; it shall still fear, but be wasted and shrivelled, if thou hast the folly to fly. Onward, upward ; there lies the path of life and of benediction. Backward, downward; there lie the blackness and the foulness of the pit.

And it seems to me that there is a great sickness, the sickness of fear and the sense of an approaching travail, stealing now through the heart of society. The world is sick at heart, because the time of its change, of its breaking out into a new and higher mode of thinking and living has come. I think that men are very, very weary of the shock of interests and of the clash of arms, and are quite sure that such a world and such a life as they see everywhere around, have the stain of the dust upon them, and not the light of heaven. They are very hopeless of any lofty progress under the inspiration of the ideas which have framed the institutions and have guided the development of modern society; or rather, for the real forces lie deeper, which have been shouted as the battle-cries of the parties who think that they have charge of the progress of the world. There seems to be a great sadness in the heart of the chief spiritual and intellectual leaders of our day. There seem to be multitudes in all the social spheres saying to themselves, the world has been groaning and travailing for ages, and is this the birth that is to gladden humanity? Is this the salvation that cost such infinite sacrifice? Is this the fruit which is to satisfy the heart of Christ? Mr. Browning's Pope is not the only man in these days who is asking, " Is this thing that we see salvation?"

And there seems, too, to be a fearful foreboding

that a time of trial, of searching and purifying is at hand; that great organic changes are in progress; that the time has come when the demon of self which has torn and convulsed society must at least be cast down from his supremacy, while Love, heavenly Love, must have freer access and larger room to help, to heal, and to save.

This is the great enlargement of heart and of thought of which all others are but harbingers: the opening of the spirit of man and of the spirit of society to receive in its fulness the Gospel of the Kingdom; to rise by faith to fellowship with the purposes and the hopes of God; to believe in the transcendent power of that love which redeemed, to rule and to bless mankind. Things looked at in one way, from one side, seem sadly bare of promise; looked at from another, they are vivid with hope. Nothing is more wonderful in history than the swiftness and the thoroughness with which great moral changes accomplish themselves, when the time of fear and strain, which is the time of enlargement, has come. Old things, which seemed to be strong as the everlasting hills, break up and vanish. Society organises itself to-day on what was yesterday an " impossible ;" and men wonder at their faithless fears. We may be on the eve of such a revolution now. "The times are out of joint," the world's heart is sick and sad. The timorous and faithless, and those that love this dreary twilight, may live to see the whole system of things, which to them seems permanent as the frame of the Creation, break up around them; while they and the world are lifted through the wreck by a force which they have no heart to believe in, and no gauge to measure, to levels that are nearer heaven.

VI.

THE LORD IS MY LIGHT AND MY SALVATION.

"*The Lord is my light and my salvation, whom shall I fear? The Lord is the strength of my life, of whom shall I be afraid.*"—Ps. xxvii.

I THINK that this is the Psalm of Psalms. All the elements of vital force with which these Psalms are charged, are here in their highest power. When it was written, or why it was written, we know not. But we know that David, when he wrote it, must have been lifted into the sphere of the purest and most intense experience of which the human spirit can be the subject; and yet—and this is the mystery of the Psalms, and the secret of their spiritual power— it is a region into which the aspiration of the poorest, the weakest, the most burdened human heart can follow him, nor is it closed against the most trembling human step. Reading these words, or rather singing them,—for they were made to be our songs in this house of our pilgrimage,—we seem to be borne up, as the Prophet says, "on eagle's wings" into this upper firmament, which David calls the pavilion, the tabernacle of the Most High. We catch the glow of the Psalmist's inspiration; his joy in God enters into us, and stirs a kindred passion. " The Lord is my light and my salvation," we, too, find ourselves singing, " The Lord is the strength of my life, of whom shall I be afraid ?" A poor, stammering, trembling mortal, the creature of a day, crushed before the moth; who thought himself yesterday but as a worm or as a beast before God, is caught up as he hears the Psalmist singing in the height. Something within expands and glows as he soars : he feels that he, too, can bear part in this blessed music ; that this God is his God as well as David's ; that he also is the child of Christ and of the resurrection, a free citizen of the eternal celestial world.

If they are our best and most blessed helpers who lift us into a world which lies beyond and above the round of our common tasks, and the dusty paths along which we daily plod, who give to us a new sense of things unseen, open for us new springs of faith and hope, and teach us to "count them blessed which endure," what shall we say of these Psalmists, who, through thousands of years, have furnished an unfailing fountain of strength and inspiration to some of the strongest, the noblest, and the most aspiring children of our race ? These Psalms are like the cells of a battery of vital force, which generate the current that is always permeating the tissues and the nerves of Christian society—conductor of a throbbing, thrilling, exuberant, victorious life. The life is not in them ; they are as the cells which store and transmit it. To open one of David's Psalms when we are sad and weary, overpressed in life's battle, or overworn by its pain, is like touching a stream of magnetic force ; it bathes all the being with its soft, tender, yet stimulating and energising flood. The strain is relaxed, the pain is soothed, the nerveless arm is braced again, the fainting heart grows strong and glad ; something has entered into us from a Divine fountain, which makes us sharers of the strength, the joy, and the hope of God.

I have spoken of exuberant, victorious life. Who does not catch in this Psalm the note of exultation ? It is the word of a man who, at the moment at any rate, felt that his joy was over-abounding. " More than conqueror," is the cry that rings through these triumphant words. He felt that there was with him, within him, a strength which all the malignant forces in the universe were powerless to cope with—and to an oriental the malign element in nature always seems fearfully strong ; he knew that his foot was firm on the everlasting rock, against which the gates of hell must rage in vain.

The man who wrote this Psalm was no novice in the school of discipline. The cry of a soul in anguish was to him no unfamiliar utterance. "*Deep calleth unto deep at the noise of Thy waterspouts; all Thy waves and Thy billows are gone over me,*" had often broken from his lips. But from the rock to which his God had lifted him, he could watch the great sweeping billows shatter themselves in foam and perish, while he sang, "*And now shall mine head be lifted up above mine enemies round about me, therefore will I offer in His tabernacle sacrifices of joy, I will sing, yea I will sing praises*

The Lord is my Light and my Salvation. 117

unto the Lord." There breathes through this Psalm just that sense of the over-mastering power, the over-abounding fulness of God's grace and love, which rings out in the exulting language of St. Paul, *" The law entered that the offence might abound. But where sin abounded, grace did much more abound ; that as sin hath reigned unto death, even so should grace reign, through righteousness, unto eternal life, through Jesus Christ our Lord."*

I have said that in these Psalms, and in this most especially, David enters into the very loftiest region of experience which can be reached by a human spirit. He climbs to heights beyond which man cannot pass ; he becomes partaker of the strength, and enters into the joy of God. But it is the peculiar glory of the Bible, that these heights do not seem to place men like David beyond the sympathy of the poorest and the weakest of their human brethren. There is nothing, here or anywhere, in the Bible which cuts off the humblest and the feeblest human soul from the very noblest and loftiest of our race, in their most exalted moments of vision and of joy. High as these men may soar, the world of the common daily life of the great mass of mankind is not cut off from them. They are not by themselves in a heavenly region, while the great world beneath them grovels, according to its nature, in the dust.

Men like Moses, Isaiah, David, Paul, and John, draw men to them, and with them, as they rise. They speak of heavenly things, they behold the heavenly vision, they pass within the shrine where they gaze on the splendour of the Uncreated Light, and see with open face the unveiled glory of the Lord. But the most lowly and undisciplined human intellect finds their thoughts within the range of its comprehension, and their vision not altogether beyond its sight. Lofty as are the themes with which this Psalm is conversant, profound as is the human experience which it unveils, it has yet been the pilgrim-song through ages of multitudes of the poorest, the lowliest, the most oppressed and downtrodden of our race. From how many a house of bondage, from how many a prison cell, from how many a den of human suffering and toil, from how many a hospital ward, from how many a pauper's death-bed, from how many a rack of torment or blazing pile has the song gone up to heaven, "*The Lord is my light and my salvation, whom shall I fear? The Lord is the strength of my life, of whom shall I be afraid?*"

And this is the distinguishing glory of Christianity, that its poor have the Gospel preached unto them, and are as much within reach of the understanding of its mysteries, as much within the clasp of the arms of its love, as the wisest, the noblest, the most instructed of mankind. The bread which nourished its Prophets, Psalmists, and Evangelists, is "the bread of God which cometh down from heaven," and it is freely offered as the gift of God's grace and love to the poorest and hungriest prodigal who tramps the wilderness, or gathers husks from the troughs of swine. It is the bread of the Father's house for each and for all of them, for all are children of the great human family which the Father seeks to reclaim and to restore. It is the bread which is their primal and natural nourishment, the hunger for which never quite dies down in the most self-abandoned outcast's heart.

The Bible has no esoteric and exoteric doctrine. It has no higher truth which can only be appreciated by an elect and cultivated circle, while its lower and poorer truths satisfy the herd of the great uninstructed mass of mankind. There are no Scribes in the scheme of the kingdom which was developed by the Master, though the Christian Church is full of them. In all these later ages they have been the worst enemies of the kingdom ; they have hidden the key of knowledge, which is the Name of the Father, and thus have shut out the poor. But the genius of Christianity is against them. Perhaps what seem the most formidable and menacing signs of these times to our timorous apprehension, are really, at bottom, but the throes of the truth as it is in Jesus, as it struggles to cast them out.

But this is what all heathen religions in the end inevitably develope—even where, like Brahminism, they do not start with it—an inner truth for the doctors, the discerning, meditative disciples, and an outer truth which is good enough for the great mass of the poor. The wise, the scribe, the disputer of this world are sure to take possession of the truth which is embodied in a heathen religious system, as they have taken possession of Christianity ; and they are sure to keep possession, while in Christianity there is a force which casts them out. It is only God's word from God's own lips, which is nigh, equally, to all the children of our race; so large, so broad that the most eagle-eyed intelligence can find no bound to it; so simple, so vital, so like homely daily bread that the wayfaring man, though a fool, can possess himself of all its treasures, can grow "*wise unto salvation*" by it, "*and rich unto life eternal.*"

It is of the very essence of Christian truth that it should be so. He who gave it, who came to bear witness to it, though the first-born of every creature, the brightness of the Father's glory and the express image of His substance, God of God, Light of light, was the friend and familiar comrade of publicans and sinners. "*The common people heard Him gladly.*" The multitude thronged His steps and hung upon His words. "*Never man spake like this Man,*" they cried, because He told them of heavenly things, things which might strain a seraph's intelligence, in such a fashion that the poorest might apprehend them; because they felt themselves drawn by the teaching into the fellowship of God's perfect and everlasting truth. Indeed, it was the wise ones who understood Him least: "*I thank Thee, O Father, Lord of Heaven and earth, because thou hast hid these things from the wise and prudent, and hast revealed them unto babes.*" The Lord stands apart from all other teachers in having nothing to reserve for an inner select circle of disciples. There is no inner, no outer, there is no nearer, no farther, with God. "*The Word is nigh thee, in thy mouth and in thy heart,*" is God's message to every human soul.

In holy and beautiful harmony with the Lord's word, is the word of His Psalmists and Prophets. It is not the rich man's word or the poor man's word, the wise man's word or the ignorant man's word, the holy man's word or the sinful man's word; it is for man and to man, every when and everywhere. In all possible states and in all possible conditions it finds and lays hold upon man; it raises, redeems and saves him. We talk sadly about the wide diversities, the sundered, alienated classes of society: the upper ten thousand in their luxury and splendour, the lower ten million in their squalor and rags. From one point of view it is profoundly sad; it is a burning stain on our Christian civilisation. But from another, a higher and truer point of view, the differences dwindle and vanish. High and low, rich and poor, scholar and fool, prince and beggar, touch their highest, and touch the same height, when the music of a Psalm breathes from their lips, or when the word of a Prophet stirs and kindles their spirits. It needs the culture of a scholar to search out the hidden wisdom of the philosopher's gospel; it needs the special training of a priest to deal with the mysteries of a ceremonial faith: from the ignorant herd the one is hopelessly hidden, from the unclean, unsanctified mass the other. But I fancy that priest and laic, scholar and fool, prince and peasant stand all together, simply level, in that one grand, divine, eternal equality which is possible for man, when they sing with the Psalmist : " *The Lord is my Shepherd, I shall not want. He maketh me to lie down in green pastures: He leadeth me beside the still waters. He restoreth my soul; he leadeth me in the paths of righteousness for His name's sake. Yea, though I walk through the valley of the shadow of death, I will fear no evil: for Thou art with me; Thy rod and Thy staff they comfort me. Thou preparest a table before me in the presence of mine enemies: Thou anointest my head with oil; my cup runneth over. Surely goodness and mercy shall follow me all the days of my life; and I will dwell in the House of the Lord for ever.*"

"THE LORD IS MY LIGHT." It is just light which fills the Scripture, while the world without the Bible is, as the Bible says, "a dark place." The Scripture reveals man in the sunlight; in the sphere of joy, of vigour, of fruit. The world and life are dark indeed, without God. Dark is just the word which describes it. Let us consider for a moment how darkness works. Sow a seed and shut it up in a dark cellar: the darkness does not absolutely kill it. The germ starts, the blade, the stem, perhaps the bud; but they are weak, pale, contorted; there is no strength, no beauty, no fertility. It is but the ghost of the plant that you see there, yet still it is the ghost, the pale image of the perfect organism. But when the bud strives to bloom and fruit you see that its vital power is exhausted: it droops, drops, and lies dishevelled and fainting in the dust. If you

The Lord is my Light and my Salvation. 123

want form, if you want colour, if you want to see the red blood glowing, if you want beauty, vigour, fruit, you must have sunlight. Not light simply, the light diffused in the atmosphere, but sunlight, hot, flashing from the fountain; it is this that quickens germs, it is this that ripens fruits.

And the aspect, the bearing, the tone of these Psalmists, is that of men who lived in the sunlight; who had their vigour full in the springs, and all their faculty awake and abroad. They were men in whom the life was vivid; the blood bounding in the veins, the light flashing in the eye, the step elastic and joyous, with onward, upward pressure. They were men who saw their way through all the dangers and difficulties which environed them; who saw the home above all the obscurations and perturbations of this earthly sphere; who had no doubt about the present, no dread about the future, because God was with them, because the Hand that ruled all things was manifestly and for ever on their side. I think that it is this sense of sunlight upon our path, and on our hearts, which in these days we chiefly miss. This earth is becoming a dark place, I fear, to a great multitude; for the sense of a living Presence in the Creation, and around man's daily paths and tasks, which was as sunlight to the Psalmist, seems to be fading out of the world.

There is something unspeakably dreary to me, in the aspect of the world which some of our wise ones would make for us; a world from which one day they will be in an agony to escape. It is a world of dull, dead necessity; all things in it, and man among the things, moved by a blind, impassive force, which works, how no man knows, and to what end no man knows. It rules with the same calm, unconscious might, the clouds that float through the heavens, the straw that swirls before the breeze, the sweep of a comet, the transit of a planet, the path of a storm, and the surge of a tide. We but meet it again, we are told, in a higher stage, in the intuitions of a philosopher's brain, in the decisions of an apostle's will, in the " Here stand I " of a martyr's conscience, and in the yearnings and claspings of a tender, sympathetic heart.

It is all settled firmly and finally, they tell us, in the very frame-work of our constitution, what we shall will and what we shall do; while what we take for the play of our freedom, is but the fluttering of the needle ere it settles to the pole. And it is all fixed equally, we are assured, for the world. Purity, heroism, a man's purpose, a woman's tenderness, a child's trust, a nation's loyalty, a church's charity, are all, at bottom, mere mechanical movements of the great world-system around and within us; in which our lives are but the spindles that twist the threads. And then, when the little force that sets us in motion and keeps us in motion is expended, we are so much dead, waste matter, which Nature dissolves, that she may work it up in new forms for some other use. Freedom, responsibility, resurrection, immortality, a Kingdom of Heaven—it is all the dream of a vagrant imagination. Eat, drink, sleep, toil, suffer, perish, sums up, according to their philosophy, the destiny of mankind. A dark world, I say, profoundly dark, profoundly sad;[1] a world in which the buds of promise drop fruitless from the boughs, and man has nothing left in the end but to make his moan over the decree that dooms him to life.

It is no answer to say that many of the men of our time who have lost the hope of immortality, are among the wisest, best, and most high-minded among us. We are living still, thank God, in the sunlight of Christianity, and they drink in influences which strengthen, purify and cheer at every pore. They cannot, as yet, do what they will, get rid of their Christianity. But try to forecast the character of the world which these presumptuous seers—seers, not of God, but of Nature—would make for us in the end, if they could work their will; feel how dread it is, how chill, how empty of duty, of service, of sacrifice, of devotion, of all that kindles joy and quickens hope; and then turn and listen to the hymn, "*The Lord is my light and my salvation, whom shall I fear? The Lord is the strength of my life, of whom shall I be afraid?*"

It is like coming out of a dark, damp cavern into the sunlight; it is like exchanging the contact of

[1] Can anything be sadder than the closing sentences of Mr. John Morley's beautiful and appreciative notice of the late John Stuart Mill, in the "Fortnightly Review" for June 1873?—" Alas! the sorrowful day which ever dogs our delight followed very quickly. The nightingale that he longed for fills the darkness with music: but not for the ear of the dead master; he rests in the deeper darkness wherein is unbroken silence."

obscene, loathsome forms for the song of birds, the breath of flowers, the hum of joyous life, and all the noonday splendour of the world. If you want the light on your lives, if you want to be glad and strong, if you want deliverance from the terrors that haunt the darkness, if you want a firm footing, a clear path, a steady progress, the light brightening as you press on, if you want health, if you want life, come out into the sunlight of the gospel. "*Yet the Lord will command His loving kindness in the day time, and in the night His song shall be with me and my prayer to the God of my life . . . . Why art thou cast down, O my soul, and why art thou disquieted within me? Hope thou in God, for I shall yet praise Him, who is the health of my countenance, and my God.*"

"THE LORD IS THE STRENGTH OF MY LIFE."

Substantially this is the same doctrine which Christ delivers: "*I am the true vine, and my Father is the husbandman. Every branch in Me that beareth not fruit He taketh away; and every branch that beareth fruit, He purgeth it, that it may bring forth more fruit. . . . As the branch cannot bear fruit of itself, except it abide in the vine, no more can ye, except ye abide in Me. I am the vine, ye are the branches: he that abideth in Me, and I in him, the same bringeth forth much fruit; for without Me ye can do nothing.*" John xv. 1-5. *The strength of my life.* The stem that bears it, the root out of which its vital juices spring; that which makes it part of a living organism, whose ground, whose form, whose life is in God.

The Lord is my Light and my Salvation. 127

Its ground, the solid foundation on which it rests, is God. The joy of David in God is really a joy prophetic of the age of the Incarnation. It was God manifest to him, not yet in the flesh, but by human speech, human guidance, human care, human love, whom he knew, and in whom he rejoiced; the Being who in the Man Christ Jesus "became flesh," and is evermore present with mankind. The strength of our life as its sure, firm, and enduring foundation is this Gospel of " God manifest in the flesh." If this be a dream, if we have "followed cunningly devised fables" in believing it, then our life is rootless and fruitless as a herb in the sands of the desert. But if this be a reality, the life of the man who believes is as a house built on a rock; or rather "*like a tree planted by the rivers of water, that bringeth forth his fruit in his season. His leaf also shall not wither, and whatsoever he doeth shall prosper.*" The life of Christ, the death of Christ, the resurrection and reign of Christ, are the source to us of perpetual renewing. If death overshadow us, if fear distract, if sorrow distress, the Lord, if we turn to contemplate His cross and passion, and to search the mighty mystery of His love, puts heart of strength into us. Believing, we can "*count them blessed which endure.*" He is the strength of assurance, of firm standing ground, of victorious force. "*This is the victory that overcometh the world, even your faith.*"

And He is the strength of growth, of vital progress. Humanity, in a high sense, began to grow, to make living and lasting progress, when the Gospel of the Incarnation was first proclaimed in the world. And the people who before the Incarnation were most clearly in the line of progress, were the people whose life and all whose national institutions were prophets of the Incarnation; who but for the coming Emmanuel had absolutely no place or function in the scheme of human history. Cut off from living communion with Christ, the higher life of men and of peoples grows faint and feeble, its fruit poor and rare; at length all fertility dies out of the trunk that bore it; it becomes dry and withered, meet fuel for the final flame.

It is just the cutting off the life of the Christian world from Christ, who quickens it and feeds all its springs, which seems to me to be the most deadly danger of our times. A resolute attempt is being made by the school of philosophers which is strongest for the moment among us, to root Christianity henceforth in man, and not in God. The Christian graces, it is allowed, are very noble and very beautiful; self-denial, self-devotion (within limits), charity, purity, integrity, are all excellent and commendable. But suppose that we treat them henceforth as entirely flowers and fruits of the human stem; suppose that we cultivate humanity and leave divinity alone; we shall be surprised, we are told, to see how grandly they will grow.

It is just the intensity of my conviction that we shall find, and soon, that they will not grow cut off from Christ, but will wither like cut flowers, and will leave us all grey and bare, which makes me cling so tenaciously to the truth which breathes its music through this Psalm. Man was made for Divine communion. Christ is the root which bears man's regenerate, celestial life. Cut the communications of the soul with the spiritual world, or let them wither and snap, and then through the trailing tendrils the very life-blood of the spirit will drain away. Cast off fear, that fear which makes us men restrain prayer before God, turn from Christ as your great exemplar, close the eye to His beauty, harden the heart to His love—it is the suicide of the spirit. The current of life is choked at the fountains, the light is quenched in the everlasting night.

But " *The Lord is my life and my salvation, whom shall I fear? The Lord is the strength of my life, of whom shall I be afraid?* " He is the strength of the life, for we live in Him. " *Jesus said unto Martha, I am the resurrection and the life; he that believeth in Me, though he were dead, yet shall he live; and whosoever liveth and believeth in Me shall never die.*" " *Our life is hid with Christ in God, and when Christ who is our life shall appear, we also shall appear with Him in glory.*" " *Therefore my heart is glad, and my glory rejoiceth; my flesh also shall rest in hope.*" Why should a living man complain? What on earth or in hell shall he fear, when, after all is torn from him, he has life, an eternal future, and God? Here is strength to endure; here is strength to overcome. The endurance may be hard; the discipline may be long, and terribly sharp and

K

stern. But life abides through it, life grows by it; life has royal prerogatives and compels its tributes. They will but enrich and adorn the child of discipline, the heir of promise, when he passes up to sing the song with new exultation, where there streams all round him, and glows within him, the sunlight of the celestial and eternal world. *"Wait on the Lord, then, and be of good courage, and He shall strengthen thine heart; wait I say on the Lord."* *"When my father and my mother forsake me,"* when all earthly helps must fall from me, *"then the Lord will take me up."* Even into the valley of the shadow of death, I can pass with a song, *"O death, where is thy sting? O grave, where is thy victory? The sting of death is sin, the strength of sin is the law; but thanks be to God who giveth us the victory, through our Lord Jesus Christ."*

"THE LORD IS MY LIGHT AND MY SALVATION, WHOM SHALL I FEAR? THE LORD IS THE STRENGTH OF MY LIFE, OF WHOM SHALL I BE AFRAID?"

VII.
GOD'S GREAT WORLD.

" He brought me forth also into a large place."—II. Sam. xxii. 20.

A SOUL in anguish is a soul in straits, in narrows; in a place too small for it, in which it strains and writhes and beats against the bars, in vain. That is anguish—the prison bars tight about us, while we pant for freedom, light and joy. Man is a large being, and he needs a wide world to live in. Sin shuts him up in a small world; a prison-house, and iron-barred. It is a grand, free outline which God sketched at the first of a human being. So grand, so free, that there is but one hitherto who has been able to fill it up to its full form—Himself.

David was a man of this royal proportion. Such men need the universe and eternity to live out their lives. If the all of David was the little span of his mortal life, and the square inches of his kingdom, his life is one of the saddest sights that the sun ever shone upon. A glorious wealth of faculty, trained under the strain of terrible trials and sufferings, and trained for the dust. The lives of such men are the grandest arguments for immortality. If a malignant demon be not the Lord and Master of the universe, such a life as

David's must one day be brought out into a larger world than this.

David as a youth had roamed on the mountains. He had fed his flocks on the wolds of Canaan. He had lain many a night under the canopy of the solemn Syrian sky, burning with stars. He had lived, too, the life of an outlaw in the mountain fastnesses. He had made his lair, like a hunted beast, in their murky caves. He had watched the gates of the hills when the dawn began to flush the pallid sky; he had seen from some lofty crag the sunlight flash in one glorious moment over a slumbering world. I picture him shut up night-long in some close rocky cavern with his bandit troop around him: men of rude lips and rude life,[1] vexing the weary hours with their coarse oaths and jests. The air foul, stifling; the moral atmosphere of the outlaws' den fouler and more stifling still.

I think that I see him stealing out in the first cool gleam of the morning, faint, sad, weary— shut up with such comrades to such a life. But the fresh breath of the morning wind stirs his languid pulses; the blood bounds through his throbbing veins. He treads the well-known path to some rugged peak which shoots up into the calm, clear air above him. As he climbs he sees the mists seething in the valleys beneath. The horizon around him widens. Peak beyond peak in the dim distance begins to blush under the kiss of the coming sun.

---

[1] I. Sam. xxii. 1–2.

God's Great World. 133

A glorious sense of freedom possesses him. A baptism of power descends. His soul expands with his horizon. Life seems larger; its trials dwindle; its powers and destinies grow. As he rises above the mists and shadows in which his lair is buried, and climbs to the clear summit, the sun kindles a cold, dead world to vivid and glorious life. He sweeps his flashing glance over the broad landscape. The mists retire their routed masses from the plains beneath him; the broad, soft uplands, and now the valleys are unveiled. The blue ocean gleams softly in the distance, and melts into the violet mist which encompasses all.

He realises with a kind of rapture how wide the world is, how glorious. He knows that there is something yet larger, more glorious, stirring within. We can imagine the shepherd poet as he grasped all this, as he drank in new strength and courage, new joy and hope, from the vision of the infinite wealth and splendour of the world, bursting into strains of lofty exultation, and pouring forth his most splendid and joyous psalms. With what intense passionate fervour would he bless the name of the Lord, his shepherd, his friend, the man of his counsel, the guide of his pilgrimage, who had led him up to that mountain summit to unveil to him the glorious vision, and to kindle within him a glad hope of the future of his being, when he should emerge at last from a darker night on to a loftier summit, lit by the glow of a brighter dawning, and sweep the horizon of a wider world. *" Therefore my heart is glad and my glory rejoiceth; my flesh also shall rest in hope. For Thou wilt not leave my soul in hell, neither wilt Thou suffer Thine Holy One to see corruption. Thou wilt show me the path of life; in Thy presence is fulness of joy; at Thy right hand three are pleasures for evermore."*

"*Thou hast brought me out into a large place.*" The first thought which I offer in illustration of the sentiment of the text is this:

1. Sin brings the soul into straits, into narrows; sooner or later, anguish, the intolerable sense of straitness, is its inevitable result. It was no mere joy over landscape breadth and beauty which drew this burst of praise from David's lips, but rather the free world of grace and love into which he had been led forth by the Lord. The *promise* of sin is always freedom, the *experience* is always bonds, the prison-house, the rack. To our first parents the tempter cunningly opened the vision of liberty; a larger life he would offer to them, a larger world. He knew the imperial pretensions and powers of the being with whom he was dealing. He knew that mere pleasure would have but poor attractions for him, unless it also fired his imagination with visions of larger, freer, bolder life. The fascination of transgression to the young lies mainly in this direction. The round of quiet duty seems to them narrow and poor. Outside there are broad, gay, seductive regions, wooing the young prodigal's steps. It is long years before the sinner, searching, pining for the substance of his vision, finds that the promise was a mere

mirage of the desert, luring with its cool proffer the thirsty pilgrim to his grave. The prodigal saw a brilliant world there beyond deserts and oceans. As he journeyed thither, with all his wealth about him, his path was spanned by a radiant bow of hope. It was long years, perhaps, before he found the devil's promise fulfilled in rags, in husks, and the sties of swine.

But the first temptation is the key to all temptation. "*Now the serpent was more subtle than any beast of the field which the Lord God had made. And he said unto the woman, Yea, hath God said, ye shall not eat of every tree of the garden? And the woman said unto the serpent, We may eat of the fruit of the trees of the garden, but of the fruit of the tree which is in the midst of the garden God hath said, ye shall not eat of it, lest ye die. And the serpent said unto the woman, Ye shall not surely die; for God doth know that in the day ye eat thereof, your eyes shall be opened, and ye shall be as gods, knowing good and evil.*" Whether this be the revealed history of the outward pilgrimage of humanity or not, it is at any rate the revealed history of the inner moral development of mankind. God only could have furnished this key to the inner life of His child. "Go to," was the suggestion; "spurn these narrow bounds to which this cautious, selfish Creator would confine you; you were made for a wider theatre; explore your world; be master in your own house of life."

So the temptation ran. "*And when the woman saw that the tree was good for food, and that it was pleasant to the eyes, and a tree to be desired to make one wise, she took of the fruit thereof and did eat; and gave also to her husband with her, and he did eat.*" It was the vision of wisdom and freedom which enchanted them, which enchants us all, when the blood is hot, and the tempter is near. The sentence came, "*Because thou hast hearkened unto the voice of thy wife, and hast eaten of the tree of which I commanded thee, saying, Thou shalt not eat of it; cursed is the ground for thy sake; in sorrow shalt thou eat of it all the days of thy life; thorns also and thistles shall it bring forth to thee, and thou shalt eat the herb of the field. In the sweat of thy face shalt thou eat bread, until thou return unto the ground; for out of it wast thou taken; for dust thou art, and unto dust shalt thou return.*" The sentence disenchanted them. For them, at any rate, the spell was destroyed for ever.

But the prodigal's folly repeats itself in every age and in every life. Man must buy his own experience, and in the hardest market. No brother can buy vital knowledge for his brother; no mother for her child. The experience of anguish is inevitable. The broad, free way is the path of the commandment. The man who transgresses passes at once into straits. They narrow as he advances. At length they close on him and crush him, and cast him out a wreck to meet the destinies of eternity.

I say that all sin inevitably narrows, cripples, and destroys the freedom and energy of the human powers. You may judge of it for yourselves. Look round you on the men who are living evil lives, contemptuous alike of God and of His laws. How does it tell upon them? Watch them through the years. Do they become larger, freer, more joyful, more hopeful men? Does the service set a stamp on their brow which is their seal of honour? Do men love them, trust them, work for them, pray for them? Does life's outer gate, as they draw near to it, wear to them more visibly the splendour of the portals of heaven? You know them,—some of them,—the devil's most zealous, most loyal servants. And you have watched them grow more selfish, more lustful, more wretched, year by year. You know the mark which their master puts upon their countenances; you know little of the weariness, the disgust, the loathing of life, which he puts within their hearts. You know something of the misery of their present, you can forecast somewhat of the horror of their future. Measure by their life and lot the worth of the devil's promise, to lead you out "into a larger place."

And this process is inevitable. For sin dulls the edge of faculty, and rots the very fibres of aspiration and of hope. There is not a faculty of man's being which the devil has power to train by his service; there is not a noble desire or hope which he has the means of drawing forth and of directing to its end. Even to that desire of freedom which lends the chief fascination to transgression, he has nothing to offer but dreary, deadly, damning captivity. Man's powers, made to range in the free, broad universe of eternal things, bending themselves on objects which perish in the using, get weak, tremulous, crippled, and are stricken at last with a paralysis which is the beginning of death. Young men, if you want to dull the use of every faculty, to dim the clearness of every perception, to foul every spring from which a living joy can flow, make your own world, the world of your own schemes and ambitions, your own vanities and lusts, and live in it. But if you want expansion, exhilaration, inspiration, life, come out into the large free world of the truth, the righteousness, and the love of God.

But not only does the love of evil destroy faculty, and rob a man inch by inch of the beautiful and joyous world in which he was born to live, and whereby he was meant to educate his powers, but it tells on the man himself; it weakens and finally destroys the very spring of his life. God's sunlight, the living light of God's countenance, is just as essential to the true nourishment of a man's inner life, to his full manly growth, as the light of the sun of this world is to flowers. The man who by his self-willed folly, his vanity, avarice, or lust, draws a veil between his life and God, who has no care to know God, no power to commune with God, no joy in the love of God, dooms himself to an inward wasting and pining, a manifest and conscious decay. His life is poisoned in the spring; joy is quenched, hope is dead. A great famine arises in that world for which he has exchanged his Father's broad dominions. What is there to live for? is the question which strikes ever more loudly on the tympanum of the inner ear; and if I die, what then? "*A certain fearful looking for of judgment.*" The soul in straits, writhing in its anguish as they grow straiter daily; moaning the moan of the hopeless, to whom life brings no solace, nor death.

I suppose that the most horrible doom which can be imagined is that which a weird poet has pictured. A man shut up in a room which defies utterly his efforts to escape from it, from which he sees that escape is absolutely hopeless, and which is so constructed by cunning mechanism that it narrows daily its dimensions by hardly perceptible degrees. Sides, roof, floor, by hair-breadths, but with awful certainty, approach each other, and close on the poor tortured wretch within. He sees his prison contracting, he knows that it must crush him, but he has time to realise and brood over the whole terrors of his doom, and to moan and madden as the bars tighten with horrible deliberation, and pound him into a mass of bloody clay. One dares not dwell on it, it is too terrible. It is the picture which the watchers on high daily look upon,—souls in anguish, in the tightening bars of the prison-house of sin.

But, "*Thou hast brought me out into a large place.*"

II. Redemption, God's mercy in Christ, brings us out into a large, free world.

It is difficult, no doubt, to trace the precise allusion here. Is David contrasting the straits of the exile with the power and freedom of the king? Or the narrow, murky caves where the hunted outlaw had his lair, with the broad, free mountains where he wandered when the danger had passed by ? Or does he compare the sense of liberty and joy which possessed him, when he had heard the word of the Divine forgiveness, with the strain and the anguish which he had known when he had been groaning under the conviction of shameful as well as guilty sin ? We cannot tell ; the sentiment is true through the whole scale, and most certainly truest of the last.

It describes the whole contrast of the ways of sin and the ways of God ; the sin-born sorrows, and the heaven-born joys of life. To hear the word of the Divine forgiveness, to feel the light of the Divine smile, to run in the way of the Divine commandment, to take up the Christian cross with all the sorrows and burdens that it lays upon us, and all the joys and glories that bud from it, is like being brought out of a prison into a large, free, and glorious world. There is a sense of liberty, of young strength, of immortal life in the soul that has seen Jesus, which is like coming out of the close, murky valley into the free air of the mountain, with a broad land lying gleaming beneath, and beyond, the blue, boundless sea. It is just a hint, no more, of God's large provision for our being with all its appetites and powers.

That we may understand this better, let us consider more fully.

1. The largeness of the world which God has built to be our home.

2. The largeness of the commandment which God has given us in His Son.

3. The largeness of the future which God has opened to us in eternity.

1. The largeness of the world which God has built to be our home.

"*The works of the Lord are great, sought out of all them that have pleasure therein.*"

With what intense delight did David describe them. And none of those who take no pleasure in God can find the delight, which God intended man to take in the contemplation of His world. There is something in the vastness of Creation, in the stern and awful certainty of its law, which has a tendency to oppress mankind. The heathen peoples were distinctly conscious of it. The modern man of science, measuring and mapping the spaces of the universe, and cataloguing the infinite variety of its forms, seems to me to manifest the same experience. The grand and stately march which he is ever beholding, oppresses him. He is prone to become a fatalist, and to give up all the higher and diviner aims of life. One of our very ablest men of science has publicly declared that if any one would wind him up as a watch, and so arrange it that he might always go right and never go wrong, he should regard it as an unspeakable gain. That is, in other words, he pines to lay down his freedom—a pining which he shares with the Hindoo.

David felt nothing of this. The beauty, the magnitude, the splendour of the universe filled him with gladness. I suppose because he felt so vividly that, vast as it was, it was a kingdom which his Father ruled, and of which he was the heir. Surely there is something inspiring in this boundlessness of Creation, in the new fields of beauty and wonder which everywhere open upon us, and will open upon us through eternity. But it is a fountain of joy of which the pure-hearted only can drink in its fulness. Sin simply destroys the faculty by which it is God's purpose that we should take in all the delight of His universe, while our being endures.

There is no limit to the field in which our trained faculties are to expatiate, no bottom to the spring from which they are to drink perennial draughts of joy. "*Eye hath not seen, nor ear heard, neither have entered into the heart of man, the things which God hath prepared for them that love Him.*" If the dry tree, the marred Creation, be so glorious, what shall be the splendour of the new Creation, purged from every stain of evil, and flashing back from its clear mirror the radiance of the face of God? And God is training us to behold it. He asks us to love and to trust, He schools us to delight in His ways, that we may tread at length those shining pathways, may read the thoughts of which the new heaven and the new earth will be the unveiling, and master all that may be meant by the ineffable vision, when "*the creature itself also shall be delivered from the bondage of corruption, into the glorious liberty of the sons of God.*"

We ought not to be swallowed up with over-much

sorrow, with such a world as this around us, which is but the vestibule of that which shall then burst upon our sight. Many of our sorrows, no doubt, touch us too deeply for such consolations. But how much of the fret and the strain of life would pass from us, if we gat ourselves up more often to some Pisgah summit, and measured the largeness and the glorious beauty of our world.

2. The largeness of the commandment which God has given us in His Son.

"*The grace of God, which bringeth salvation, hath appeared unto all men, teaching us that, denying ungodliness and worldly lusts, we should live soberly, righteously, and godly, in this present world. Looking for that blessed hope, and the glorious appearing of the great God, and our Saviour Jesus Christ.*"

By "the commandment" I mean the whole of God's self-manifestation to man. "*I have seen an end of all perfection, but Thy commandment is exceeding broad.*" We have in Christ a truth whose ultimate depth we can never explore. Man has a boundless capacity. He was made to seek, to hunger for the infinite truth, the infinite good, the infinite love. In Christ this Infinite is revealed. Man's word man can measure. He can gauge it, and mark it with the stamp of his praise or censure, but here is a Word which gauges, which searches, and which censures him.

Oh! what blessed rest settles on the spirit when it has got from Christ its lesson of duty. A word from the lip, a lesson from the life of Christ comes to the weary, halting, doubting soul, like the touch of the angel to imprisoned Peter. The bars break, the chains drop, the captive walks forth free. And as he walks he sings, "*Thy statutes are my songs in the house of my pilgrimage.*" Men sing when they are sound in strength, and love their work. And those whom God brings forth have found a sure guide, a clear light, a straight track through all life's snares and pitfalls, a track which runs broad and firm through death, and is lost only in the pathways of heaven. "*Oh, how I love thy law! it is my meditation all the day.*" .... "*How sweet are thy words unto my taste, yea, sweeter than honey to my mouth. Through Thy precepts I get understanding; therefore I hate every false way.*"

But there is something that man needs from God yet more than guidance. He wants a large forgiveness, a large love. "*Blessed be God who hath not turned away my prayer, nor His mercy from me.*" The fifty-first Psalm opens some of the deeper depths of David's experience. It speaks of the large home of love and joy into which God brings out the forgiven and justified soul. The one thing which is deadly to a human spirit, is God's frown. The one thing which is quickening, is God's smile. The man who knows the joys of God's salvation, the blessedness of him "*whose iniquity is forgiven, whose sin is covered,*" seems to find all things possible. There is literally no bound to his aspiration and hope. "*Beloved, now are we the sons of God, and it doth not yet appear what we shall be; but we know that when He shall appear, we shall be like Him, for we shall see him as he is."* Like a bird escaped from the snare, he soars and carols. Like a captive fresh from his dungeon, he strains with almost mad delight his recovered powers.[1] Being justified by faith he has peace with God—the perfect peace. It is a free, large, boundless forgiveness, an infinite, an everlasting love. Sin is not pardoned only, it is abolished. Where sin abounded, grace "overabounds." Where sin reigned unto death, there grace reigns through righteousness, unto eternal life, through Jesus Christ our Lord. Everywhere exuberance; exuberant power, exuberant compassion, exuberant love. *" O the depth of the riches both of the wisdom and the knowledge of God, how unsearchable are His judgments, and His ways past finding out." " All things are yours; whether Paul or Apollos, or Cephas, or the world, or life, or death, or things present or things to come; all are yours; and ye are Christ's ; and Christ is God's."*

" Thou hast brought me out into a large place."

3. The large future which God has opened to us in eternity.

There are sorrows which, as I have said, touch us too deeply for Nature's consolations. But there are none which are beyond the solace of the Divine commandment. There is no trouble known to man, there was none known to Christ, whose springs of consolation are not in the Divine word. For one moment it seemed that man might know an anguish

[1] The excesses of fanaticism, in the early ages especially, are largely connected with this joy of deliverance.

beyond the reach of even heavenly solaces. But the answer came, the help, before the cry had reached heaven's gate. *"Father, into Thy hands I commend My spirit,"* revealed the depth of the Saviour's trust, the perfectness of His rest in God. The music of His coronation anthem broke upon His ear, as He passed to the justifications and the compensations of eternity.

David had a vision of this. *"Deep calleth unto deep at the noise of Thy waterspouts, all Thy waves and Thy billows have gone over me." "Why art thou cast down, O my soul? And why art thou disquieted within me? Hope thou in God; for I shall yet praise Him, who is the health of my countenance, and my God."* Asaph had a vision of it. *" I cried unto God with my voice, and unto the Lord I made supplication: . . I remembered God, and was troubled; I complained, and my spirit was overwhelmed. Will the Lord cast off for ever? Will He be favourable no more? Is His mercy clean gone for ever? Doth His promise fail for evermore? Hath God forgotten to be gracious? Hath He in anger shut up His tender mercies? And I said, This is my infirmity, but I will remember the years of the right hand of the Most High. Nevertheless, I am continually with Thee, Thy right hand upholdeth me. Thou shalt guide me with Thy counsel, and afterward receive me to glory. Whom have I in Heaven but Thee, and there is none upon earth that I desire beside Thee. My flesh and my heart faileth, but God is the strength of heart, and my portion for ever."* Paul had a vision of it. *"Our light affliction, which is but for a moment, worketh for us a far more exceeding and eternal weight of glory; while we look, not at the things which are seen, but at the things which are not seen; for the things which are seen are temporal, but the things which are not seen are eternal."*

Man, as I have said, is a being of royal proportions. It needs eternity to work out fairly the problem of his life. God surveys that horizon; get thee up into the mountain, stricken one, and survey it too. There are those who rebel against this appeal to eternity. We ought to see here and now, they say, the meaning of all that we are called upon to endure. But as matter of fact, life does not explain itself, and never has explained itself, within the limits of the present. The men who persist in making it explain itself within these bounds, if they are in earnest about it, grow morose or go mad; or if they are weak of heart, they give up the hope, and settle down quietly to a life like the brute's.

But God will be satisfied with no less than eternity, to work out his plan, for you, for me, and for mankind. *"Wherefore gird up the loins of your mind; be sober and hope to the end, for the grace that is to be brought unto you by the revelation of Jesus Christ."* Give up the effort to make your life explain itself here. Let no darkness, however drear, terrify you. Let no temptation, however fierce, amaze you. Let no cup of bitterness, however intense, wring one moan from your lips. What is a moment's gloom to the eternal sunlight? A moment's pressure to the eternal triumph? A drop of bitterness to the great ocean of everlasting joy?

Bessed be God that He has a world so large into which to bring forth His pilgrims of the wilderness, sore pressed by the burdens and strained by the travail of life—a world where "*our sun shall no more go down, nor our moon withdraw itself, where the Lord shall be our everlasting light, and the days of our mourning shall be ended.*" There we shall be ashamed of the very memory of our sighing, as we gaze on the glory which the sorrows of this life have revealed.

Nor need we wait till then for the solace. There have been those here who could "count them blessed which endure." This world has Pisgahs, whence a clear eye may survey the length and the breadth of the promised land; and where we may long for death, that our feet may press that blessed shore. These words are the true hymn of the pilgrim. The whole course of our lives, if Christ be our Captain, "the Captain and the finisher of our faith," is the fulfilment of the promise suggested by the text. In Christ, God is ever seeking us, to bring us forth from the narrows, the straits, in which we have entangled ourselves by sin, and from which no power in the universe but that of His grace can deliver us, into the broad world of "His salvation."

But the narrowest passage still lies before us, the sharpest strait, the keenest anguish, when we stand face to face with grisly Death. "*But though I walk through the valley of the shadow of death, I will fear no evil, for Thou art with me, Thy rod and Thy staff they comfort me."* It is but a moment's passage, through a sharp anguish, to a world where the sunlight is eternal.

I once came back to the daylight after long wandering in subterranean caves. While I live I can never forget the vision. Words cannot paint the splendour of colour which seemed to blaze on the bare rock under whose arch I issued forth, as the sunlight caught the mosses and lichens, or shot a shaft of glory into depths of shade. The sun was shining there as it had been shining for ages. It was no other sunlight than had life-long gladdened my sight. But it seemed to me as if at that moment the veil of Creation had been lifted; as if for the first time I had seen Light. Once again, I thought, I shall see that revelation. Light, to which even this blaze of splendour is but murky vapour, will one day burst upon my sight, when I emerge from the straits, the anguish of my night of travail, and in my flesh, in the eternal sunlight, I shall see God.

" THOU HAST BROUGHT ME OUT INTO A LARGE PLACE."

VIII.

THE PILGRIMS.

" For they that say such things, declare plainly that they seek a country."—Heb. xi. 14.

LITERALLY a fatherland. The writer means that here we suffer, toil, and hope, in exile; the Father's home, the kingdom of our perfect and eternal citizenship, is beyond. Thus, too, St. Paul; "At home in the body, exiled from the Lord." And who that aims at the higher life is at rest and satisfied, in the inmost heart of him, with anything which he can see, or hope for, or dream of as possible, in such a world as this? It is a strange, sad life, which asks the heaviest sacrifices of its noblest children, and inflicts on them the keenest pain. There would be no key to it—no possible means of understanding such a history of sacrifice and suffering as this chapter records, and which every faithful soul through all the Christian ages repeats—if God Himself had not come down to live it, that He might make it visibly the vestibule of an eternal life; wherein all that is dark will be revealed, all that is wrong will be righted, and the sufferers for righteousness' sake will be justified and glorified for ever.

I confess that this is the very core of my theology ; that is, of such notions of the nature, methods and purposes of God, as I have been able to work out from my experience of life, and my study of His word. It would all be dark to me, utterly, hopelessly dark, if I did not believe that the travail of life and of the Creation is, not watched and pitied only, but shared to its uttermost depths of pain, by the Lord.

There are those, no doubt, who find life very pleasant, and their course very prosperous, and very satisfying to all the desires and cravings which are as yet awakened within their being. But they have not yet begun to live. They are out of the concord of all the great ones of the world through all the ages ; and if they rest there they must look downward and not upward for the true comrades of their spirits ; they will find their true kindred in the end, not among the saints or the angels, but among the brutes.

But most of us, I imagine, if we were to utter the deepest judgment of our spirits, would say, I would not live alway, at least such a life and in such a world. If I must live for ever, my God! let it not be under this burden, with this fleshly clog, amid these wailings and moanings, this sadness, this conflict, this sin! Let me not drag on this double, discordant nature, the hand on the gate of heaven, the foot on the threshold of hell ; every moment a care, a strain, a terror—for " if the righteous scarcely be saved, where shall the ungodly and the sinner appear?" and with which shall I stand? No, if I am to live, if this burden of existence under such stern conditions is one which I may not lay down, let me live under simpler, purer, more home-like conditions, in a world which shall meet instead of mocking the deepest needs and yearnings of my spirit, which shall help instead of marring the fair unfolding of my powers; in which my heart shall not be wrung by the sadness around me, nor torn by the strife within; and in which I may be able to believe with calm confidence that I am the child of a benign and blessed Creator, and that He made me and means me to be blest.

I suppose that these, or something like these, are the terms which we should be disposed to lay down, if we could make a treaty with heaven as to the conditions of our existence; or if the question were submitted to us, whether we would elect to live on or to be struck out of the book of the living for ever. We should be disposed to demand some such conditions as these for a life which is never to die. Well, the Gospel means and the Bible declares, that the God who made us has laid down these conditions for us. This is the life, yea, fairer than this, fairer than anything of which our finite faculties can at present dream, which He who laid this burden of existence upon us has ordained, and for which, with wise, firm, fatherly foresight, He is training us in His Son.

There would be no honest possibility of escape from the conclusion, either that a malign spirit has made and rules this sad, suffering world, or that opposing spirits of equal power are struggling for the possession of the world and of the soul, if the Bible had not revealed this life distinctly as an education. Like all education, it is inevitably full of toil, and care, and pain; but these have their explanation, their only but ample explanation, in the life of which this is but the vestibule; where they are who have fought the battle and borne the strain before us, and whence their voices flow down, as peace streams down on the soft, calm evening air,

>Mortal, they softly say,
>   Peace to thy heart.
>We too, yes, mortal,
>   Have been as thou art.
>Hope-lifted, doubt-depressed,
>   Seeing in part;
>Tried, troubled, tempted,
>   Sustained as thou art.

Or in words of sublimer and more far-reaching strain, "*These all died in faith, not having received the promises, but having seen them afar off, and were persuaded of them, and embraced them, and confessed that they were strangers and pilgrims on the earth. For they that say such things declare plainly that they seek a country. And truly if they had been mindful of that country from whence they came out, they might have had opportunity to have returned. But now they desire a better country, that is an heavenly; wherefore God is not ashamed to be called their God, for he hath prepared for them a city.* . .

... And these all, having received a good report through faith, received not the promise; God having prepared some better thing for us, that they without us should not be made perfect."

Let us consider, in developing the meaning of this passage,

I. The universal experience of the great spiritual leaders of our race; the men who have left their mark, not so much on the outer history, as on the inner beliefs, the thoughts, feelings, desires, imaginations, and aspirations of mankind. These are the real fathers of history. And how much we know of them. Some divine instinct seems to have moved them to reveal the deepest secrets of their lives. The men who have been the mightiest builders of the outer structure of society, the conquerors, the founders of empires and of dynasties, we seem to know but outwardly. Nebuchadnezzar, Cyrus, Alexander, Cæsar; how little we know of their inner lives. Cæsar has left to us a biography well nigh as ample in bulk as the confessions of St. Augustine. But from one end of his great work to the other, there is hardly a word which unveils to us the secrets of his inner life. It is all about the outer world in which he was a master workman, perhaps, the world's master workman; but he has left no mark on the spiritual development of mankind, and he has left not a hint about the method of his own.

But Abraham, Moses, David, Paul, Augustine, Alfred, Bernard, Dante, Luther, Cromwell, how much we know of them, how largely the secret history of their being is laid bare! We seem to pass into the sanctuary of those toiling, suffering, struggling, aspiring spirits, and to hear their wailings and their pæans of victory. As we listen their life passes into us, and becomes God's quickening breath to stir the feeble pulses, and kindle the languid aspirations of our own.

Is there no higher hand manifest here? Is it by chance that we have this full record of the inner lives of the great ones who have lived most deeply and purely from within, and whose lives bear most directly on that which concerns the spiritual quickening and development of mankind? And their experience is uniform. It is all set in the same key. It is all charged with deep dissatisfaction with the present condition and order of things, regarded otherwise than as the school discipline of the spirit; and with intense faith in and longing for a world in which the beliefs that are crossed and the hopes that are crushed by the sin, the wrong, the pain which fill this earth with wailing, shall be justified and crowned; a world which the ever blessed God shall not be ashamed to own as His creation, and in which He shall see, not the tears, but the joy and the glory of His sons.

At the head of this great line, the men of faith (and the men of faith have been the fathers of the ages), stand the patriarchs, whose lives in their mere outer form were symbolic for all time. I have spoken of the men of faith as the true fathers of human development. Who are the men who have influenced most mightily the beliefs, aspirations, and efforts by which, in all ages, human society truly grows? He had a deep insight into the secrets of man's heart and of the heart of society, who said, I care not who makes laws for men, if you will let me make their songs. The feelings, the thoughts, the sentiments, the interests, the hopes, the fears, the pleasures, of the daily lives of men, in the larger sense, make history. The political master workmen construct the theatre, but the form and pressure of that humanity which is to play its part upon the stage, are determined from within.

And who are the men who stimulate and mould most mightily this inward development? Surely the great believers; the master thinkers, prophets, poets, whose faith is their strongest and grandest power. Moses and Paul stand above Cyrus and Cæsar as true fathers of human development; though Cæsar's be "the greatest secular name in history." And what is the key-note of such lives? It was no specially devout student of this chapter of the Hebrews, who said of the poets what is true of the whole order,

<blockquote>They learn in suffering what they teach in song.</blockquote>

Patriarchs, prophets, apostles, preachers, fathers of the Church, their life is one. They found all things here "jangled," "out of tune and harsh;" while the principle of order which they saw working could only complete its mission in heaven and eternity.

"Perhaps," said Plato of that perfect Republic of which he dreamed, " some image of it remaineth for us in the heavens." And so too these great ones of old declared plainly "that they sought a country." "*And now they desire a better country, that is an heavenly. Wherefore God is not ashamed to be called their God, for He hath prepared for them a city.*"

I have said that the lives of the patriarchs were symbolic. They were types which set forth what God meant to be the character of all faithful lives, all lives which strive to rise to sympathy with Him, to the end of time. And they were literally and palpably "*strangers and pilgrims on the earth.*" The lords, by the very firmest of all titles, of the land of promise, they held in actual possession not a grain of its dust—yes, some grains; the graves where they buried their dead: "*And Abraham stood up from before his dead and spake unto the sons of Heth, saying, I am a stranger and a sojourner with you; give me a possession of a burying place with you, that I may bury my dead out of my sight. . . . . And after this, Abraham buried Sarah his wife in the cave of the field of Machpelah, before Mamre; the same is Hebron in the land of Canaan. And the field, and the cave that is therein, were made sure unto Abraham, for a possession of a burying place, by the sons of Heth.*" Pilgrims even in their own land, the land of promise, dwelling apart in their tents on the mountain pastures, mixing themselves up but slightly with its interests, rarely entering the congress of its social and political life. Their only direct association with it a profoundly sad one, the graves of their dead; yet profoundly significant, it pointed to a more wealthy and glorious land of promise, where the dead live again, and the lost are restored.

And this prophecy of the life of faith, history has amply fulfilled. The faithful ones in all ages have been and must be the pilgrims, "confessing that they are strangers and sojourners on the earth." Their faith lays hold on a divine idea of life and of human progress. Looking round them, the confession is wrung from them, "this is not divine; I see here an enemy's work: the divine things here —and there are divine things here in rich abundance, it is not the devil's world—are the things that are budding, not the things which bloom and fruit. They are the things that are swelling with the promise of a future far-off summer, not the things which the sun of this world quickens to rapid and brilliant maturity, parent of as rapid and foul decay." *Our life is hid with Christ in God.*" " *We are buried with Him.*"

The higher that we rise in the contemplation of humanity, and observe the men who are most closely enshrined in the homage and love of their fellows, the more plainly do we meet with lives whose meaning and end this world cannot explain to us. Such lives, if this world were all, would present to us that type of character and conduct to which some profound instinct compels our homage, as a miserable abortion; we see in them promise broken, purpose frustrated, hope destroyed, with a thoroughness, a ruthlessness, which might kindle grim joy among the fiends of hell. I can conceive of nothing sadder for heaven, more joyful for hell, than the lives of earth's noblest pilgrims, if the true Canaan, of which God spake to their spirits, were here upon this earth. The pleasures, possessions, and crowns of this world they have not striven for. Its prizes they have not cared to grasp. They have asked of earth only a standing ground, that they might do steadily, constantly, their God-appointed tasks.

Room to stand upon, was all that the patriarchs asked of the earthly Canaan. It is all that the faithful ones in all ages look for and care to receive. And the end of it cannot be here. "*God is not ashamed to be called their God, for He hath prepared for them a city.*" Were there no home, no fatherland, where this great faculty can bloom and fruit, where this lofty hope can burst in joyful and blest fruition, it would all be shameful together; the universe would be one vast field of desolation, and the Being who made and who rules it would be either a fool or a fiend. But God is not ashamed to be called our God. "*Here we have no continuing city, we seek one to come;*" "*A city which hath foundations, eternal in the heavens, whose builder and maker is God.*"

II. Let us consider the confession out of which this condition springs. "*They confessed that they were strangers and pilgrims on the earth.*"

That is, they do not find here the elements of a

home, a final condition of life and relationship in which they can rest, and work to the full strain of their power. Always there is the image of a more perfect life, and a more perfect world, beyond.

Why? Why cannot they find rest in such homes as this world can offer to them? Why cannot they be content with such work as it proposes for the exercise and discipline of their powers? Is not the earth bright enough? Are not fields and flowers, and clouds and stars, fair enough to satisfy the keenest passion for beauty? Is not love rich enough? Are not homes blessed enough? Does not life offer a field large enough for the free play of our energies? Is not the world full, if we will seek them, of springs of interest and joy?

It is through no blindness to the beautiful in Nature, the lofty in thought, the blessed in love, that the men and women of faith "say such things," have been saying them for ages, are saying them still. Perhaps such see far more that is good and beautiful here, and thank God for it more profoundly, than many more easy and self-satisfied men. But they say that things and beings here are made upon a scale which the life of a larger world alone can justify. They say that rich as the world is in beauty, and life in interest, there is no room here to work out life's profoundest problems, no time here to reap life's richest harvests, no sphere here in which to realise life's purest and loftiest dreams. They say that the beauty which delights, the pleasure which gladdens, create a thirst, a heartache for beauty more perfect, for pleasure more intense and pure. They say that as man rises in knowledge, in culture, in fineness of perception and desire, he feels himself more and more out of tune with this earthly system, which constantly crosses what is best in him with disappointment, and stings what is noblest with pain.

Man is so organised that things, persons, memories, hopes, may become to him as part of his very being. And he knows it. God has given to him "discourse of reason," "looking before and after," and he knows that that which is other than himself may become part of his life. And yet he is powerless to assure the possession of it from moment to moment, while his one certainty is that he must lose it soon. God has made him thus, to love intensely, to clasp tightly what is dearer to him than dear life, and God gives to him no right to control it, no power to refuse it to disease, and pain, and death.

Made infinitely more sensitive than the brutes, and more dependent on all around him, he is as much at the mercy of the accidents of the Creation, and may at any moment, and in a moment, see "all his pleasant things laid waste." The more tender his nature, the more keen his sympathy, the more quick his apprehension, the more intense his passion, the more does pain—hopeless, desperate pain if this be all—dog his steps. As he rises higher in his development, the more varied, manifold, and imperative as are the needs and relations of his life, the more do they seem to be part of a larger scheme than this earth has room for, and the more does life seem full of buddings of power and promise which never bloom in this world, far less fruit.

We start in life with great hopes, with conscious stirrings of great powers. But what is life, if we are shut up to the present, but a constant discovery of limits, nay, a constant narrowing of limits, until we move consciously in a very narrow and disenchanted world ? Do we see this blighting of promise, this frustrating of hope, anywhere else in the Creation ? or is it man only, to whom it is a source of keen agony, who has to lift this cup of sadness to his lips ? Shall we not rather say that God kindles the imagination, paints the vision, in life's young spring, and then leads His pilgrim forth into the hard, bare wilderness, where visions vanish under the blinding glare on the level lines of sand ; that there He trains the soul's muscles by stern, sharp exercise, and then shews to the veteran pilgrim his vision once more, beautified and glorified, when the wanderings are ended, and there gleam in the dim distance the blue mountains of the Fatherland ? If life has no sphere beyond in which it may work out its possibilities at large, man's life is the saddest thing in the vast Creation, and the Being who made it and who blighted its promise, is an Almighty tyrant, and not a God.

But this is after all the mere surface of the matter. Powers undeveloped, faculties crippled, hopes blighted, promise cut back to the quick, these, with a being like man, capable of suffering so keenly,

The Pilgrims. 163

capable of living so joyously, so blessedly, are strong arguments for immortality. But there are deeper reasons than these.

What should we think of a god who should make a world full of cripples, and watch them calmly as they crawl and writhe through life? Yet thus it is with all of us, if this be all. There is a deadly poison in the blood. It infects every child of Adam. *"There is none that doeth righteousness, no not one." "All have sinned, and come short of the glory of God."* It is the testimony of human consciousness, as well as of the Divine word. And the poison is in our blood by no act or volition of our own. There is a dread mystery behind the doctrine of original sin. We are born to sin and to suffer. Orthodox theologians insist with bland satisfaction, that if a man be damned eternally he has himself to thank for it. He was warned, the way of safety was pointed out to him, he would not escape. It pleases them to forget the tremendous pressure which is against man from the beginning; how by no act of his own he brings a lustful nature with him into a sinful world, to live a life on whose conduct hang the issues of eternal pain or eternal bliss. Unless we may give a larger range and a longer day to the ministries of God's grace and mercy than our theology finds room for, then it is an awful thing to live a human life in a world which was made and is ruled by the Christian's God.

And the noblest of men are the most intensely conscious of the working of this deadly virus. "*O miserable man that I am,"* cried the foremost man of his time, *"who shall deliver me from the body of this death?"* Such men confess that they are strangers and sojourners, because they—made as they are, believing as they cannot help believing, aspiring as they cannot help aspiring—can never rest, can never find a home, in a world of which the devil seems to share the dominion, and in which every good and beautiful thing that it holds is stained somewhere with the slime of sin.

No! God did not mean us to go crippled and numbed for ever, or to wear out a miserable shred of existence, moaning and wrestling with tremendous evils, and then perish and leave them reigning still. What sort of god were he who should cause generations to be born to sin and to suffer, haunted by thoughts and hopes of righteousness, and let them find at last in dying, that while the sin is a dread reality the righteousness is a dream? But "God is not ashamed to be called our God, for he hath prepared for us a city." This life of ours would be the burning shame of the great universe, if there were no city of habitation, for which it is the high school of discipline, and where its dread problems will find blessed solution, prepared for us on high.

And look at the world. Is it a world in which spirits that "trail the clouds of glory as they come, from God, who is their home," should try to find a rest? Do not our eyes fill with tears as we see the sweat of its agony, and hear the moans of its pain? Read the visions of the prophets; study the dreams of the poets, and then turn and look on life. Be bold. Lift the veil. See the selfishness, the folly, the malice, the hate, the envy, the lust, the tyranny, which make fair regions of this world a very hell to the eyes of the angels—a hell of discord and pain.

What sort of a world is it in which you, busy men of the world, do your business day by day? How much that is heaven-like comes across you? How much baseness, cowardice and greed, that sicken the very soul within you? But the world is mending, you say. Yes, it is mending; it must be mending, else Christ were dead in vain. And it seems to me that they must be blind to the most explicit testimony of history, who do not see that it is mending mainly through the operation of that spirit of thought, and care, and ministry for others, which the patriarchs were taught to cherish in their lonely life in Canaan, —they knew that they were to be blessings as well as to be blessed,—and which Christianity has made the law of life for human society. And yet when one sees the beggary, the luxury, the wantonness, the selfishness, the misery, that abound still even in Christendom, the cry, "How long, O Lord, how long?" breaks from our writhing lips. Prophets prophesy, and God promises, a world in which righteousness shall reign, peace shall flourish, truth shall shine like sunlight, and love shall weave its holy and blessed bands around every heart. Look round and see the world which sin has given us in its stead.

I have said that sin has made this earth hell-like. But in reality that is just what it is not. If it had been hell-like, man would have made it into hell long ago. No! Heaven has a hold upon it, a firm and blessed hold. The world is full of heroisms, too; silent, noble heroisms. Sufferings and sacrifices demanded and consecrated by love, irradiate the poorest dens, and hallow the coarsest and most uncultured hearts. It is a strange weltering confusion. Highest heaven, deepest hell are represented here, and here they fight out their battles. But is this Babel of confusion the end which the God of order, of beauty, of life, has wrought for through these infinite ages? Has the whole Creation been groaning and travailing in pain, since the morning stars sang together over the young world, and is this that we see around us, and which saddens *us* even with our dull hearts, is this the birth that is to gladden God? No! "OUR FATHER, WHICH ART IN HEAVEN, HALLOWED BE THY NAME. THY KINGDOM COME, THY WILL BE DONE ON EARTH AS IT IS DONE IN HEAVEN!" And it will be done, as the outcome of all this travail of man and of Nature, in the new heaven and the new earth wherein dwelleth righteousness.

This leads me to say some words in brief on—

III. The state in which we are told that this experience is to issue at last. "He hath prepared for us a city," a place of citizenship, a fatherland, a home, on high.

I shall have more to say on this subject in the closing portion of this volume; here it will be enough to affirm that a fundamental proposition of Revelation is surely this, that life is the training school of the Kingdom, that earth is the vestibule of heaven. There was a Man on earth once who had suffered as no other man has ever suffered. Scarred more deeply than all other men by the thorns and the spears of life; wasted by toil, consumed by zeal, bowed down by burdens of shame and pain, He died the saddest death that man has ever died; and then He rose from the dead and reappeared in a radiant, triumphant form, master of all the forces of the universe, throned on the great high throne of the Creation, to reveal what, to such a life as His, is the function and ministry of death.

The risen, blessed, and glorified Christ, with the marks of the Cross and Passion still on Him—the harvest of life's experience, the fruit of all its pain and travail, gathered and garnered for ever—*is* the Apocalypse. The central image of the book is the key to all its visions. "*And I beheld, and, lo, in the midst of the throne and of the four beasts, and in the midst of the elders, stood a Lamb as it had been slain.*" I have heard the Apocalypse spoken of as the natural history of moral principles. It paints the struggles and triumphs of the Love that died on Calvary, to redeem the world.

And you must pass with the seer within the veil, you must gaze, as through the Apocalypse it is given you to gaze, on the radiant throng who surround the throne, you must hear the rustling of the palms which their victories have won for them, and catch the jubilant notes of the hymn which they learned on earth with sobs and tears; you must see the holy city, new Jerusalem, coming down from God out of heaven; you must watch, not the birth, but the bridal of Creation, when the bride, the Lamb's wife—that is, man, tear-stained, toil-worn man, you, me, if we have learnt the pilgrim hymn—purified and perfected by life's tremendous discipline, shall join with Christ in the fruitful marriage of eternity; and then you will understand, as an Apocalypse only can give you to understand, why God is not ashamed to be called your God, and what manner of city He hath prepared for your habitation there.

The life of the risen Christ is the key to it all; and the vision of the world where "*they who came through great tribulation, who washed their robes and made them white in the blood of the Lamb,*" "*are before the throne of God, and serve Him day and night in His temple.*" "*Beloved, now are we the sons of God.*" Be it ours to live the life of sons, "*Blameless and harmless, without rebuke, in the midst of a crooked and perverse generation; among whom*" be it ours to "*shine as lights in the world, holding forth the word of life.*" "*Now is our citizenship in heaven.*" The home, the fatherland, is not far away. At any moment on the wings of faith we may rise into its serene, unclouded regions, refresh ourselves with a vision of its order, and stir our pulses with the breath of its song. And thence also "*we look for the Saviour, the Lord Jesus Christ; who shall change our vile body, that it may be fashioned like unto His glorious body, according to the working whereby He is able even to subdue all things unto Himself.*"

IX.
THE NOBLE ARMY OF MARTYRS.

" And ye became followers of us, and of the Lord; having received the word in much affliction, with joy of the Holy Ghost."—I. Thess. i. 6.

"MAN can do without happiness, and instead thereof find blessedness," writes the foremost man of genius and the sternest moralist of our times. I suppose that he means to describe something of the nature of the experience of these Thessalonian Christians, and probably he would acknowledge that the greatest human teacher of the lesson was the man who wrote these words. Paul's life as an apostle, preached this sermon as no moralist could preach it; and Paul's life was but a faint echo of a greater life, in which the idea was wrought out with divine completeness—the Man of Sorrows, and yet the most blessed Being in the universe, *" God over all, blessed for evermore."*

If a man cannot understand how far blessedness transcends and is independent of mere happiness, and how "many afflictions" may be perfectly consonant with much joy of the Holy Ghost, the joy that man shares with Christ, he may be a Christian by courtesy, but he knows little of Christian experience. Many a heathen has looked more deeply than such an one into the mystery of godliness, and has fuller fellowship with the mind of the Lord. This is the great Christian idea of a fruitful human experience : "*Much affliction, with joy of the Holy Ghost.*"

The calling of a son of God confers no immunity from sorrow; but it opens beneath and through the sorrow, a spring of over-mastering, and to such a man as Paul, transporting joy. It is a great mistake to suppose that Paul's views of a Christian experience can be summarised in the terms, present pain, future joy. Paul while he lived, worn and burdened as he was, was the most blessed man living in the world who has left to us any record of his life; he was the man into the fellowship of whose spirit it would have been most worth your while and mine to enter; the man whose life-work was the noblest, the most faithful, the most glorious, which was done on the earth in his day; while it has left altogether the deepest mark on the higher culture and progress of our race.

The Cæsars, where are they? The world has received the legacy which they handed down and has forgotten them; their names have passed into the custody of the scholars. They have left the strongest traces upon the world they ruled; their mark is stamped where it never can be effaced. The Roman empire is the matrix of European civilisation; but for the great majority of us moderns, as men, the Cæsars are little more than shades. But Paul is living among us as vivid and masterly as ever. His word at this moment is worth more to us, and can do more for us, than all the rescripts of the masters of Imperial Rome. And why? For the same reason which makes his Master's word more profoundly a word of life to us. He pleased not himself; he fulfilled a Divine commission; he followed Christ in the regeneration, "with much affliction and joy of the Holy Ghost." It is the man who can bring some regenerating power to bear on his age, who is shrined most lovingly in the homage and reverence of mankind.

It is the secret of the noblest power, the purest blessedness, and the most vivid hope—following Christ in the regeneration; that is, in the work of building up and restoring on earth what sin has destroyed. You may rush hither and thither in search of the true good of your being, and you may hew out many a goodly cistern to yourself. It is all vanity of vanities, till you have found and follow Him. Paul lives still so vividly in the midst of our modern world, because Christ, whom he followed and whose chosen organ he became, still lives, an abiding presence in our midst.

It was Christ in Paul who lived that life, and who left that record. The men, however mighty for the time they might be, who drew their inspirations from the ideas and ambitions of the hour, have vanished; or at best they have left but fossil skeletons of their lives for the curious to study; while these men, who followed Christ, in whom Christ was living, by whom Christ was speaking, are still amongst us, because Christ is amongst us; and they are to this day, though after the flesh the world knows them no more, His chief organs of influence on mankind. Three hundred years ago Paul shook Christendom, as mightily as he shook heathenism and Judaism in his day; and perhaps the day has yet to dawn when the living influence of St. John will be fully felt in our world.

I. Followers of us, and of the Lord.

"*Brethren, be ye followers of me, even as I also am of Christ.*" "*Brethren, be ye followers together of me; and mark them which walk so as ye have us for an ensample.*"

There is something startling, and, indeed, it seems almost awful, in such words as these. A man of like passions with ourselves, dares to propose himself as a mark for imitation to men and women who were seeking to be followers of incarnate God. But Paul does not shrink from it—"*followers of us, and of the Lord*"—and his life course amply sustains his words. But who dares to echo them now— who would not shudder at the thought of setting himself forth as a model of Christian perfectness, an image of Christ, by which, being close at hand, to dim eyes the original might become the better known?

And yet the world is not without its Christ-like ones in any age; men and women who seem, not to be baptized only, but penetrated and possessed, by the spirit of the Lord Jesus. Their lives are as out of tune as was His, with the ideas, the habits, the aims, of the busy world around them; while in tune, as was His, with the life of the unseen throng who "*do the Father's commandments, and hearken to the voice of His word*," here and on high. But there is nothing, on the whole, more wonderful in the world's spiritual history, perhaps, too, in the spiritual history of all worlds, than the measure in which it has been given to men and women like ourselves, with no special opportunities and advantages which are not also within our reach, to be and to live like the incarnate Son of God. The Lord does not shine on high in unapproachable isolation, like the sun in the firmament. As the first among peers, the elder brother among brethren, a bright particular star amid a cluster of constellations, He leads the marches of the great human host, with which He has cast in His lot and mixed up His life for ever. This likeness of living men to Christ is a sermon of hope to all of us, and it opens a great vision of what educated and perfected humanity shall be in Heaven.

But where are the points of likeness? Whence did Paul derive his right to say to the churches, Ye became followers of us, and of the Lord? Out of such Christian experience as he here records, "*I live, yet not I, but Christ liveth in me, and the life which I now live in the flesh, I live by the faith of the Son of God, who loved me and gave Himself for me;*" and out of such passages of his history as the twelfth chapter of the Second Epistle to the Corinthians chronicles: "*Therefore I take pleasure in infirmities, in reproaches, in necessities, in persecutions, in distresses, for Christ's sake; for when I* am weak, then am I strong." "*And I will very gladly spend and be spent for you; though the more abundantly I love you, the less I be loved.*" The speciality of the likeness lies in this power of self-sacrifice; the power to lose all selfish thought and consideration in tender care for his brethren and for mankind.

It may seem a strange truth to this age of keen, intense competition, when the commercial idea rules so absolutely that nations are chary of moving in any cause, however righteous, except their own interests, in the narrowest sense, are very plainly involved. But it is well worth one's while to take note of the fact that these men, whose lives have been so noble, rich, and fruitful, who in a great sense are living still among us, whose presence the world with righteous instinct will not suffer to vanish, had absolutely no thought of any interest but Christ's, and were ready at any moment to lay down their lives on the altar of sacrifice, if by death, they too, like their Master, might win a blessing for mankind.

We are not likely, any of us, to become altogether as Paul, even by the most intense study and admiration of his character, but we may follow him as he followed Christ; and it may help us to live a little less selfishly, and to be more bold and large in our ministry to our fellow men, to see where such a life as his was rooted, and what was the secret of the mighty power which he, and such as he, have wielded over men. It is to have no self-will, to be absolutely open to the will of God.

It is a hard saying—no self-will; about which some will be ready to ask, "what on earth does it mean? Are we to have no will of our own, no thought and care for ourselves and those belonging to us?" God forbid! Paul had a very mighty will of his own, and had to express it and to bring it to bear, again and again, in defiance of the whole secular and religious world of his time. But he had purified the current of that will by deep inspirations of the heavenly air which a man breathes in prayer, and in meditation on the word and the ways of God.

It was his own will, and yet not his own; it had been refined and moulded into harmony with a higher will; he willed what was also the will of God. "*I live, yet not I, but Christ liveth in me.*" He had laid his spirit bare to the stream of Divine influence; and just as the blood gets purified from its carbonic dross as the vital air breathes through it in the lungs, so the will of Paul—those desires, aims, hopes, loves, which are the springs of action—was purged of the acrid leaven of self by wrestling, conquering prayer; the prayer that God would search him to the most hidden depths of thought and will, and purify him, and would use him as an instrument for the fulfilment of His own holy and blessed purposes, making the instrument keen and strong, no matter how fierce might be the furnace fires; the prayer, above all, that God would strengthen him to follow his Master in the path of self-denial and self-sacrifice, and teach him to find the true delight and glory of his spirit in spending himself in the service of mankind, like God.

Do not think, I pray you, that a man must adopt formally the calling of an apostle or an evangelist, to enter into the fellowship of such a life as this. There have been very daring and successful soldiers, very able and masterly statesmen, very prudent and prosperous merchants, the deepest thought of whose hearts has been, "I am not my own, I am bought with a price, and I am bound therefore to glorify God with my body and with my spirit, which are His." Hard as it may seem, it is the beginning of peace to say it, and to try to live it. You may have your own way, and rule as absolute lord in your own little kingdom; other wills may feel themselves compelled to bow to your will, and you may exult in the sense of your power to sway them at your pleasure; but you will find yourself in the end miserably heart-sick and weary of your own way, when you have got it. While, on the other hand, you may give up your own will, deny yourself, and make it your steady purpose and effort to care for the welfare of others, to bear their burdens, to lighten their cares, and to minister to their joys—which is none the less beautiful and heavenly because philosophers call it by a fantastic name in these days—and a glow of heavenly peace and joy will pass into your spirit in the effort, and will abide there as a foretaste of the joy that you will share with God, with Christ, and with the great assembly and church of the Firstborn, in heaven.

"Followers of us, and of the Lord," said Paul, because he followed Christ so boldly, so utterly;

because none of the things which the men of this world strive for could lay their chain upon his spirit, neither did he count his life dear unto himself, if he might finish his course with joy, and the ministry which he had received of the Lord Jesus to testify the Gospel of the grace of God. The likeness to Christ lay expressly in the power of self-sacrifice; in the large, loving, ministering heart which could renounce its dearest, yea, even its eternal hope, if men might but be blessed. And this is to grasp perfectly the difference between blessedness and happiness which the text expounds to us, and to the consideration of which in fuller detail we will now proceed.

II. They entered into this fellowship by receiving the word "with much affliction, and joy of the Holy Ghost."

Confession, or profession as we call it, is in these days cheap work: so cheap that it is difficult to find any true gauge of its reality. Then it was dear work, and at any moment might cost dear life. It is not good to be out of fellowship with the struggles and sufferings which have won for us prosperity and peace. How many a stout citizen in past ages has stained his own hearth-stone with his life-blood, that you may sit with your dear ones around yours, no man daring to make you afraid. An age which feels no fellowship of spirit with the martyrs is not a noble age, is not a blessed age, however the elements of material prosperity may abound. Christian brethren, ask yourselves what you have in common with the noble army of martyrs, in your peaceful, happy homes, with your ample resources, with your wide circle of friends and kindred, and your prosperous, life to which your religion just adds an ornament of grace and a crown. Remember the men who won the inheritance for you; consider at what cost they won it, and at what cost they kept it; and understand how receiving the word with much affliction, may be one very constant condition of the purest joy of the Holy Ghost.

We learn from the narrative in the 17th chapter of the Acts of the Apostles, that Paul had troubled work at Thessalonica. "*The Jews who believed not, moved with envy, took unto them certain lewd fellows of the baser sort,*" and stirred up a persecution against him. They expelled him from Thessalonica, and not content with that, followed him with their persecutions to Berea. We gather from the epistle that the persecution was prolonged, and that the Thessalonian Christians had literally to take their lives in their hands, when they professed themselves the disciples of the Lord Jesus.

We read about this calmly, and as almost matter of course. But strain your imagination to realise these "afflictions." Feel the cords tightening round your limbs, and the blood beginning to start under the strain; see the glaring eye of the African lion blazing on his victim, and his savage jaws opening to champ his prey; hear the hiss of the red-hot iron, or the swing of the executioner's axe; and then bethink you in the last dread moment, of a gentle wife, a brave boy, a tender girl, whom you are leaving helpless in the hard world, obnoxious to the same doom. Does it seem to you, as you realise it, that you could lift your head, and utter the name of Christ with your last breath with passionate devotion? Yes? Then you can understand how martyrs taste, as none perhaps but martyrs can taste, "*the joy of the Holy Ghost.*" But which of us is brave enough? Whose faith is strong enough? Wonder not that the joy of the Holy Ghost seems well-nigh to have died out of our churches, and that to the world's keen eye our religious life looks cold and gloomy as night.

A second source of the "much affliction" of the Thessalonian Church, was the utter rupture of all the bonds of kindred, friendship, and social relation, and the loss of the means of earning even a modicum of bread. It is evident from the second epistle that there was deep poverty in the Church, and an unusual number of utterly dependent members. Many of them, we may be sure, sank at once from a position of affluence to penury and distress, and were in danger of literally starving, and of seeing those dearest to them starve, because they could not bring their lips to deny a Name which they were bent on magnifying—because Christ had laid on them the obligation to confess Him, whatever might be the cost. They had to break up their homes, to separate themselves from friends and kindred, to betake themselves, many of them, to menial occupations, to forego all the prizes which they had been trained to strive for, and to make themselves objects of universal distrust and scorn. They received the word with much affliction, as England received it at the Reformation, and continued to receive it through the Revolution; as Hindoos, Chinese, Africans and South Sea Islanders receive it to this day.

"*And others were tortured, not accepting deliverance,*" is a record which might be written of any age of the Jewish or Christian Church. Christ, who died for the world, has ever in the world men and women not a few who are ready to die for Him, to endure any extremity of torture rather than deny that they love Him, or silence even for a moment the murmur of His name upon their lips. Christ's great love for man has kindled man's great love for Christ, which is the joy and glory of the world of spirit. The history of earth's martyrs—and all religions can boast them—is the noblest epic of this world; the history of Christ's martyrs is perhaps the noblest epic of heaven.

And this which I have described is independent altogether of the sorrow which springs out of the stern struggle against world and flesh and devil, to which a disciple of Christ devotes himself; the bitterness of which is expressed from his constant failures, his sense of the disloyalty of his own heart to the Saviour, his beggarly propensity to run after the gauds and prizes of the moment, and to let the things not seen and eternal go. In the great fight of afflictions—fight against the world, fight against the ruling powers—no fight so hard, so long, so stern as this. They received the word with much affliction; they plunged into a sea of troubles when they gave themselves to the Lord; and they knew, as none but those who can face that sea of trouble can know, "the peace which passeth understanding," and "the joy which is unspeakable and full of glory."

That we may understand this better, let us notice—

1. That the purest joys of a man's life are strangely independent of his surroundings. What he *has* in the way of pleasures and possessions is literally nothing in the account; what he *is*, and what he has in the inward treasure-house, is all in all. Take the simplest and most familiar illustration, into which all can enter. If two persons love each other with passionate devotion, to be near each other, even in penury and toil, is pure bliss ; to be separate, even in wealth and splendour, is pure misery. Those who truly love would far rather have the fellowship of toil and struggle, than the separate inheritance of all that this earth could yield of possessions and delights.

Once, at any rate, it seemed so to you, my reader; and those were not your worst days. The fellowship of kindred souls is the purest joy that is known to mortals. The dinner of herbs where love is, is not simply *better* than the stalled ox with strife: there is absolutely no comparison. It is not that the one is a higher pleasure than the other. The one is pure joy; the other, except to the basest natures, is pure pain. In truth, man cares nothing about his surroundings when his soul is glad within him, and can sing through its conflicts and toils; they vanish utterly, as the night fogs at the kiss of the sun.

2. This will help us a little way, and in a wholly right direction, to understand "*the joy of the Holy Ghost.*" It is the joy of the man who has found the true Lover and Lord of his being, whom he can serve with perfect loyalty, love with passionate devotion, and obey with supreme delight. It is the joy of the lonely widowed soul which has discovered its kindred; of a sick man who feels within himself that the spring of his life is healed, that his vigour and vital energy are restored. The earth does not gladden more when the morning sun flashes his light on her bosom, than does the soul rejoice when the light of the heavenly sun first touches it, and it passes out of darkness into warm, bright day. Circumstances are nothing. "I have found Him whom my soul loveth," is the cry; and nothing can kill, nothing can even dash, the joy which that consciousness quickens within.

Man can glory in infirmities, in distresses, in necessities, in persecutions, if they but bring him more fully into the sphere of Christ's fellowship and love. These men were so filled with the joy of God's salvation, that I question not that it was a matter of glorying with them if they were called to suffer, that they might show how much they loved, and how much they were beloved. This explains the constant language of the apostles about glorying in tribulation, and counting it all joy if they were called to suffer for Christ. Their joy was so exuberant that they were ready at any moment to put it to the test of the keenest pain. All love delights in sacrifices, yea in sufferings, for its object. Suffering ceases to be pain if love consecrates it ; it becomes a holy and blessed offering, and it tends ever to the increase of love.

And let the careless reader understand, that the choice in life is mainly between suffering with joy of the Holy Ghost, and suffering without it. Do not let the devil cheat you into the belief that the choice is between an easy, merry, careless, pleasant lifecourse, and the struggles and sorrows of the Christian, lightened and sweetened by the joy of the Holy Ghost. Life is no merry march, or holiday pastime for any of us ; but the true agony of life must be with those who are without God and without hope in the world. God sets no such choice before us as the pleasures of sin and the pains of godliness. The choice, as I have in the next discourse set forth more at large, is simply between the sorrows of sin and the sorrows of Redemption; the one embittered by the frown, the other illumined by the smile of God.

There is sorrow with a curse in the heart of it, and sorrow with a blessing ; sorrow with the devil for a comforter, and sorrow with God for a friend ; sorrow with the fiends for comrades, sorrow with Christ as the elder brother of the spirit ; sorrow with hell at the end of it, and sorrow with heaven. Here is your choice, the only choice which the Lord leaves you. Choose at once, for the sorrow comes hastening on. Escape is blankly impossible, but you may meet it with a smile of welcome, with a song of triumph. Fiercely as the storm may beat, this anchor at any rate will hold. "*It is a faithful saying that if we die with Him we shall live with Him;*" "if we suffer, we shall reign." How faithful, they know full well "*who received the word with much affliction and with joy of the Holy Ghost*," and have passed up to the recompenses of eternity.

X.

THE TWO SORROWS.

"For it is better, if the will of God be so, that ye suffer for well-doing than for evil-doing."—I. Peter iii. 17.

MUCH of this first epistle of Peter is occupied with the consolation of sufferers—the suffering sons of God. It was written to Hebrew Christians; Peter himself being a Hebrew of intense national sympathies and of marked national character. The suffering sons of God involved an idea which was not a little perplexing to one who had been trained in the Hebrew school. " Let the wicked suffer, let the saints be happy," was the formula which came most readily to Hebrew lips. It expressed the notion of the right order of things which ran through all the national literature, and it was deeply ingrained in the popular heart. A far truer and nobler philosophy of life is to be found, by those who will search for it, in the Hebrew writings; but the first Psalm contains the pith of the ideas which were popular in the Hebrew, as in some other and more modern, religious philosophy.

Peter was a man of the people, and his ideas ranged naturally with the popular views of his time. Paul too was a Hebrew of the Hebrews, but he had been trained in a higher and more thoughtful school. Perhaps it is not too much to say, that there was something in the nature of Saul of Tarsus, which enabled him to look more deeply into the mystery of sorrow, than could the strong, rough fisherman of Galilee—a man by nature of simple ideas, simple habits, and simple hopes. Paul's nature was much more complex and profound. The acute thinker, the accomplished scholar, the intensely sensitive and sympathetic man, he had in him an instinct which prepared him for a life of toil, sacrifice and suffering, in ministry to his fellows. Under no conditions could life have gone with him simply and easily; his was a nature to fathom to its very depths the mystery of the Passion and the Cross.

Into the mind of Peter these ideas would seem to have wrought themselves but slowly. He took upon himself to rebuke the Master, when first He unveiled the Cross before his sight. "*Then Peter took Him, and began to rebuke Him, saying, Be it far from Thee, Lord; this shall not be unto Thee. But He turned and said unto Peter, Get thee behind Me, Satan: thou art an offence unto Me.*"

The need of the suffering continued to be veiled from him. He it was who would take the sword to spare his Master the agony by which a whole world was to be saved. "That be far from Thee, Lord," he was saying again, when he drew the sword to smite the captors of Jesus; and we may be sure that his voice was not the least loud among those who uttered the lamentation, "*We trusted that it had been He which should have redeemed Israel, and this is the third day since these things were done.*" The prophesied resurrection seems quite to have passed away from his thoughts. The women's words were to the apostles "but idle tales, and they believed them not." He had much to learn about the meaning of Calvary. "*O fools, and slow of heart to believe all that the prophets have spoken; ought not Christ to have suffered these things, and to enter into His glory?*"

Peter, beyond all men, profited by the baptism of the day of Pentecost. He stands forth a new man from that hour. It was as though a veil had been lifted from around his spirit, and the light of the truth which through the Lord's words had been dimly struggling into his mind, had flashed on him in all its brightness. From that moment the Lord's counsel was quite clear to him. As plainly, as grandly, as Paul, he deals in this epistle with the mystery of sorrow; and he connects, as clearly as Paul, the sufferings of the saints with the sufferings of their Lord: the disciple suffering with the Master; the limb sharing the experience of the Head.

The suffering sons of God! "*It is better, if it be the will of God, that ye suffer for well doing than for evil doing.*" "*Wherefore let them that suffer according to the will of God, commit the keeping of their souls to Him in well doing, as unto a faithful Creator.*" Perhaps the true children of God, the faithful, the Israelites indeed, felt, not unnaturally, that when their Messiah should appear, he would release them from the cloud of sorrow and bring them out into the serene daylight of peace and joy. Who should be happy in this universe, if not the pure-hearted, the gentle, the loving, the patient, the believing! Must there not be some flaw in the constitution of the Kingdom of God, if such are left to be a prey to sorrow, wounds, and death? "*For thy sake we are killed all the day long, we are accounted as sheep for the slaughter,*" describes but a poor heritage for sons.

Doubtless they thought that when the Kingdom of Heaven should come, their long night of agony would be ended, and that the dawn of the day of triumph would be in the sky. One hardly knows which would be sadder, their heart or their Master's, when He announced that He had not come to send peace upon the earth, but a sword. It is stern work to meet an enemy's weapon; but it is infinitely sadder to trouble the convictions and to blight the hopes of a friend. This sadness in its fullest measure fell to the lot of our Lord. He knew that his friends were looking for rest, comfort, and honour; He knew that the heritage which He would leave to them would be exile, distress, and shame. "*In the world ye shall have tribulation,*" was all that He could say to them about the present; and a sharper pang must have shot through His heart than through theirs, as the sorrowful words dropped from His lips.

They accepted the lot bravely. "That be far from Thee, Lord," "That be far from us," was the natural cry of their spirits. "It is a Kingdom of Heaven; the children of the Kingdom cannot be doomed to such a lot as this!" But when the lot mastered them, when they found that the Lord meant in sober sadness that they must go cross-bearing through life, they accepted it heartily. Their teachers even stirred them up to accept it joyfully, as a full communion of experience with Christ. This is the whole tenour of Peter's epistle. "*Beloved, think it not strange concerning the fiery trial which is to try you, as though some strange thing happened unto you; but rejoice, inasmuch as ye are partakers of Christ's sufferings; that when His glory shall be revealed, ye may be glad also with exceeding joy. If ye be reproached for the name of Christ happy are ye; for the spirit of glory and of God resteth upon you: on their part He is evil spoken of, but on your part He is glorified.*"—I. Pet. iv. 12–14.

It is a constant theme in the writings of Paul, who in handling this subject grows "very bold," as he says of Esaias, and prays, "*That I may know Him, and the power of His resurrection, and the fellowship of His sufferings, being made conformable unto His death; if by any means I might attain unto the resurrection of the dead.*"—Phil. iii. 10–11. Let us consider,

I. The suffering of the children of God which is according to the Divine will. Let us look a little into its springs. There are three which I specially note:

1. The struggle against the current of the world without them.
2. The struggle against the world within them.
3. The burden of their ministry to mankind.

1. The struggle against the current of an ungodly world.

We *talk* about this in these days, they in theirs had to do it. The world's current is in some sort with us, with our beliefs, our endeavours, our aims. Christian ideas have wrought themselves, in a measure which is easily under-estimated, into the texture of the life of modern society. The world can do very well with a moderate measure of unselfishness and unworldliness; though Paul would still be counted as a madman were he in the midst of it, and the Lord would be cast out of its camp again. Such thorough devotion to the heavenly life, such utter contempt of the world's current maxims and prizes, would be as darkly distrusted now as it ever was. The men of the loftiest strain find their lot a lonely one still, but none the less are they the leaven of society. Yet belief in the facts and ideas of Christianity, is according to the course of the world among us; and a certain amount of self-denial, of attention to religious duties, and care for others, is accounted decent and respectable.

Easy, prosperous Christians, whose leading idea is to make themselves safe for eternity, had better be quiet about their burdens and sufferings; the world only laughs at them. But if a man *will* live godly in Christ Jesus, if he *will* look into his Master's experience, and try to understand what God means by life ; if he *will* bear witness, by a holy conversation, that the works of the world are evil; if he believes in his soul that the only life is the love of God, that it is not worth while to win a fortune or a throne, if a shadow were to steal between the soul and the light of God's countenance in winning it, that all the world cannot harm a man if he stands where God has placed him, and is about His work ; if he holds the following of the Lamb here to be the one condition of following Him there ; then life will be one long, stern struggle. Daily he will have to arm his soul for a battle, and his most familiar scenes and associates will furnish both the field and the foes. His life will seem to them a mystery, a dire mistake. Many will smile and sneer, vote him faint-hearted, and jostle him aside as they press on to the prize. He will have constantly to rein in his powers from a race in which he might win if he cared to contend. Living apart from the world in spirit, above the world, he must pay the penalty of many a heart-ache, many an hour of sharp anguish, many a moan in the ear of heaven, which the Father understands, How long, O Lord, how long! Unloose me, and let me free !

2. The struggle against the world within, which it is harder still to endure.

There was one who had endured at the hand of the world, because of his unflinching fidelity to Christ, all that is here set forth, " *Of the Jews five times received I forty stripes, save one. Thrice was I beaten with rods, once was I stoned, thrice I suffered ship-*

wreck, a night and a day I have been in the deep; in journeyings often, in perils of waters, in perils of robbers, in perils by mine own countrymen, in perils by the heathen, in perils in the city, in perils in the wilderness, in perils in the sea, in perils among false brethren; in weariness and painfulness, in watchings often, in hunger and thirst, in fastings often, in cold and nakedness."—II. Cor. xi. 24–27. But I think that he opened a deeper depth of sorrow when he wrote the words,—"*I therefore so run, not as uncertainly; so fight I, not as one that beateth the air; but I keep under my body, and bring it into subjection, lest that by any means, when I have preached to others, I myself should be a castaway.*"—I. Cor. ix. 26–7.

There are no true disciples of Christ who would not thankfully endure any amount of outward pressure, if they might but be free from the inward strain. It is there, on the neck of the unruly powers and passions, that the yoke chiefly galls. "Without, fightings," "within, fears," and the fears by far the worst. "*Unite my heart to fear Thy name,*" and I can bear all the rest. But deliver me from myself,—this vain, shallow, passionate, lustful, envious, hateful self, and then let the world do what it will! Are there any true children of the Kingdom, true soldiers of the Cross, who would not readily yield themselves into the hand of malignant power to work its will upon them, if the fountain of bitter waters might but be healed for ever within?

Here is the great struggle of the Christian life. "*Mortify, therefore, your member which are upon the earth, fornication, uncleanness, inordinate affection, evil concupiscence, and covetousness, which is idolatry . . . But now ye also put off all these; anger, wrath, malice, blasphemy, evil communication out of your mouth. Lie not one to another, seeing that ye have put off the old man and his deeds, and have put on the new man. . . And above all these put on charity, which is the bond of perfectness."*—Col. iii. 5-14. All the rest were easy work. But day after day this battle has to be renewed. Old enemies, again and again beaten, again and again rise up in full force and renew the struggle. We think perhaps that we have won a great victory, and slain some passion or lust which had been tormenting us, for ever. The soul faints and sickens to find it rising again in full strength at the very next occurrence of temptation, and to see that the old round of conflict and self-crucifixion has to be retrod. It is not only the beaten combatant in life's battle who is tempted to cry, " *O miserable man that I am, who shall deliver me from the body of this death?*" The victory is so costly that it wrung from Paul the same moan, checked ere it rose to heaven by the joyful outburst, " *I thank my God, through Jesus Christ my Lord.*"

3. The burden of their ministry to mankind. We have read the history of Paul's outward troubles and struggles. Consider the significance of what follows : "*Beside those things that are without, that which cometh upon me daily, the care of all the churches. Who is weak, and I am not weak? Who*

is offended, and I burn not?" And again, *"For though I be free from all men, yet have I made myself the servant of all, that I might gain the more. And unto the Jews I became as a Jew, that I might gain the Jews; to them that are under the law, as under the law, that I might gain them that are under the law; to them that are without law, as without law (being not without law to God, but under the law to Christ), that I might gain them that are without law."*—I. Cor. ix. 19–22.

The man who gives himself to be the world's servant and minister for the Lord's sake, opens his heart to a cloud of cares and sorrows, from which he might, if he pleased, keep far away. It is hard, stern work, this caring for the world. It is the sphere of activity in which he may enter most profoundly into the Master's experience, and feel something of the weight of the Intercessor's, the Mediator's burden, which well-nigh crushed His heart. If it does not crush us, it is because the chief weight is upon the Master still. Moses felt it when he interceded for the people, and staked his life, and more than his life, on his intercession. *"And Moses returned unto the Lord and said, Oh, this people have sinned a great sin, and have made them gods of gold; yet now, if Thou wilt forgive their sin; and if not, blot me, I pray Thee, out of Thy book which Thou hast written."*—Ex. xxxii. 31–2. And Paul, *"I say the truth in Christ, I lie not, my conscience also bearing me witness in the Holy Ghost, that I have great heaviness and continued sorrow in my heart. For I could wish, that myself were accursed from Christ for my brethren, my kinsmen according to the flesh."*—Rom. ix. 1-3.

There are those living now who are simply spending *life* in their daily ministry, and are serving their fellow-men at the cost of all else that man holds dear. And who is worthy of the name of a disciple who refuses this ministry to man? It was for this purely that the Master came. "*The Son of Man came not to be ministered unto, but to minister, and to give His life as a ransom for many.*" "*As My Father hath sent Me into the world,*" He said to His disciples, "*even so send I you.*" It is the Christian life. "*Ye are not your own; for ye are bought with a price. Wherefore glorify God in your body and in your spirit, which are His.*"

But the burden sometimes presses crushingly. The hardness, the unthankfulness, the impenitence of men, will bring bitter tears from loving and unselfish hearts. The work, too, will often seem quite hopeless. "*Master, we have toiled all the night, and have caught nothing,*" will constantly be our complaint. "It is all useless; the righteous perish; I am left alone," we cry like Elijah, and then fling down sword and shield in the wilderness, praying that death may come swiftly and release us from the burden and the pain. Suffering according to the will of God! There is no release from it. It lies enfolded in the conditions of our life as Christians. We cannot refuse it if we would; we dare not if we might.

Here is one side of the picture—certain suffering in the Christian life. Is this the only side? Is all the sharpest suffering endured by the children? Are they the only afflicted and burdened of the world? It would be a strange world if it were so; a strange Kingdom of Heaven. The rebels alone happy, the children always in tears! It was not a very deep view of life which Asaph presented: "*I was envious at the foolish, when I saw the prosperity of the wicked. For there are no bands in their death, and their strength is firm. They are not in trouble as other men, neither are they plagued like other men. . . . . . . Their eyes stand out with fatness, they have more than heart can wish.*"—Ps. lxxiii. 3–7. Or Job: "*Wherefore do the wicked live, become old, yea, are mighty in power? Their seed is established in their sight with them, and their offspring before their eyes. Their houses are safe from fear, neither is the rod of God upon them. Their bull gendereth and faileth not; their cow calveth, and casteth not her calf. They send forth their little ones like a flock, and their children dance. . . . . . They spend their days in wealth, and in a moment go down to the grave. Therefore they say unto God, Depart from us, for we desire not the knowledge of Thy ways.*"—Job. xxi. 7–14.

There is another side to the account, to which we will now turn—

II. The suffering evil-doers.

1. We have seen what comes of swimming against the current; the struggles and shocks to which a man dooms himself, when he sets his face fairly against the evil which is in the world, resolved, by God's strength, to stem it, and to live after a pattern shown

to him from a higher sphere. Let those who do not like the prospect set their faces with the world, swim with the current, and care chiefly for worldly success, and see how it fares with them. I am not uttering words carelessly, or for the mere sake of effect, when I say, that I suppose that the unhappiest men upon this earth, on the whole, are its princes, its nobles, and its millionaires. There is nothing which so palls as the pomp of high station, nothing which so wearies the soul as the monotony of success. Dives had his good things here, and Lazarus his evil things. But even here, Dives was the cursed man, with all his pomp, Lazarus the blessed man, with all his rags and wounds.

"Sinners may escape the rod," we sing sometimes thoughtlessly. Do you find that they escape it? Does this sum up your observation of their lives? How many wretched sinners, men and women, whose life is a burden and a curse to them, are to be found wherever a human company is congregated? How many in the poor bare cottages, poor and bare through drink and lust, which lie all round our happy homes? How many in our great banking houses, our palaces of commerce, our squares and parks where the rich of this world chiefly dwell? The jostle, the strain, in swimming with the current, is just as hard as in swimming against it; nay, harder, for of all the strains that a man has to bear, the most exhausting, the most agonizing, is that which he has to endure when his heart is set with its whole energy and passion on a purely worldly success.

You may be inclined to doubt it. Ask lunatic-asylum keepers what light they can throw upon it; or read the memoirs of those familiar with the secret history of courts. But let a man win the eminence on which he has set his heart, and which has become his one aim in life; his miseries but begin. Who has not heard some selfish schemer, who has struggled on to a grand position, begin to groan at once over the care and distress which it brings? Paralysis too is none the more endurable for gilding; and a wrangling family can make the finest house a hell. I know a young man who, by a sudden stroke, made a splendid fortune, and the dread of dying in a poor-house is beginning already to cast its dreary shadow over his life. Sinners escape the rod! I think that the devil takes care that they shall feel it to the quick, and it is not oil that he rubs into the wounds. If it is pain that you shrink from, take not the devil's yoke upon you; you will not find rest with him.

2. It is stern work, no doubt, to stem the current of an unholy nature, to tame rebellious passions, and to compel them to own a master's hand. It is a long, hard struggle, this conflict with passion, and it ends only in death. Well, if you shrink from the prospect, indulge the passion, give it full swing, and see how it will be then. "*Rejoice, O young man, in thy youth.*" Take thy fill, eat, drink, and be merry; the reckoning is at hand. Is there any horror like that of a worn-out profligate's premature old age? The dull eye, the trembling limbs, the confused brain, the stammering tongue, the brand "beware'

set upon his brow, the soul settling down the while into a darkness that may be felt. Or in other forms, let selfish, jealous passions have full sway. Do not fight them, do not master them; let them alone until they have mastered you. Is there any small hell upon earth more complete than the home that they will make for you? Set it down in your scheme of life that you are not to deny yourself for wife, for children, for kindred; that it is their place rather to deny themselves for you; and how much joy or profit will your daily intercourse with them yield? How far will their love solace your toils, lighten your burdens, and welcome you home when weary to the sweetest rest?

It is a hard battle, no doubt, to which in God's name I call you, the battle against passion, lust, and self. But there is one thing harder, infinitely harder, to which the devil is calling you—indulgence. Loose the rein, and your course will be a swift and stormy one to the nether darkness and the pit.

3. The burden of ministry. "Well," says the self-centred, worldly-hearted man, "at any rate I can escape that. If I live to myself, I can at least avoid that sea of care." Yes, you can avoid that. It is a field of experience from which a man can keep himself, if he will. It is the purely voluntary suffering, the will must go with it, and it is most completely according to the will of God. You can escape it if you please; you cannot be forced into it against your own will; and you can take a wretched heartache with you through life, for want of some noble and ennobling work.

I have said that probably the unhappiest men in the world are to be found among its wealthiest. And the reason lies here. It is not simply that riches and honours bring cares, breed strifes, and gender satiety. It is that it is so hard for rich men not to trust in uncertain riches ; and hearts trusting in this world's wealth, cannot help aching for a better trust and a nobler treasure. They cannot help aching, I say. You can help giving ; you can help ministering ; you can help devoting yourself to the good of others ; but you cannot help the heartache which a life of selfishness brings. The heart aches for that which it was made to possess and to enjoy. It is God's law of life. No man shall rest save in that which God ordained to satisfy him. And the sharpest of all pains, the most intolerable of all pressures, is that of a heart pining for its true God-given work.

And now in the light of these principles let us,

III. Consider the affirmation of the text. What we have before us in life is clearly the choice of the kind of suffering which we will endure. Escape we cannot. "*Man is born to trouble, as the sparks fly upward.*" Suffer man must, with a nature like his, in a world like this. Let the worldly-hearted take notice of the essential condition of man's life in this world. There are the two sorrows—the sorrow of the righteous, the sorrow of the unrighteous; the sorrow of the self-centred, the sorrow of the self-sacrificing ; the sorrow of the self-controlled, the sorrow of the profligate ; the sorrow of the world, the sorrow of the Kingdom ; the sorrow of Christ, the sorrow of the fiends. There they lie, the two burdens. Your choice is between them. Lift one you must, bear one you shall. God grants no immunity to you or to any other man. Choose ; the choice is before you, and now ; and consider, as you weigh them in the balance, that—

1. The one inspires, the other emasculates the spirit.
2. The one has pure joy in the heart of it, the other pure agony.
3. The one ends in glory, the other in shame and the everlasting night.

1. The one inspires, the other emasculates the spirit.

The sorrows and struggles that come to a man in fulfilling the will of God, are like strong exercise on the mountains. They make him strain and pant, but they make him glow; they brace, purify, and exalt his power. Deep down in his inmost soul he knows that suffering thus he is doing the thing for which God made him, and that all his powers have found their work. He knows that in this battle the everlasting strength is on his side. He knows that however hardly he may be pressed, however sharp may be his moan, there is One watching with sure, Almighty hand who will never suffer him to be lost.

And he is at one with himself. His heart says, It is well. And a man can bear anything if he be but heart-whole; if there be peace and unity within. I see the suffering sinner slinking along the world's pathways, unable to look up, unwilling to look round, afraid to look within; no Hand beneath him in the struggle, no Presence beside him in the storm. He has no vision of a future to animate and inspire him; he spends his strength daily and for nought; the inner man becoming weaker, sadder, wearier, more heart-sick of it all; until, but for the dread of something after death, he would be ready for the suicide's plunge into the dark river, and the haunted rest of an unhallowed grave. Suffer according to the will of God, and drink in fresh inspiration daily. Suffer according to the will of the flesh, and watch the daily weakening of your noblest powers, the withering of your fairest hopes, the darkening of your brightest visions, as your soul settles down into the night.

2. The one has pure joy in the heart of it, the other pure agony.

Strange as it may seem, the hour of a spiritual man's sharpest suffering is often the hour of his sublimest joy. Why? Because the Lord is with him, drawing the weary form to His bosom, resting the aching head on His heart. Songs in the night! The night of sorrow bright with song! It is not only the sense of the Divine strength which inspires the sufferer; it is the sense of the Divine love that makes him blest. We can bear anything when a loving heart is beating beside us. And shall we faint "under the light affliction" when the very heart of love is gathering us to its embrace? Nay, "*Most gladly therefore will we take pleasure in infirmities, in reproaches, in necessities, in persecutions, in distresses, for Christ's sake, for when we are weak then are we strong."* The sufferer knows that he is growing into the love of his Father, his Saviour; and is tasting the water of a living fountain, which will be welling up through eternity.

In the heart of the sinful sufferer there is the germ of pure agony. It is hopeless suffering, and that is the anguish of the fiends. There is nothing to make it tolerable. "My punishment is greater than I can bear," said the first flagrant sinner. It is the character of all unhallowed suffering; it must break down the strongest strength, it must wear out the most resolute will at last. Suffering without hope! It is the anguish of the pit. And your suffering in sin, loving it and cleaving to it, is of this essence. The sharper it becomes the more dire the agony, the darker, the more horrible the despair.

3. The one has its end in glory, the other in shame and everlasting contempt.

Men are willing to suffer for a crown, to struggle for a prize. What would life be without its future? No matter what burden you may bear, what moan you may mutter, if *"this light affliction, which is but for a moment,"* is working for you *"a far more exceeding and eternal weight of glory."* It will matter little when God lifts up your head with honour, in the day of the manifestation of His sons. Nay, it will matter much. " *Ye are they which continued with Me in my temptation, and I appoint unto you a kingdom.*" These sufferings will be the theme of the most blessed communion, the seeds of the purest joys, the most radiant glories of eternity. These, who have suffered according to the will of God, shall awake to everlasting life, and those, who have suffered according to the will of the flesh, shall awake to shame and everlasting contempt.

Fellow sinner, fellow sufferer! We are the heirs of the same bitter inheritance of sorrow through sin. Will you have God's light upon it, God's love in it; or the devil's darkness, the devil's curse? Suffer you must. Escape you cannot. But, oh! see to it, see to it, that when your hour of anguish comes upon you, you have God and Christ upon your side.

XI.
THE SACRED DARKNESS.

" Who is among you that feareth the Lord, that obeyeth the voice of His servant, that walketh in darkness and hath no light? Let him trust in the name of the Lord, and stay upon his God."—Is. 1. 10.

Is it by chance, think you, that the prophecies of Isaiah are laden with such a burden of sympathy with the sufferings of Messiah, and with such dark foreshadowings of the agony and bloody sweat, the cross and passion, the death and burial, in which, to the eye of sense, that mission of love would end? Of all the sacred writers, it is Isaiah who paints the most pathetic pictures of the Man of Sorrows, and of the Life of Sorrows. The thorn crown and the bloody spear, though the mist of ages intervened, were not hidden from his sight. There were moments when there crossed his vision a splendid heroic form, the form of a conquering king, crushing his foes beneath the wheels of his triumphal chariot, as he thundered on amid universal acclamation to the empire of the world. But there lingered before his sight the form of another King, with the stain of tears upon His cheek, and the drops of bloody sweat upon His brow. He was pallid, worn with watching, weak with hunger, emaciated by a life of conflict and pain. He was crowned, but the thorns of His crown pierced Him; He was robed, but in the mocking purple with which He had been invested by His insolent guard. There were throngs of His subjects round Him, but they cried out, Away with Him, away with Him; and they dragged Him at length through a brutal, jeering rabble to enthrone Him on a cross. The King whom Isaiah saw was "*despised and rejected of men, a man of sorrows and acquainted with grief, and they hid as it were their faces from Him, He was despised, and they esteemed Him not.*"

And the prophet paints it all as one who *saw*, and whose soul was filled with shame, with anguish, and with unutterable pity, at the spectacle. The men who lived with Messiah and who beheld His passion, have not left to us such pathetic records as these. This greatest and most far-seeing of those who "*spake beforehand of the sufferings of Christ, and the glory that should follow*," dwells with peculiar tenderness on His lonely and forsaken lot, on the cup of human anguish of which His soul alone knew all the bitterness, and of that desert path, the whole gloom and horror of which He alone explored. Was is by chance, I say, that this royal prophetic spirit was led to fathom these depths of Messiah's sorrow, and to strike thus early the sad key-note of His history? Or had he himself tasted this cup of bitterness? Had he himself, in his finite human measure, been "despised and rejected of men; a man of sorrows and acquainted with grief"?

The Sacred Darkness. 207

Ah! it is the sorrowful who alone can comprehend the sufferers. It is those who have passed through the high school of discipline, who alone know the meaning and can gauge the measure of human grief. Isaiah knew beforehand the fellowship of his Master's sufferings; he was led by the same Hand through the same depths. He had passed through that which fitted him for vivid sympathy with One, who after a life of Divine ministry was left to agonize on the Cross alone. He was of that elect band of whom the Saviour spake—they are the peerage of earth and of heaven—who can drink of the cup which Messiah drank of, and can endure the baptism with which He was baptized. And in painting, with a touch whose pathetic tenderness remains unrivalled still, that mystery of sorrow—the sorrow of sorrows of earth's history, and of heaven's—he was but painting out, as the Spirit taught him, the outlines of a tragedy, which he knew to be all too possible by the witness of his own sad heart.

He was an old man, a very old man, when he wrote this grand Evangelic poem, which opens with the blessed commission, the true beginning of the Gospel, "*Comfort ye, comfort ye my people, saith your God. Speak ye comfortably to Jerusalem, and cry unto her, that her warfare is accomplished, that her iniquity is pardoned, for she hath received of the Lord's hand double for all her sins. Hark! A voice crying in the wilderness, Prepare ye the way of the Lord, make straight in the desert a highway for our God.*" He was drawing near to the end, and it was destined to be a bloody end, of a long and illustrious career, as the first statesman as well as the first prophet of his time. Isaiah's statesmanship, as revealed in his prophecies, is a mine of political wisdom which has yet to be fully explored.

I am not, of course, unacquainted with the very strong body of criticism, which would connect this latter portion of the book of the prophecies of Isaiah with a much later writer, living in the midst of the events on which these prophecies mainly bear. It has always seemed to me utterly impossible, to explain away the grand prophetic element in the book by any such hypothesis; nor has any argument which I have met with appeared to me conclusive, or anything like conclusive, against the received ideas. I think, too, that the most recent criticism, as is constantly the case after a period of sceptical frenzy, seems to be setting in the direction of the old opinion once more.

I take this book then to be Isaiah's work, and the work of an extreme old age. He had lived to *"serve his own generation according to the will of God."* Paul was not more intensely, more passionately devoted to his ministry, than was Isaiah to the service of the profligate and degenerate age and people among whom God had cast his lot. There can be little doubt, I imagine, that he had been the mainspring of the reformation which has made the name of Hezekiah illustrious in history. The hope which he had nursed in his heart, and which his splendid imaginative faculty had enabled him to pourtray, in colours which remain still the most vivid pictures of a golden age of peace and blessedness in the world's literature, was realized for a moment, and then faded from Jewish history for ever.

Hezekiah, to whom he had been the stay and the staff, both in his reformation, and in the formidable political difficulties of his reign, died, and the impious Manasseh occupied his room. The people who had suffered rather than wrought the reformation, when Manasseh gave the word, swiftly cast off the yoke which it had laid upon their passions, and rushed to such daring excesses both of idolatry and profligacy, as cast even the reign of Ahab over Israel into the shade. The twenty-first chapter of the second book of Kings records the shameful history. Every possible act of apostacy which the chosen people could commit, they indulged in with eagerness. And to sum up all, it is said that Manasseh "*seduced them to do more evil than did the nations whom the Lord destroyed before the children of Israel.*" Of those nations it is said the land "*spued out its inhabitants,*" because of their horrible vices; and this explains the ruthlessness of the warfare of the Israelites in their invasion of Canaan, as the picture of the people under Manasseh which is here painted, explains the ultimate horrors of the captivity.[1]

Isaiah watched the reaction; he was at this time some fourscore years old. And he watched it with worn and weary heart. He saw the torrent of im-

---

[1] Compare Lev. xviii. 24-30.

piety sweeping away every wreck of that which he had once hailed as a glorious and lasting revival in the Jewish State and Church. It seemed as though the doom of the people were already sealed, as if the hope of their regeneration were for ever dead. No! not for ever. The old prophet rebuked his faithless heart. Not for ever. God lived, and the word of God. "*All flesh is grass, and all the goodliness thereof is as the flower of the field. The grass withereth, the flower fadeth, but the word of our God shall stand for ever. O Zion, that bringest good tidings, get thou up into the high mountain; O Jerusalem, that bringest good tidings, lift up thy voice with strength. Lift it up, be not afraid, say unto the cities of Judah, behold your God.*"

The great hope, with which the word of the Lord had been laden since the first days of man's transgression, could not die. So the old seer betook himself to vision. All around him was black as Erebus. But in the far future there was a golden gleam on which he fixed his sight. It widened as he gazed, and all the glory of the Kingdom of Heaven was unveiled. It was there before *his* sight, as it had been from the beginning before the sight of God. As real as the scenes of impiety, impurity, and blood which filled him with horror, was this golden, glorious future for Israel and for the world. And then he wrote the vision; his last legacy to his people before he was "sawn asunder" by the fiendish barbarity of the king.

He wrote out at large this most magnificent of

visions, this chain of prophecies of the glory and blessedness of Messiah's reign, which for splendour both of imagination and diction is probably unmatched in any literature; and he left it to God to guard it, and to fulfil its promise in His time. *"Whereas thou hast been forsaken and hated, so that no man went through thee, I will make thee an eternal excellency, the joy of many generations. . . . Violence shall no more be heard in thy land, wasting nor destruction within thy borders; but thou shalt call thy walls Salvation, and thy gates Praise. The sun shall be no more thy light by day, neither for brightness shall the moon give light unto thee, but the Lord shall be unto thee an everlasting light, and thy God thy glory. Thy sun shall no more go down, neither shall thy moon withdraw itself, for the Lord shall be thine everlasting light, and the days of thy mourning shall be ended."*

The man who could see that through the miseries and horrors of Manasseh's reign, had found, as far as man may find, the key to "the sufferings of Christ and the glory that should follow;" and he had won nobly the right to be heard, in speaking to all who are called like Christ to pass through great darkness, in doing the Father's will, and in finishing His work. *"Who is among you that feareth the Lord, that obeyeth the voice of His servant, that walketh in darkness, and hath no light? Let him trust in the name of the Lord, and stay upon his God."*

Let us study the character of those who are visited with the experience described in the text.

Two features stand prominently forth ; the pious mind, the godly, Christ-like life.

1. The pious mind. "*Who is among you that feareth the Lord?*"

It is the most constant description of piety in the Old Testament. The fear of the Lord was the sign of the godly character, and the strength of the godly life. It describes, under the conditions of the elder dispensation, the spirit and the attitude of the man to whom the mind and the will of God were not only substantial, but supreme realities in the conduct of his life,—the man who set the Lord always before him, and who knew, in his secret soul, that the one great concern of life was to stand right with Him.

God was a very living presence with the Jewish people. He had not begun to fade into an abstraction, under the manipulations of the Scribes and priests. He had been seen, at least the blinding splendour which veiled His presence had been seen, by their fathers, and His voice, the voice of His law amid mighty thunderings, had been heard. His arm had been visibly bared, and again and again it had wrought wonders both of judgment and of salvation in their midst. They remembered all the great and terrible works which He had done before their eyes, the redemption which He had wrought for His servants, and the destruction which He had dealt to their foes. Thus God became a very living presence in the midst of them ; One whose "well done" carried with it the support of an Omnipotent hand, while behind His frown waited hell and death. And the fear of the Lord grew to be a very vivid and mighty principle of action in Israel, on which men were not afraid to stake possessions, fame, and life, for time and for eternity.

Nor is the Old Testament fear inconsistent in any wise with the love, of which we read so much in the words of Christ and of His apostles. "*Perfect love casteth out fear*," it is said. Truer word could not be spoken. But love casteth out fear by absorbing it into itself. Slavish fear it destroys utterly, but holy fear it adopts and cherishes. The perfect filial love is a love which has this holy fear in the heart of it; it is more fearful of wounding the Father's love, and grieving the Father's heart, than of anything else in this wide universe. The loving fear, the fearful love, is the divine passion in "the children of the Highest"—deep reverence, trembling awe, perfect, tender, trustful love.

The men described in our text are the lovers of God rather than of the world; men to whom it is matter of daily anxious concern to please Him, who have Him in all their thoughts, who take their daily mercies from His hand with the light of His love upon them, who sweeten their daily toils and struggles by the thought of His sympathy and care. To them the wealth of the universe would be literally no compensation for His frown; for them a world in arms could bring no shadow over the sunlight of His smile. They make Him "*the Man of their counsel*," their "*Chiefest among ten thousand*," their portion, their shield, their strength, and their exceeding great reward. "*Who is among you that feareth the Lord?*"

2. He will manifest his fear by a godly, Christ-like life.

"*That heareth the voice of His servant.*"

I think that in this passage, by "the servant of the Lord," Isaiah means the Messiah. It is the term which He constantly employs to designate Him. In chapter xlii. 1, the words, "*Behold My servant whom I uphold, Mine elect in whom My soul delighteth,*" can refer to no other. And again in lii. 13, the words, "*Behold My servant shall deal prudently; he shall be exalted and extolled, and be very high,*" introduce that matchless picture of Messiah's sufferings and spiritual triumph, on which in the introduction to this discourse I have dwelt at large. And I think that there is a very rich suggestion here. The men who obey Messiah's voice are the men who can sympathise with Messiah's mission. "*I call you not servants, but friends.*" They seek to make their lives, within their limits, the images of His life in the world. It is very significant that "fearing the Lord," and "obeying the voice of His servant," are here spoken of as synonymous. This means that he who has an eye for God will also have an eye for Christ. He who feareth the Father obeyeth also the Son, and recognises Him at once as the "Sent of God." Two beautiful instances of this are recorded by St. Luke ii. 25-38. Simeon knew the infant in a moment, and sang his *Nunc dimittis.*

And Anna the prophetess, entering the temple, burst forth into praise.

These are the Christlike men and women who are spoken of in the text, the men who obey the voice of Christ's mission, to whom He saith in all ages, "*As My Father hath sent Me into the world, even so send I you.*" They are not afraid of self-denial and sacrifice ; they do not shudder at the cross, which has been consecrated for them by the Lord. They believe in self-denying, self-sacrificing ministry; they are able to live, not for themselves, but for mankind. They are able to urge on their self-denying course, as Isaiah did, through a host of oppositions, and at peril of possessions, position, and even of life. They feel it to be a natural thing, a thing to be expected, and for which they are bound to be prepared, that the better they serve the world the less they should be appreciated by it, the more they should be a mark for the slings of its hate and the shafts of its scorn. They are sure that the better they serve their Heavenly Master, the more thoroughly they must be content to let the prizes of this world go. No man can hear Messiah's voice in the inner chamber of his spirit, without entering into Messiah's ministry to man. And no man can enter into that ministry without taking all things which he had held as gain, and counting them " but loss for Christ;" without taking the cross and bearing it patiently, until at life's outer gate the angels lift it, and present the cross-bearer to be crowned. "*The Lord God hath opened mine ear, and I was not rebellious, neither* turned away back. *I gave my back to the smiters, and my cheek to them that plucked off the hair. I hid not my face from shame and spitting. For the Lord God will help me, therefore I shall not be confounded: therefore have I set my face like a flint, and I know that I shall not be ashamed. He is near that justifieth me."*—Isaiah l. 5–8.

. This was the key-note of Messiah's mission. What man is there among you that heareth it, and is prepared to tune his life to this Divine pitch? Which of you feels this to be the heavenly life, the truly beautiful and glorious life? "*I am crucified with Christ: nevertheless I live; yet not I, but Christ liveth in me: and the life which I now live in the flesh, I live by the faith of the Son of God, who loved me, and gave Himself for me.*" Which of you encompassed by perils, and with death in sight, would cry, "*None of these things move me, neither count I my life dear unto myself, so that I might finish my course with joy, and the ministry which I have received of the Lord Jesus, to testify the gospel of the grace of God.*" "*Who is among you that feareth the Lord, that obeyeth the voice of His servant, that walketh in darkness and hath no light? Let him trust in the name of the Lord, and stay upon his God.*"

II. The condition of experience described in the text.

"*Who walketh in darkness, and hath no light.*"

The first question which occurs is, What has such an one to do with darkness? With God's smile shining as sunlight above, whence and how this gloom? The path of such a man as we have pictured, must, one would say, be bathed in sunshine. Can there be darkness when God, the living God, is in presence with a human soul? This is but part of a greater question, How could the well-beloved Son, He in whom the Father was ever well pleased, grow up before Him *"as a root out of a dry ground, without form or comeliness,"* and with no beauty that man, beholding Him, should desire Him? His splendour, fresh from heaven, should surely dazzle every eye, and his beauty enchain every heart!

And how could He who even unto death, a death of lingering torture and shame, did the Father's will and finished the Father's work, pass through a horror of great darkness in the very crisis of His obedience, when He bowed His head and said, "It is finished," with lips stiffening in death? *"My God, My God, why hast Thou forsaken Me?"* was an exceeding bitter cry from the lips of One, who had come to that hour of agony that He might do the will of the Father and glorify His name; whom not even that horror of darkness could tempt to cast the cup, the dregs of which were yet undrained, from His hand. There was darkness over the whole land—that we can well understand; but whence this infinitely denser gloom which overshadowed Incarnate God?

I am not about to attempt to answer this question directly. My concern here is rather with those who are like-minded with Christ, and who pass through the same darkness. The consideration of their case may cast some light for us on His. But at any rate I am anxious that you should see that the darkness of such is no isolated experience; it is part of the fellowship of the sufferings of the Lord.

Let there be no confusion between this darkness, and the gloom in which a man buries himself by conscious and wilful sin. I do not mean to say, that it is not as dense, or as hard to bear. It may seem denser and harder to bear. But the two things belong to quite separate worlds; as distinct as are the sorrow with which one mourns a friend, and that with which one bewails a sin. And this is where Job's friends went so dismally, so shamefully astray. They saw him walking in darkness and having no light, and they concluded that the shadow of some great secret transgression had fallen over his soul. They were wrong, utterly wrong. The shadow of a great folly, so gross as to be a sin, was rapidly falling over theirs. The darkness of which Isaiah writes is at any rate not the misery which springs out of the consciousness of flagrant transgression. It is not the outward and visible sign of sin hidden and cherished in the heart. These are God's children, obeying the voice of His Christ, who pass through it. We must search elsewhere for its springs.

1. The plainest and most palpable source of it, is the seeming frustration of our holiest and most unselfish purposes, a dreary want of success in what seems to us our best and most Christ-like work.

We can hardly shake ourselves free from this

The Sacred Darkness.

judgment of *success*. The right thing must succeed, we say. We reiterate it to ourselves with emphasis and earnestness, and we demand of God that it shall succeed. And we are right. The right thing must succeed, and we have a right to demand of God that it shall succeed. And if we can wait and see "the end of the Lord," we shall see the success. But here our faith fails. Verily we " have need of patience." Of how much sad miscarriage in life is impatience the root! But our cry is, " Now, Lord, all is ready; the work is faithfully done; now crown it with success." And God seems inexorable to our prayers. He wants two things to succeed, the work in the world, and the work of patience in us. And He will not measure His day by ours. Then the shadow begins to fall. In proportion to the strength of the strain, and the vividness of the hope, is the coldness, the darkness, the drearihood of the night in which it all seems to be lost.

Isaiah had staked all on that Reformation. He had wrought at it with passionate ardour. He saw it grow to beauty and grandeur under his hand. Then it perished, and not even a wreck was saved. "Is it all a mockery?" the faithful are tempted to cry. "Are these godly principles, these heavenly hopes, but a dream that lures us to our ruin? Is it the Lord or a mocking fiend who rules the disorder of this lower world? Or am I all wrong? Am I, pretending to be a servant of the Lord, and to obey the voice of His Christ, but a self-seeking, self-centred hypocrite? Have I dared to put my hand to an ark too pure for my unhallowed touch? Has the work failed because God will not have the help of such as I am?" Then a horror of great darkness falls over the spirit. It despairs of itself, its own salvation, the world, the Church; dense darkness has covered it all, and the gloom is broken by no gleam of light.

2. We may be passing through very heavy pressures of affliction; and, missing the comfort, the hope, which we think God should bring to us, we cry that we are forsaken; perhaps we are cheated into believing that all which was brightest in our past was a delusion or a lie. We are prone to lay down, unconsciously, methods for God. We frame to ourselves a notion of how He ought to help us, and when. But "His ways are not as our ways, neither are His thoughts as our thoughts;" and He makes us feel it. It is a part of our education which is most essential, and in the process of the discipline we seem sometimes buried in gloom. We see others hopeful even under crushing calamities. We hear songs in the night, but we cannot stir ourselves to sing. "There must be something wrong," we say, "or we should not be left to struggle thus, without a vision of the Divine Deliverer; we should not be left to suffer thus, without the presence of the Divine Comforter. No! it is all a delusion; the Lord deals not thus with those whom He recognises as His children. I have been cheating myself with a hope which God refuses to justify. Let me shrink back into the darkness, it is the element which most

suits me. God neglects me, has forgotten me; let me wither in silence and die."

Much of the sense of darkness in times of great strain and sorrow, is due to the morbid condition of mind and body which is generated at such seasons. The mind is overwhelmed; the nerves are overstrained. They ache for rest and find none. They search for the Father's bosom on which to cast their weariness, and He seems to be hidden. It is the eye which is dim and misses the signs of His presence. It is the ear that is dull and fails to catch the whispers of His sympathy and love. And so we make our faithless moan, "'*My way is hid from the Lord, my judgment is passed over from my God;*' and this is the very moment when I most need Him, when the vision of His face and the touch of His hand alone can save me from despair!"

3. But the main source of the darkness which sometimes buries the most pious and faithful under its pall, is the shadow of their own sinful nature, which at moments it seems to them hopeless even for God to attempt to redeem. Was it not the weight of the world's sin, realised at that moment in its full horror, which drew the cry "*My God, My God, why hast Thou forsaken Me?*" from Divine lips? Just in the measure in which we realise the grandeur of the vocation, and the glory of the destiny, to which we are called in Christ, will be the conviction in moments of depression that it is too grand, too glorious, to be ours. "Ah, Lord God," is the moan of our spirits, "I am undone. Sin is too deep-

rooted, too tyrannous, even for Thy grace. How poor, how beggarly, is my faith, my love, my hope. '*I am a worm, and no man.*' Were there a spark of the true Divine life in me, it would be shining now with a visible lustre. Were I Thine, Thou wouldst turn my darkness into day."

Those who have entertained a high and strong assurance concerning their calling to salvation, are often visited with seasons of darkness, peculiarly dense and drear. It is as though the living soul had become a cold corpse, no pulse of love, no glow of hope, no flash of joy, no breath of prayer. All dark, dark—the darkness and coldness of the dead. It comes from mysterious, unfathomable springs, this rayless darkness of an intense believer. But the springs are fed by the great chaotic sea of evil that surges up from black depths in the Creation ; and which sometimes, in the world and in us, seems to defy the power of even the re-creating breath of the Spirit of the Lord.

III. The text tells us of the believer's trust and stay.

"*Zion saith, The Lord hath forsaken me, and my Lord hath forgotten me.*" The Lord saith, "*Can a woman forsake her sucking child, that she should not have compassion on the son of her womb ? Yea they may forget, yet will not I forget thee.*" Hast thou not known, hast thou not heard, the Name of the God of Jacob ; what He is, what He has promised, what He can do ? Cling to that Name ; though it be with the wild, agonizing grasp of desperation, still cling.

However restless, however joyless, however hopeless your spirit, rebuke "your infirmity," and consider the Name of the Most High. Stay yourselves on Him. That is, hold to your duty, the duty next to your hand, in the strength of God. What you know to be right, though you see no light upon it, cleave to. Blind men even can feel their way. Dark as it may be, there will always be waymarks in the path of duty, which you may feel for, and keep the road. Say to your murmuring soul, "I can do without peace, I can do without joy, I can do without hope, for a time ; but I cannot do without duty. I cannot cast away sword and shield, and fly. I cannot turn craven or sluggard. Fight I will, while my arm can strike a blow ; and till my right hand forgets its cunning, I will work. That I know to be my vocation. The devil shall not tempt or frighten me from it. And for the peace, the joy, the hope, the light, that shall be as God wills, in time."

That is the true wisdom for one who is in darkness, to keep firm in the broad highway and await the inevitable dawn. Night is not the inevitable thing ; "there shall be no night there." The dawn is inevitable, for God lives, and God is light. What if He is breaking your idols, your cherished plans, your much loved work, which may be filling the place which He only can occupy to the full in your heart ? What if He is forging your character by strong hammer strokes of discipline ; welding your patience, bracing your courage, nerving your hope, kindling your love ? Trust in the Name of the Lord through it all, stay yourselves on your God, and wait.

You know how they pass the finest clay through the hottest fires; the clay which is able to take the softest impression, and to receive the most delicate hues. Again and again they heat it; in each furnace it loses some grossness, and becomes at length pure and fine and rare. Do souls of men want no annealing; can they spare the purging fire? I think that sometimes, when the grossness has all but vanished, and the purity is all but perfect, God passes them once more through a hotter furnace, that they may gain the last touch of Divine completeness, and may bear the finished lines and hues of those who, like their Master, being perfected by sufferings, have won the place beside Him on His throne. This may be the last great darkness that shall oppress you, the season of the final discipline. I think that I have known such cases. The eminent in holiness and fidelity to duty, passing through a season of profound depression, when the clouds were on the eve of rolling away for ever. When the Master cried out of His hour of darkness, "*My God, My God, why hast thou forsaken Me?*" the prelude of His coronation anthem was already hymned on high!

And further, let him that walketh in darkness and hath no light, trust in the name of the Lord, and stay himself on his God, because "*light is sown for the righteous, and gladness for the upright in heart.*" It is *sown*. That means that darkness—night, storm, and winter, are between the seed sowing and the harvest. Nevertheless the harvest comes. Be not weary in well doing ; never mind what it may cost, never mind how dull and dreary it may seem. It is right, it is God's will, cleave to it. These are seeds of light that you are sowing ; if God lives to fulfil His purpose, they must fruit one day in glory. They must. All earth, all heaven, all hell cannot stay it, or rob the faithful sower of his harvest. Darkness must be transitory, day must be eternal. Darkness is of earth and time, day is of heaven and eternity. God is light, and light must chase the gloom in which a loyal soul may be for the moment buried ; unless the devil is the eternal lord and master of the universe, and the fiends are to sing over the wreck of the Creation a " Chaos restored."

Times and seasons are and must be in God's hand. *When* the night shall end, *when* the light shall shine, rests absolutely and inscrutably with Him. But it does *rest*. That the night shall end, that the day shall shine, is as absolutely sure as that He is Lord and Ruler of the world. We have no right to question His providence if the night be long, and the gleam of dawn in the sky be dim and far. We can leave our times in the hand of Him, who hath given to us His well-beloved Son, as the pledge of His faithfulness, as the proof of His love. But if we are to believe that the darkness in which a believing soul may be plunged, can prolong itself through eternity, we should have the right to say that God is a fiction, and the Bible is a lie. Brethren, it cannot be. It is a long, long night, the night of earth's history, but at evening time there shall be light, for beyond the night there is God, and God is light. Long as your struggle may be, dark as your night, keen as your pain, the dawn of the everlasting day will break around your head with unclouded splendour; and that darkness, which now threatens to engulf your being, will but illustrate and intensify the radiance of eternity.

XII.
THE SACRED JOY.

"As the sufferings of Christ abound in us, so our consolation also aboundeth by Christ."—II. Cor. i. 5.

THESE words fathom a depth of human experience which can only be touched by those, who seek in the life of Christ the key to the mystery of pain. There is a suffering which is common to man, which is the heritage of the race of Adam; and for man there is, in respect of such suffering, consolation in God. There is a suffering which belongs to life under its highest conditions in this world, which is known in its fullest measure to the purest and loftiest natures—God's priests and kings. The kings who live delicately, who wear soft raiment, and are the regulating wheels in the machine of State, wear golden diadems. The kings whose toil of brain forecasts, and whose toil of spirit clears the way for human progress, whose work lies far in advance of the great host which struggles on in their tracks, and who in the course of generations get recognised as the master-spirits, wear mostly the crown of thorns.

There are men who work purely from an inward necessity. They *must* speak the word and do the work to which some inward pressure moves them. Fame, wealth, power, all the ends for which the mass of the workmen are striving, kindle them not. Whether men will hear, or whether men will forbear, whether men will applaud their work, or whether men will ban it, whether a throne or a prison awaits them, they must say and do what they have been set to say and do; their springs are within and on high. The outward world for them adds nothing to the impulse, while it steals nothing from the sanctions, of duty. They seem to sit on high, above the din and the dust of to-day's battle—" in heavenly places," the apostle calls it—so calmly, so steadily, so far above the reach of earth's perturbations, do they accomplish their work. That work may lie in the midst of the throng of the world's activities; they may be princes, statesmen, captains, inventors, philanthropists; but their springs of thought and action flow down from distant celestial fountains, and are strong and constant as the river of God. The world rarely comprehends them till they have passed up from it—the greatest of them hardly till they have been dead for generations; till it has struggled on to the standing ground which they won for it, and left to it as their legacy. Then in the mists which settle over the past, the forms of the great leaders loom grand and colossal, and they, being dead, receive almost worship as demigods, who, living, knew but rare moments of happy and honoured rest. The lives of such men are full of a suffering which the mere man of this world never tastes; full, too, of a Divine glory and joy which are equally beyond his range.

The life of our own great Alfred, for instance, was a life of ceaseless effort and intense endurance. He was a martyr life-long to an agonising disease, and yet he measured out his day and his night through the years of a stormy reign with minute exactitude, so as to be able to devote the whole of it, with the severest completeness, to the service of man in the fear of God. Could one see his likeness, one would expect to find it seamed all over with the lines, not of thought only, but of constant, intense, and often agonizing effort; as they may be seen on the brow of Dante, another of the great suffering friends of mankind. It is not easy in these days to enter believingly into the experience of such men, who belong mostly to the formative ages of history; though he who *will* live godly in Christ Jesus, in any age, may know something of the fellowship both of their sufferings and of their joys, and be able to understand the strength of the self-renouncing purpose which made them find their life in their work for men.

And it was work which brought mostly no pay, no honour, but rather shame, anguish of soul, and peril of death. Could they have been content to be selfish, and to live like the world around them, power and wealth would have been easily within their reach. But because they must needs work for the world, and live for the world, they must needs also suffer for the world. In proportion to the keenness of their sympathies, the strength of their love,—and these are always the keenest and strongest in such natures,—was the pain and the sorrow which every day they were called upon to endure. You, who live much out of yourselves can understand something of their experience. You whom a large paternal heart binds tenderly to your children, whom a friendly heart binds tightly to your friends; you, who are called daily to self-denying offices of duty and sympathy, and who sorrow more over the pains and woes of others than over your own; you know well how the most cherished things on earth are springs of sorrow as well as of blessing, how each fresh love is a fresh duty, and each fresh duty a fresh pain.

It is no question at all of external losses and bereavements. It is no question of internal anguish through consciousness of guilty sin. It is a pain which belongs to the spirit when the spirit is at its highest; a pain the reason of which we must ask, not of man, but of God. This world can neither explain such lives, nor justify such endurance. Festus, the able man of the world, must always esteem such a man as the Apostle a madman. The foremost man of all the world in his day, a man of whose empire over the minds of men Cæsar's empire was but a shadow, lived, while Cæsar played with the world's sceptre, as he thus describes: "*For I think that God hath set forth us the apostles last, as it were appointed to death: for we are made a spectacle unto the world, and to angels, and to men. We are fools for Christ's sake, but ye are wise in Christ; we are weak, but ye are strong; ye are honourable, but we are despised. Even unto this present hour we both hunger, and thirst, and are naked, and are buffeted, and have no certain dwelling-place; and labour, working with our own hands; being reviled, we bless; being persecuted, we suffer it; being defamed, we intreat: we are made as the filth of the world, and are the offscouring of all things unto this day."*—I. Cor. iv. 9-13.

• Who can explain it? Who can justify it? Who can show that it is the way of the blessed life and of the eternal glory? He only who, *"being in the form of God, thought it not robbery to be equal with God; but made Himself of no reputation, and took upon Him the form of a servant, and was made in the likeness of men: and being found in fashion as a man, He humbled Himself, and became obedient unto death, even the death of the cross. Wherefore God also hath highly exalted Him, and given Him a name which is above every name: that at the name of Jesus every knee shall bow, of things in heaven, and things in earth, and things under the earth; and that every tongue should confess that Jesus Christ is Lord, to the glory of God the Father."*— Phil. ii. 6-11.
" Beloved, think it not strange concerning the fiery trial which is to try you, as though some strange thing happened unto you: but rejoice, inasmuch as ye are partakers of Christ's sufferings; that, when His glory shall be revealed, ye may be glad also with exceeding joy. If ye be reproached for the name of Christ, happy are ye; for the spirit of glory and of God resteth upon you: on their part He is evil spoken of, but on your

part He is glorified. But let none of you suffer as a murderer, or as a thief, or as an evil-doer, or as a busybody in other men's matters. Yet if any man suffer as a Christian, let him not be ashamed, but let him glorify God on this behalf."—I. Peter iv. 12-16.

I think that these considerations will fairly introduce us to that inner experience of suffering to which Paul here directs our thoughts, and which contains within itself the spring of perfect and eternal joy. "*Blessed be God, even the Father of our Lord Jesus Christ, the Father of mercies, and the God of all comfort; who comforteth us in all our tribulation, that we may be able to comfort them which are in any trouble, by the comfort wherewith we ourselves are comforted of God. For as the sufferings of Christ abound in us, so our consolation also aboundeth by Christ."*—II. Cor. i. 3-5.

And let us first understand that the suffering of which the Apostle speaks is not accidental, it is a suffering which is according to the will of God. These men of whom I have spoken have been among the world's divinest men: the men in whom the instinct of humanity has recognised most of a divine spirit; while Paul, in whom the outline of this life was most completely filled up, stands plainly manifest to every eye in the forefront of history. And God, strange as it may seem, seeks to multiply such men, not to diminish their number; to fill up, not to disband the noble army of sufferers for mankind. We are distinctly called to the fellowship of Christ's sufferings. "*Know ye not, that so many of us as were baptised into Jesus Christ were baptised into His death? Therefore we are buried with Him by baptism into death; that like as Christ was raised up from the dead by the glory of the Father, even so we also should walk in newness of life. For if we have been planted together in the likeness of His death, we shall be also in the likeness of His resurrection: knowing this that our old man is crucified with Him, that the body of sin might be destroyed, that henceforth we should not serve sin."*—Rom. vi. 3-6.

The mission of Christ was to call all men into this inner sanctuary of spiritual life, the sanctuary of sorrow; and to fill the world with men and women who have mastered the divine art—the art of suffering for the good of others, and for the glory of God, which is the good of all. It is the diviner form of human life which we are now studying: the form to which it becomes us all to pray that in Christ we may be conformed.

Let us consider the nature of the suffering which is to be regarded as a sharing of the suffering of the Lord.

I have said that it is distinctly to the fellowship of Christ's sufferings that we are called by the Gospel. He suffered for us, that we might suffer with Him, a suffering which should be not unto death but unto life. The popular evangelical theology expresses it thus: He suffered to spare us suffering, He bore the penalty for us, He endured for us the sharpness of death, that we might evade the penalty and escape the pain. That He suffered for us in a way of which no independent suffering of our own, in the strength of our own will, could have supplied the place; that He won for us by suffering for us a standing as justified souls before God, and a place in the school of spiritual culture which no art or effort of our own could have won, is most surely and deeply true. That the full effect of His suffering on our behalf, in our stead, can only be realised by those who can suffer with Him, is another and deeper truth which will be clear to the most earnest students of the Word of God. We are to suffer under the sense of sin in a spirit kindred with His own hatred of it, and sorrow over it. We are to "die unto sin." We are to be crucified with Him as to the old man of sin, that we may live unto Him, and to God through Him, in the newness of His risen life. Our entering into the spirit of His death is the condition of our entering into the spirit of His life. Our entering into His suffering is the condition of our entering into His glory. We must watch, weeping, by the cross, if we would sit reigning on the throne. The fellowship of His sufferings is to be among the chief experiences of our Christian calling; to be understood in its fulness at last when the struggle is over, when we cast our crowns before His feet, and enter into His joy for ever.

1. Among the chief elements of this sorrow, surely we must reckon the spectacle of the misery of mankind. Even on His throne it was a constant burden on His heart. On earth He wept as He beheld it. He, the Almighty One, on whom the Everlasting

The Sacred Joy. 235

Father had laid the help of the world because He was "*mighty to save*," wept bitter tears as He moved among the signs of the world's misery and woe. And the Christian, like Christ, is bound to consider it, to feel the pressure of the burden of it, and to make it a charge on his soul to lighten it, and to open springs of consolation in this desert of death. Ah! my friends, what sad, sad sights do the walls conceal from us as we walk along our streets! Take one that I know, and that could be multiplied by millions. There is a brute in a human form, drunk as no brute ever was, who has just reeled home from the gin palace. The door of his house shuts upon him, and there he is lord. His poor, toiling, patient, God-fearing wife is beaten, kicked, and almost killed. His children run shrieking into corners to bury themselves from the sight of a father, and from the touch of his murderous hand. The wages which should have bought them their Sunday's dinner have been squandered to work them all this misery; and you may hear the poor mother, if you listen, crying out to God for pity on her little ones, for help against the beast or fiend whom the laws have made the absolute tyrant in her home.

It is but one of the manifold forms of human misery which abound, but I think it one of the very saddest. And think you that Christ does not see this and pity it profoundly? It filled His heart with a pain which brought Him to the world to help it; and His soul still travails, His spirit still strives and is grieved, when broken human hearts cry out of such deep misery to Him. There are wider aspects of the sorrow, the anguish, of Christian society, in which pauperism, vice, woe, seem to have planted themselves so deeply that no husbandry of ours can uproot them ; but these I must pass by. The anguish is there, multiform, many voiced, and the burden of it presses on the Saviour's heart. He expects us to share it, that we may help Him to heal it. There will be but cold welcome in Heaven for the man whose heart has not often groaned over the miseries of the human world. The love of Christ is a fountain of deep and tender sympathy for humanity. These are also *our* brethren.

2. The deadly nature of evil.

We cannot cheat ourselves into the belief that it does not much matter ; that sin is a taint in the blood which will work itself out in time. We cannot repeat the soothing formulary, God is good, and, as He is omnipotent He will make it all right for all at last. We have looked at sin in the light of the sacrifice of Calvary. By that cross we have learnt how terrible it seems to the eye of God ; how deadly it must be in the heart of man. Those who have followed the Lamb by that bloody road to Golgotha, hear His dread words ringing in their ears, as they realise the guilt of mankind, "*If these things be done in the green tree, what shall be done in the dry?*" A profounder interest is awakened in all that concerns the higher welfare of mankind, when we measure all that it has cost. Those dearest to us press on our hearts with a yet heavier burden ; we know what dread questions are awaiting their decision, that there is a word spoken which will be a savour of life unto life or of death unto death to their souls.

The truth which Christ has revealed to us, shews life and man in an aspect unspeakably solemn. "*Knowing therefore the terror of the Lord*"—having the fear of God, and of all that God has made known, before us—"*we persuade men.*" We take the burden on our spirits, for we know what sin is, and whither it is driving souls; and woe is unto us if we fail to make the witness clear. God sends us, as He sent His Son, to bear witness to the world, to convince it of sin, of righteousness, and of judgment; and if the witness of the Spirit in us be not full and clear, if we are found false witnesses of God, the blood of souls will He require at the faithless watchman's hand.

3. The resistance of the will of the flesh to the best efforts and influences; its determination to reject the things that will heal and save. It was this that made the Master the Man of Sorrows. This was the bitterness of His grief over doomed Jerusalem. "*O Jerusalem, Jerusalem, thou that killest the prophets, and stonest them which are sent unto thee, how often would I have gathered thy children together, even as a hen gathereth her chickens under her wings, and ye would not.*" . . . "*If thou hadst known, even thou, at least in this thy day, the things which belong unto thy peace! But now they are hid from thine eyes.*"

To see a man perish within reach of rescue, to

see a shipwrecked sailor dashed in pieces on the rocks, where, had there been but a brave heart and a strong arm, he might have been saved, is one of the most piteous of spectacles. Imagine the spectacle which the world is presenting to the eye of Christ each moment—this moment, while the thought passes through your brain. "*Ye will not come unto Me that ye might have life*" is His sad, pathetic complaint of mankind. He knows that He can give life to the seekers, to those who open their hearts to His claim, and to the tractive force of His love. And yet for want of a call, a cry, a movement of the heart towards Him, He sees Death making havoc of His world. He calls, He pleads, He promises, and He knows that it is in the very tenderness of love ; and He sees the men to whom He offers life and glory scout and shun Him, as though He offered shame and death. His love is cast back scornfully ; His blood, shed in mercy, that blood which stays the sword which is sweeping above the world, is trampled carelessly under foot ; the devil gathers willing troops to follow him to anguish and ruin, while Christ finds but here one and there one who will follow the Captain of Salvation to eternal glory. "*Were there not ten cleansed, and where are the nine?*" is the question which is always wrung from the sad lips of Charity.

> Oh ! shame beyond the bitterest thought
>   That evil spirit ever framed :
> That men should know what Jesus wrought,
>   Yet feel their haughty hearts untamed.

The Sacred Joy.

And the disciple of Christ, the minister, as each one of us is bound to be, of His grace and truth, has the burden pressing ever upon him, as he fulfils his ministry in a scornful and gainsaying world.

We preachers know that we are setting before our fellow men "life and blessing;" that if they will hear the word, while they go forth to battle and discipline, stern both of them and searching, they go forth to a joy unspeakable, a life diviner than the life of the seraphim, and a final glory of which the Lord gives the measure in the words, "*Father, I will that they also whom Thou hast given Me be with Me where I am; that they may behold My glory, which thou hast given Me: for thou lovedst Me before the foundation of the world.*" And yet we know there are multitudes who will not have it; who hear the words, as of old, but who do them not; who talk idly when the day is ended, of the service or the sermon, and then, on the morrow, get up to toil and moil, or perhaps to trifle through the week, with hardly a higher aim than have the beasts that perish. And some will do worse, will gamble, and drink, and cheat, and wanton, and make their homes wretched and their business a snare to souls, and do more harm and wrong in one short week than a lifetime can repair.

And is not all this dull, dead weight of the world and the flesh on the aspirations and purposes of the human spirit, a heavy sorrow to every Christ-like nature, as it is a burden to Christ up there on His glorious throne? "*Turn ye, turn ye,*" we cry with the prophet, "*for why will ye die, O house of Israel?*" Oh that thou wouldst know, at least in this thy day, the things that make for thy peace, before they are hidden from thine eyes!

4. There is the future eternal destiny. I dare not dogmatise about this, so much is wisely hidden. But the Lord spake of an "*outer darkness,*" "*a worm that dieth not,*" "*a fire that is not quenched.*" Some terrible meaning there must be in it. Will one whom I love, one in my home, one among my company of friends and comrades, doom himself to explore it? It is a dread subject. Shall there be everlasting wailing in the universe, a region of anguish over which the horror of great darkness shall brood eternally? The soul shudders at the contemplation. But agony there must be so long as there is sin. And the thought of the shame and the agony which sinners doom themselves to endure, pressed as a constant burden on the heart of Christ throughout His ministry. It was this that drove Paul forth into barbarous lands, if he might but save souls from death, and hide the multitude of sins, and the misery which sin brings forth to darken and to sadden, not earth only, but the celestial spheres.

The fellowship of the Redeemer's tears is no unknown experience to the disciple. This also he must know, if he would become partaker of the sufferings of his Lord. "*But blessed be God, even the Father of our Lord Jesus Christ, the Father of mercies, and the God of all comfort; who comforteth us in all our tribulation, that we may be able to comfort them which are in any trouble, by the comfort wherewith we ourselves are comforted of God. For as the sufferings of Christ abound in us, so our consolation also aboundeth by Christ."* There lie hidden in the pain the springs of the joy.

Let us enquire how *"our consolation also aboundeth by Christ."*

If we are called to share the suffering, we are called also to share the consolation, we are called into the fellowship of the Lord's joy and of His hope. There was a "joy set before Him," for the sake of which " He endured the cross, and despised the shame." He knew the strength of truth. He knew the tractive force of love. He knew that His suffering for man gave Him a power over man which all hearts must respond to. As the darkness of the last agony deepened around Him, He saw beyond it the vision which drew from Him the words, "*And I, if I be lifted up from the earth, will draw all men unto Me.*" He had a joy set before Him ; the joy of a sure redemption of humanity ; the joy of the eternal victories of His grace and of His love. That joy, while we lift the burden, we are called to share ; and so "*as the sufferings of Christ abound in us, so our consolation also aboundeth by Christ.*"

And these are some of the elements of the joy.

1. The God of all power and might has taken up the burden, and wills the redemption of the world.

God has come forth in Christ to undertake in person the recovery of our race. Every word, every effort of man, though it may appear to fall to the ground unheeded and unfruitful, has His will to prosper it. In working for man, in suffering for man, we have this assurance at any rate to sustain us—God is with us. Blessed be God for that assurance! It is our sure refuge from a despondency which, but for that, would easily deepen into despair. We see constantly the will of man counterworking the will of God. We see Mammon or Moloch on the throne of the world, and Christ thrust out. But it cannot be for ever; nay, it is but seeming now. There are things behind the veil of the visible, which we do not see, and which are already winning for Christ the empire over men.

Power, even almighty power, is powerless in moral conflicts. But He who is the Father of all spirits, must have a hold on them which we do not discover, must have echoes in their hearts to His name which we cannot catch—and He is with us. His eye ranges over the ages and he foresees a blessed consummation. The day *is* before Him, to whom eternity is present, when "God shall be all and in all." Christ is the God-man, "God manifest in the flesh." With all the vantage strength of His Godhead, He is working at this problem of man's salvation. And the necessities of things, the moral laws, the spiritual currents, are working together for His success.

The Saviour sustained His human heart when the burden pressed too heavily, by the thought, "*I and My Father are one.*" "*But Jesus answered them, My Father worketh hitherto, and I work. Therefore the Jews sought the more to kill Him, because He not only had broken the Sabbath, but said also that God was His Father, making Himself equal with God. Then answered Jesus and said unto them, Verily, verily, I say unto you, the Son can do nothing of Himself but what He seeth the Father do: for what things soever He doeth, these also doeth the Son likewise. For the Father loveth the Son, and sheweth Him all things that Himself doeth: and He will show Him greater works than these, that ye may marvel. For as the Father raiseth up the dead, and quickeneth them; even so the Son quickeneth whom He will. For the Father judgeth no man, but hath committed all judgment unto the Son; that all men should honour the Son, even as they honour the Father."*—John v. 17-23.

And we, when we feel unspeakably saddened by this burden of human misery and wrong, rest on the thought, "God is in Christ reconciling the world unto Himself." And it is as a rock beneath our feet. We dare to rejoice with a solemn joy, even in front of the world's wrongs and delusions, because God is in the midst of it. Where, how, we know not always. The visible church sometimes gives us but dim indications of where and how He is working. But we know in Christ that He is in our midst; that this is His elected work; that He has staked the glory of His Kingdom and the blessedness of His home on the issue of the grand experiment of freedom; and therefore, "*as the sufferings of Christ abound in us, even so also our consolation aboundeth by Christ.*"

2. There is a joy in the fulfilment of a self-denying, self-sacrificing ministry which is more like heavenly rapture than any other experience which, in this world, is within our reach. We have already, as the counterpoise of the sorrow, what can only truly be described as the joy of God. In deep sadness must much of the work be done. The world's purest and noblest spirits, in all ages, have been half-maddened by the sin and misery around them. Our two foremost men of genius at this moment are prophesying against us more or less fiercely or wildly, and are thrown utterly out of tune with their times by the sight of woes and wrongs and lies which are a deep disgrace to Christian civilisation, and which they say that Christian civilisation is making no adequate, resolute effort to cure. Alas!

> The Son of God, in doing good,
>   Was fain to look to Heaven and sigh;
> Nor can the heirs of sinful blood
>   Seek joy unmixed in charity.

But heavy as are its burdens, rich and great already are its rewards.

Man was made for this ministry. He was made in the image of God that he might be able to fulfil it. It is the healthy exercise and discipline of the soul. It makes the vital blood course merrily along its channels. Unselfish work, inspired by the love of Christ, is the soul's gymnastic culture. It lifts us too up into breezy mountain altitudes: we breathe a lighter atmosphere, we bask in a brighter sun. And the fruit is blessed. To sow the seed of the Kingdom in good and honest hearts; to hear brave, strong workmen in the Kingdom of God say, "I am what I am on earth through you," is the purest joy of a lifetime. Evil is fearfully contagious, but good is, blessedly, more contagious still. One good life obliterates the traces of many evil ones, and "*charity covereth the multitude of sins.*"

To believe this, and to watch the work growing under his hand, is the joy of the Christian workman, of which neither man nor devil can rob him. No man who has heard it, would change the blessing of the poor and of him that is ready to perish, for the wealth of Crœsus; no man who has known it, would part with the joy of being an instrument of healing and culture to toiling, suffering, struggling human spirits, to be crowned and throned among this world's kings. The Lord had the empire, "*all the kingdoms of the world and all the glory of them,*" laid at His feet. But for the joy that was set before Him He calmly put it aside. "*Get thee hence, Satan, it is written thou shalt worship the Lord thy God, and Him only shalt thou serve.*" That joy it is given to us to share with Him; it is the purest and deepest human joy, and so, "*as the sufferings of Christ abound in us, so our consolation also aboundeth by Christ.*"

And we know, about the whole of our ministry, and the suffering which in sympathy with Christ we willingly endure, that "*he which goeth forth*

and weepeth, bearing precious seed, shall doubtless come again with rejoicing, bringing his sheaves with him." We know that God is with us, and so may forecast the future. But Christ has forecast it for us, and our hope is built upon His word. He bears with evil painfully, and imposes on us the pain of bearing with it, because before His work is ended He will transmute it to good. Where now is wailing, shall be shouts of rejoicing; where now is wrong, in the end righteousness shall spring. Where now the footstep of the destroyer is planted, black and barren, on the wilderness which once was Eden, mercy and peace shall bloom in the footsteps of the Redeemer. The tree of knowledge, which has borne such bitter fruits of misery, shall be a tree of life by the everlasting river, and the leaves of the tree shall be for the healing of the nations. "*For as the rain cometh down, and the snow, fom heaven, and returneth not thither, but watereth the earth, and maketh it bring forth and bud, that it may give seed to the sower, and bread to the eater; so shall My word be that goeth forth out of My mouth: it shall not return unto Me void; but it shall accomplish that which I please, and it shall prosper in the thing whereto I sent it. For ye shall go out with joy and be led forth with peace: the mountains and the hills shall break forth before you into singing, and all the trees of the field shall clap their hands. Instead of the thorn shall come up the fir tree, and instead of the brier shall come up the myrtle tree: and it shall be to the Lord for a name, for an everlasting sign that shall not be cut off.*"
—Isaiah lv. 10–13.

Bear then, and forbear. Pity, cherish, love; yearn, as a mother yearns over her prodigal first-born, over the world which is loving and seeking destruction: your sorrow is not unto death, but unto life. Christ assures it. "*He shall see of the travail of His soul, and shall be satisfied.*" It shall be yours too to drink deeply of that cup of rapture. "*Where sin abounded grace shall overabound. Where sin hath reigned unto death, there shall grace reign through righteousness unto eternal life, through Jesus Christ our Lord.*" Christ is the surety of the everlasting triumph, and therefore "*as the sufferings of Christ abound in us, so also our consolation aboundeth by Christ.*"

XIII.

THE GARDEN BY THE CROSS.

" Now in the place where He was crucified there was a garden."—
John xix. 41.

AND it was spring, the splendid oriental spring. The flowers breathed their sweetest fragrance around the cross where their Lord was bowing beneath the load of His great agony, and was passing, God-forsaken, as man thought, and as for one dread moment it seemed even to Himself, into the valley of the shadow of death. There is something startling in the association—the Cross, the Garden ; the one, the very symbol of shame and suffering, the most awful witness of the destructive power of the sin which has laid waste the world ; the other, the brightest of the relics of Eden which the compassion of the Father has saved out of the wreck. The form, the hue, and the breath of flowers, is the purest fragment of the pristine beauty which survives to us. They bloom as fair, as fresh, each spring, as when the dew of the Maker's benediction lay like a mantling glory upon Eden ; though perhaps it is just this dewy splendour, the first bloom of the beauty of Creation, which sin has brushed off from the world. We know what fruit is when the bloom is off it. Colour, form, fragrance, are all there; but something is lost which can ill be expressed—its glory, the last touch of perfection, the glow and the signature of life. It is like the glow of health in a human countenance; it adds to it a special inexpressible charm. I think that it must have been radiant in David when he sang to his soul, "*Hope thou in God, for I shall yet praise Him, who is the health of my countenance and my God.*"

And so the pristine glow has faded from the Creation; or is it that a film has passed before our sight? At any rate, Eden is lost to us; and it is only in moments of imaginative rapture that we can restore the broken image of what has been in the past; while through the Apocalypse we gain some realising vision of all that God has in store for us, in what will be something higher than a Paradise regained. But flowers help us to comprehend it, better perhaps than anything which is left to us in this path of our pilgrimage. Nothing more brings home to us the boundless beauty, power, and love which are in Him, who made one fair world for us which we have deflowered, and who is making by His redeeming love another whose perfection shall be transcendent and eternal. The blush of spring, the glow of summer, the ruddy gold of autumn, are shed forth by the Creator in pure joy of creation. And where no eye but His, and perhaps the angels', sees them, where no human heart is gladdened by them, there He has scattered them in the wildest luxuriance.

Pure joy in beauty is manifestly a passion which is cherished on high.

Have you ever laid your face close to the herbage of a breezy down in summer, and peered into the world of wonderful beauty which the grasses, the mosses, and the lichens unveil. Nothing so fills one with the sense of the boundless benignity of the Being from whom we receive, and in whom we enjoy all the good of the present, while we trust to Him the future, as the lavish beauty with which He has clothed the Creation. And nothing in the mere creature region seems to me so full of promise of what that future will be, when, in the new heaven and the new earth, the lost harmony between man and Nature is restored. God keeps the flowers bright and fragrant around us as a memory and as a prophecy; a hint of what we have lost as mere creatures by the reign of sin, and an earnest of what the reign of Christ will one day restore. The beauty of the life which man lost by transgression, still survives in the flowers which he crushes beneath his footsteps. It was the Master, for whom the world had nothing but a cross, who said, "*Consider the lilies of the field, how they grow; they toil not, neither do they spin. And yet I say unto you that even Solomon in all his glory was not arrayed like one of these.*"

Now in the place where He was crucified there was a garden. The place of a skull was embosomed in beauty; a smile as of heaven played over its ghastly aspect. Flowers bloomed sweetly around the saddest path which was ever trodden by human footsteps; and they gleamed pale and fair in the moonlight which shone on the sepulchre, where men had laid their Lord.

We have here presented to us in the very closest association, and yet in the sharpest contrast, the darkest act of the tragedy of life, and the fairest, gayest, gladdest vision which the eye of man can look upon in his world. We will consider the contrast in detail and some of the suggestions of interest which it affords.

I. The darkest act of the tragedy of life. "*In the place where He was crucified.*" I speak of the tragedy of life. That crucifixion does not stand alone. It is but the culmination of all that good has suffered at the hands of evil, patience at the hands of force, truth at the hands of the father of lies, from the first days of the Creation until now. There is a profound sense in which the Lord was *the* Man of Sorrows. He stands on a lonely height of pre-eminence, as the chief sufferer of the human race. None could drink His cup to the dregs; none could fathom to the depth at which He knew it, the mystery of pain. But He was also the head of a great brotherhood of sorrow. Alone as the Man of Sorrows in one sense, in another, He was "the firstborn among many brethren." A great cloud of unseen witnesses was around Him when He suffered, who had all drunk the same cup of life's bitterness, and trod the same dark path to heaven.

Read the catalogue of their names and heroic deeds in the epistle to the Hebrews. These are all from the history of the chosen people ; but each Gentile nation has its elect of sorrow, whom it honours with its reverence and cherishes with its love. The Lord's martyrdom was but that of the chief martyr. There had never been an age before, there has never been an age since, in which the men whom God hath sent into the world to serve and to save it, have not been pierced with its shafts and crowned with its thorns. Very terrible is the history of all the agony which sin has inflicted on its victims; the sighing and the groaning of souls in anguish which rise ever from this earth into the ear of God. But the chief sufferers of the world after all are its saviours. If their history were fairly written, it might wring tears of sympathetic anguish from the angels in the homes of the blessed.

It is a dark tragedy which is played out here, and the end of it is inevitably a death. Sin has entered into the world, and death by sin ; and death reigns over all. Life in its highest forms is a daily dying ; the noblest men are most conscious of it, and most cheerfully accept the condition at the hand of God. And death bounds at last and completes the history. Such is man's life, such necessities are impressed on all earthly things by the reign of sin. The inevitable end of such a life as the Lord's, in such a world as this, was the Crucifixion. Evil was but acting out the ends at which it had aimed through all the ages of man's history, in slaying the Prince of Life, and burying Him in the darkness of the tomb. It was no casual or isolated outburst of the malignity of evil. Every witness for God through all the ages, had been called to face in his measure the same suffering, and to bend under the burden of the same cross.

But there was something far deeper and more solemn than the mere human suffering of the heir of a sinful race, in this passion of the Lord. It was the darkest act in the tragedy of life; the darkest, we may well believe, that the universe can ever know. It was emphatically the hour of the Prince of Darkness, but it was his last hour. His victory broke his power, and broke it for ever. That tragic element which will give the tone to the noblest lives while this sinful world endures, through Christ becomes but the prelude of a great drama, which will end at last in glorious joy. But for the moment the darkness was utter; love, Divine love, love that smiled at pain, and wounds, and death, if it might but win the redemption of the beloved, was seized in the very home which it entered on its mission of mercy, was wounded in the house of its friends, was bound, scourged, and dragged by the very brethren to whom it clung with such tenacious tenderness, to a cross of anguish and of shame.

The nature of sin was never fully known in the universe till that hour; the hour in which it seized and slew the Lord. Are there words in human literature of such profound pathos, as those in which the inspired prophet of Calvary paints the scene? The Man of Sorrows so stricken and bowed, so marred by pain, by vigils, by hunger, by temptations, and by tears, that men shrank from Him, as from one "*smitten of God and afflicted.*" But "*He was wounded for our trangressions, He was bruised for our iniquities.*" Alone, He wrestled with the burden of His anguish in Gethsemane; alone, He stood before His judges and tormentors, His dearest and most familiar friends flying from His side; one of them, the most trusted, protesting with oaths and curses, " I know not the man." Alone He trod the path to Calvary, and fell prostrate beneath the burden of His cross; while the men for whom He bore it all, and would bear the horror of the final darkness which was beginning to draw its shadow around His spirit, raged before the cross with fiendish exultation, and pierced His dying ear with the stings of their malice and the shafts of their scorn. It was Satan's triumphal hour. It was the Saturnalia of hell and of death.

He was alone. "Yet not alone, for the Father was with Him." "*Father, I have glorified Thee on the earth, I have finished the work which Thou gavest Me to do.*" And not alone, blessed be God, in another sense; not wholly out of the pale of human sympathy and love. Daughters of Jerusalem were there, weeping and lamenting. The anguish of a bursting heart was too palpable for a woman's eye to miss it. The fairest flowers which sin has spared in the human fields, are a woman's vivid sympathy and fearless compassion. And these, blessed be God, were not wholly absent. They added a higher beauty and fragrance to the flowers, which bloomed around the tear-stained footsteps of the Lord.

But, as we have said, there was a yet more awful significance in that scene, than any which could grow out of the intensity of the human suffering which it revealed. It was the hour of the Prince of Darkness in a double sense. It was not only the hour in which he could wreak his malignant will on the chief of human sufferers; it was the hour in which the Father gave full expression to His mind about transgression; in which He declared the intensity with which He hated it; and revealed the ruin which it must inevitably work on every being who submitted to it, and the death which was its necessary doom.

God was declaring by that cross, for all time and for all eternity, the deadly, damning nature of transgression. He was giving to all beings the measure of His abhorrence of it, by the anguish, the darkness, the horror of spirit, through which the Son of His eternal love must pass, if He would take on Himself its burden, that He might bear it away, and destroy it out of the living universe for ever. There is a mystery here which we shall never fathom; it is unsearchable as life, as God—God's well-beloved Son passing through God-forsaken darkness, taking on Himself all the burden of human transgression, and by one awful act of atonement bearing it away for ever. "*And He, bearing His cross, went forth unto a place called the place of a skull, where they crucified Him, and two other with Him, on either side one, and Jesus in the midst. . . . Now from the sixth hour there was darkness over all the land until the ninth hour. And about the ninth hour Jesus cried with a loud voice, saying, My God, My God, why hast Thou forsaken Me? Jesus, when He had cried again with a loud voice, said, It is finished, and He bowed His head and gave up the ghost."*—Matt. xxvii. and John xix.

It was the darkest act of the tragedy of life.

But in the place where He was crucified there was a garden.

It is a startling contrast, the last act of that awful tragedy; the garden smiling and shining all round, in all the beauty, splendour and gladness of the spring. There is a beautiful suggestion here which one loves to dwell upon. It is but a sentiment; but if we dispense with sentiment, how much of the delicate charm of Nature and the rarest joy of life would be lost. One loves to dwell upon the thought that Golgotha was a garden, and that earth's fairest, brightest, gentlest nurslings were there, mingling their smile and their balm with the trampling of furious footsteps and the cursings of malignant foes.

Very dear to Him through His lonely life-course, were the flowers which bloomed around His feet as He trod His daily path of pain, and the herbage of the mountain slope where He wrestled night-long for strength to endure. None of the beauty of the world which He had called into being, was hidden from His eye as He passed along its pathways. The word of the lilies, the birds, the cornfields, the blue sea waves, the morning flush, the evening glow, entered freely into His ear, and soothed and sustained His heart. In truth, it is mainly to Him that we owe our vision of the glory of Nature. For the men of old time there was a veil over it all. The Lord, by His advent, lifted the veil from two worlds.

It is an old question, and one of deep and curious interest, how far the modern intense delight in the beauty of Nature was shared by the ancients, and how far it is the gift of the advent of the Lord of Nature to His world. I believe that the advent of Christ has placed the whole sphere of Nature in a new and closer relation to man. Man, knowing through Christ the God of Nature, knowing the mind of Him who created and who rules it, has an altogether new and higher interest in the observation of the world.

It is said that the ancients, and heathen peoples generally, had but feeble perception of natural beauty. But this must by no means be stated too absolutely. It is true that Julius Cæsar gives us no hint that his eye had rested with delight on the beauty of those Alpine summits, which men will now traverse half the globe to look upon. But, here and there, some exquisite passages occur in classical literature, which reveal a delicate and cultured observation. And yet it is hardly for its own sake that the beauty of Nature is delighted in, even by the most imaginative writers of the ancient schools. The Hindoos probably come nearest to the moderns, in the large, joyous apprehension of the glories of their Indian home, which their literature discloses. But always there is the strong tinge of melancholy, crossing and dashing the delight, in the heathen heart.

The Christian observation of Nature is set in a new and quite higher key. Through Christ, Christian peoples have a delight in their world, which before Christ was hardly known to the elect spirits of our race. Always of old the terror overshadowed the joy. There was an awful, unfathomable mystery there, which marred all pure enjoyment. Men trembled, helpless, before the mass and the force of the elements around them; in the sweep of whose vast circuits they were too fearful to admire and to love.

The Jews had much of the Christian enjoyment of natural beauty, and for the same reason. They knew the mind and heart of the King. Moses touches the true key-note in the words: "*The Lord thy God bringeth thee into a good land, a land of brooks of water, of fountains and depths, that spring out of valleys and hills; a land of wheat, and barley, and vines, and fig-trees, and pomegranates; a land of oil olive and honey; a land wherein thou shalt eat bread without scarceness, thou shalt not lack anything in it, a land whose stones are iron and out of whose hills thou mayest dig brass. . . . A land which the Lord thy God careth for: the eyes of the Lord thy God are always upon it, from the beginning of the year even unto the end of the year.*"—Deut. viii. 7–9, xi. 12.

David's psalms complete the chord.

But the grand stimulus to observation and discovery, to that spirit of which Mr. Ruskin's "Modern Painters" is the most eloquent and brilliant expression, and which lately sent some of our ablest men of science half round the world, to catch a sight of the sun low down on the horizon in eclipse, is the sense that it is the Lord's handiwork which is around us, full charged with the communications of His mind as is His written word. At any rate, the infancy of modern science was nursed by Christianity, and to Christianity it will offer the tributes of its matured experience at last. A Comtist may smile at this as a weak superstition. He may regard the theological stage of the development of science as synonymous with the infantine, and treat it as one of the childish things from which science has parted for ever. We think that he forgets all of which the circle is the symbol. If it commenced with religion it will complete a circuit, and return, with matured intelligence and wider range of vision, to religion once more.

Men will one day see that it is the Father's counsel which they are searching out when they fathom the depths of Creation; it is the benignity of a Father's smile that they are taking in when they bask in the sunlight, when they watch the shadows play in the upper air upon the snow-peaks, or catch at even the last rosy kiss of the daylight, as it falls down the mountain slopes on a wearied world. The Lord has given to us the rightful possession of all this by His Incarnation. It was right that the flowers should bloom their bravest around Calvary. It is the Lord who feeds continually the springs of that joy which they breathe through the world.

But still the contrast stands out sharply; we will try to gather some of its suggestions.

1. Consider the impassive serenity of Nature, through all the struggle and anguish of life. There are times when this serenity becomes dreadful, and maddens men. Is there no pity there, they ask, for the throes that are rending us? Is all hard and impassive throughout the universe? Do the stars everywhere rise and set so calmly over the storm and the agony of life? It seems to us terrible that Nature should hold her accustomed order, that flowers should bloom, and stars should shine, and moonlight should flood the air, when the Lord who made, who rules the universe, was dying in the form of a servant the death of a slave. We should have watched for the signs of the universal groaning and rending of Creation, in sympathy with the groans and death pangs of its Lord. We should have expected the whole framework of Nature to shiver into fragments, and to strew the wreck as a pall upon His sepulchre. No! in the place where He was crucified there was a garden. The flowers never lifted their heads more gaily in the sun than on the morning of the crucifixion, the moon never shed a brighter flood of lustre than that which streamed over His grave.

And it is ever thus. It is part of the deep mystery of Nature and of life. A mother who has watched night long the death struggles of her darling, who in the morning has gone home, looks bitter reproach at the sun rising so calmly on her agony. The east flushes into rosy splendour, the birds carol their gayest strains, the air is musical with the hum of life, while her heart is breaking, and the night has settled over her inner world. Nature is pitiless. She quickens not a pulse in sympathy with our passion, she hushes not a song in pity for our pain. We may come forth to a new life, we may go down to dark death, she cares not. We may blow thousands of earth's best and bravest into fragments in the storm of battle; she buries them calmly, and next year she reaps her richest harvests from their graves.

And men madden under this indifference. Is it, they ask themselves wildly, the mask of the indifference of God? The pagan sees behind it a malignant demon, mocking at his pain and pouring contempt upon his life. Sympathy man pines for. He can bear extremities, if sustained by sympathy and love; but Nature knows no sympathy. Our sadness, our gladness, stir not a pulse, claim not a sigh. She attends our gay occasions with flowers and festal music; she breathes the same music, and scatters the same flowers over our graves.

2. Let us thank God that it is so.

The garden blooms on, the Cross has vanished, while the tradition of it has become the most sacred and blessed possession of mankind. The sun shone as calmly on the morrow as on the morning of the crucifixion. The quiet business of Nature goes on, unhasting, unresting; it is untroubled by the tramp of armies, by the overthrow or reconstruction of the greatest empires of the world. And God be praised for it. Pain and storm, strife and anguish, birth and death, are for time; order, beauty, life, are for eternity. The sun shines gaily on the morrow of our anguish, and we writhe under it; but the sun shines on, and we come to delight in it, and we bless the constancy which brings it forth morning by morning exulting out of its chamber, to prophesy to us of the world where the sunlight is eternal.

And Nature is right. She will not bewail our calamities, as though they were irreparable. She smiles and sings as she reweaves for us the threads of our broken purposes, or heals the bleeding tendrils of our hearts. There is infinite solace in Christ for the most burdened sufferers. "*Our light affliction, which is but for a moment, worketh for us a far more exceeding and eternal weight of glory, while we look not at the things which are seen, but at the things which are not seen, for the things which are seen are temporal, but the things which are not seen are eternal.*" Why should Nature weep and moan, and stay her benign and beautiful process, when she knows that the stroke which we think is crushing us, is a benediction, and that we have but to stretch forth the hand of faith to grasp the earnest of eternal glory?

Nature is so constant because God is so constant; so constant in His purpose to transmute our suffering into glory, our moans into songs. There is boundless hope for us and for mankind, in all that He has laid up for us in Christ. "*Eye hath not seen,* nor ear heard, neither have entered into the heart of man, the things which God hath prepared for them that love Him." And of this the sunlight and the garden, and the calm procession of the seasons, are His witnesses. He suffers them not to be moved by our changes, for He is not moved; nor are we moved, if we have faith, from Him. He sees the end to which they all are working; the far off harvest of tears and pain which they assure. He saw through the gloom which gathered around Calvary, the brightening morning of the Resurrection. The burst of heavenly music, to His ear, was already cleaving the darkness of the tomb, and pealing around the triumphal train, that attended the victim of Calvary to the throne which awaited Him on high; "*Thy throne, O God, is for ever and ever, a sceptre of righteousness is the sceptre of Thy kingdom. Thou hast loved righteousness, and hated iniquity, therefore God, even Thy God, hath anointed Thee with the oil of gladness above Thy fellows.*"

3. Consider of how much that garden around the Cross was symbolic, in relation to man and to the Lord.

"*He was delivered into the hands of men.*" Alas! that this should mean, He was delivered to wounds and to death! The first crime was one with the last crime—fratricide, the shedding a brother's blood. His brethren they were who had been raging around Him, filling the air with their mad outcries, and dragging the Prince of Life to the cross and to the tomb. But around, above, all was calm, nay triumphant. There were worlds on worlds, sphere beyond sphere, which held on their way more surely as the hour of His final triumph drew near. The plains of heaven were glowing in a more vivid sunlight, the harps of heaven were swept to a more exulting strain The great ones of the past put on their glorious forms, and pressed through the veil to greet Him. The very dead beneath the sods in which the cross was planted, stirred as His footsteps pressed them, and bursting from their tombs prepared to join the train which He would lead up on High.

There was joy, an awful joy, through the universe when that cross was uplifted. All beings in all worlds won something through the prophecy, "*And I, if I be lifted up from the earth, will draw all men unto Me.*" Should the flowers then droop and exhale corruption, when all beings in all worlds were struggling into a new and more glorious life? No! "*In the place where He was crucified there was a garden.*" And it spread forth all its brightness, and shed forth all its fragrance, as the Lord passed on to the cross, which was His pathway to His throne. And it blooms still, and will bloom on till the death day of Creation. Then the tree of life will be seen, planted by the everlasting river. Its leaves shall be for the healing of the nations, and flowers shall gleam and fruits shall glow with unfading splendour, in those bright homes which Christ hath won for us, where "*they shall hunger no more, neither thirst any more, the sun shall not light on them, nor any heat. But the*

Lamb which is in the midst of the throne shall feed them. He shall lead them to living fountains of waters, and God shall wipe away all tears from their eyes."

The homes which Christ hath won for us! Around the Cross there was a garden, by the Cross the garden was saved. The death of Christ was the life of all things. Order, beauty, hope, joy, life, were all saved by that cross from ruin, saved for the new heaven and the new earth, wherein dwelleth righteousness for evermore. Saved by the Cross. *"God forbid that I should glory, save in the cross of my Lord Jesus Christ, by whom the world is crucified unto me, and I unto the world."* Does the tongue stammer as you try to repeat the confession? Do the lips tremble? Does the heart shrink? Are you passing with averted eye by Calvary? Stay, stay! by the way you are treading lies the gate of death. No Cross, no crown, no throne, no radiant home among the redeemed in the new Creation. No Cross, no Christ, no God, no hope, no life, for man or for the world. Bend then before the Cross the willing captive of mercy. Learn the lesson of self-renunciation. Take up thy cross and follow, patient, the Master's footsteps, and then wait, wait, wait, until He shall lift thee to a bliss and a splendour which shall eclipse thy most daring dreams!

XIV.

OH! THAT I HAD WINGS LIKE A DOVE!

'*Oh, that I had wings like a dove! for then would I fly away and be at rest. Lo! then would I wander far off, and remain in the wilderness. I would hasten my escape from the windy storm and tempest.*"—Ps. lv. 6-8.

How many captive souls have breathed forth this exclamation in their anguish; how many weary pilgrims of life, with aching limbs and bleeding feet! But, alas! the wings await us only when we have fought out our battle, and have trodden the path to the edge of the dark river. Two only of our race, we are told, have been lifted, in one bright moment, out of the very midst of the pain and the strain of life into serene celestial regions, where "the wicked cease from troubling and the weary are at rest"—in another sense than that which was present to the mind of Job, when he uttered that terrible malediction on life. So when we have made our moan we must grasp our pilgrim staff again, and face the danger and roughness of the way. The wings, to bear us to the homes we dream of, where the light is for ever shining, whence the tears are for ever banished, where the soul gathers around it its elect kindred with no dread of change or death, we shall find, if we are patient, in time. These words of David are a genuine outburst of human sorrow and aspiration. It is the language which again, and again, and again, is wrung from the heart of earth's purest and noblest men.

It seems strange to those who have not looked into the mystery of God's ways, that souls should be so restless and full of a nameless and agonizing longing, in a world so rich and beautiful, and which Heaven meant to be so blessed. No small part of the mystery of human sadness is the fact, which all the inner history of life forces upon us, that the sense of it seems to be strongest in the wisest and loftiest spirits of our race. In truth it is part of the heritage of our freedom. Life might be less sad, certainly it would be less rich and less hopeful, if it were less free.

Freedom is the richest, the grandest, the gravest, but in some stages of development it is the saddest, of all endowments. The truth holds in the political and social as well as in the spiritual sphere. The well-fed and kindly mastered slave has, perhaps, an easy, indolent, reckless enjoyment of the moment, such as the anxious, toiling, careworn child of freedom rarely knows. The rich humour, the childish glee, of the negro races, has lived on through all the bitter experiences of their bondage. We might hazard a guess that few of the eager, acute, energetic whites in America can laugh such a laugh, and sing such a song, as their once careless and jovial slaves. Their enfranchisement may take the ring out of their laughter and the fun out of their nature, while it brings in nobler and more fruitful things.

All enslaved classes and races have had a bitter experience to undergo, in the first stages of their newly-won freedom. Part of the difficulty of enfranchisement, for which due allowance has not always been made, lies in the unwillingness of serfs to be free. The fact that the serfs on the estates of the Church were, on the whole, the last to be enfranchised, means, not that the Church was a hard landlord, but a kindly one. The men were kindly treated, well cared for, under easy masters, and they were in no great hurry to face the burdens and the responsibilities of liberty. Those who have regarded with intelligent eye the process of enfranchisement of serfs in Russia, note much bitter discontent and trouble as among the first-fruits of a measure which was inevitable, and is in harmony with the principles which, under Christ's auspices, guide the development of the modern world.

The last wreck of feudalism is now disappearing from our habits and institutions in England. The formation of Unions of agricultural labourers, and the necessity under which farmers and landlords find themselves laid, to recognise them and to treat with them, brings home to the one class hitherto beyond their reach, the ideas and the forces which have reconstructed the social relations of men from the very foundations, in every other region of the national life. The gloomy prophecies of trouble to the agricultural interest and to the country generally, which are freely indulged in by the class who have kept, through a great part of rural England, their day labourers in a condition which has brought shame and sorrow on the whole community, will have but little terror for those who believe that what is so simply right must, in the end, work for good to all parties concerned in it.

But it is well that the friends and supporters of this movement of the peasantry should remind them, that in taking this great step of progress as a class, in lifting themselves to a higher level, they are lifting themselves also into the region of new responsibilities and cares. They will have that which is amply worth the effort, in every manly judgment; but they will have, like all of us, to pay for the progress which they win. Something they will miss which belonged to the old life, as they stretch on to the new; and if their thought is that increase of comfort and happiness will be the immediate fruit of their movement, it is possible that they may find its first-fruits increase of pain.

For a serf, and those near to the condition of a serf, there is mostly some one who is responsible, who is bound to care that they are fed, clothed, and nursed. Enfranchise them, and they must learn to care for themselves; and *they* are not the *mass* who, in such a condition, care enough for the higher joys and hopes of freedom, to face cheerfully the burden of daily anxiety and pain that they may win it. The slave's heart is content, on the whole, with bondage, and the spectacle of the strain and the struggle through which the free have to rise to the full possession and use of their freedom, does not greatly tempt those whose nature is servile to desire deliverance from the yoke.

The truth is, that the freeman is the man who has the courage to suffer, who has a native aptitude for bearing burdens, and who holds conflict included in his idea of life. And God has made us free. He has forced our freedom upon us. We are made, whether we will or no, responsible for our actions, for our development, for our bare nourishment. The decisions of our will carry with them, whether we choose or no, issues which live on through eternity. The burden is laid upon us, and those who best measure it—who best understand what it is to be a man, with such a body as ours, in such a world as *this*, with such a world as *that* looking down upon us, and sealing life with its awful everlasting issues—feel most deeply its pressure; a pressure under which, "Who is sufficient for these things?" must often burst from the noblest and most faithful lips.

We are beset behind and before, and on either hand, by responsibilities and destinies. We are bound with iron bonds of law, till faith transmutes them into bands of love. We are free, within wide limits, to do what we will. We may rob, cheat, murder, if we please. But there our freedom ends. Laws strong as adamant, fixed as the throne of God, take possession of us and our doings. The doer of good is blessed, the doer of evil is cursed, beyond the power of earth or of heaven to gainsay.

The freeman, too, has a great load of care resting upon him, of which the interest of others is the burden. Those dear to him are cast upon him. He has, in a little sphere, to be to them as God. And the necessary limitation of his power to bless them, the miscarriage to which all his purest efforts and wisest aims are subject, the way in which his dearest plans and hopes are ever in peril of shipwreck, overpress the pilgrim, and wring this moan from him as he struggles on his way.

And then, the end! Who assures it? Who tells him with authority, that he, with his poor faint heart, his futile will, his struggling lusts, his vain aspirations, his broken hopes, his ideal always far up above him on the height, and seeming farther as he climbs, can one day be strong and glorious as the angels, pure, beautiful, blessed, and complete? Ah! all freedom has its pains and dangers, but of all freedom the grandest, the saddest for the moment, is our great human freedom, freedom to be a man in this vast, awful, unhomelike world.

And there are the birds, the beasts, the flowers, all round us, gay and careless, happy, joyous as we were in our merry spring-time; sporting in the sunlight while the sun is shining, then nestling in soft coverts, sleeping a dreamless sleep, till the new day calls them to new gifts and joys. "*Consider the lilies of the field how they grow; they toil not, neither do they spin.*" "*Consider the birds of the air, they neither sow, nor reap, nor gather into barns,*" but verily they are fed. There is something exquisitely tantalising, to over-strained men and women, in this careless ease of the Creation, happy in the moment, with no thought of the morrow; no fears, no burdens, no regrets.

It seems to us like the dream which our inspired dreamers have dreamed for us of the islands of the blessed, where the hard conditions which wring us so sharply are abolished, where skies are radiant, where earth is lavish, where beautiful forms are teeming, and unlovely things are far away. Why cannot we be as careless as that sky-lark, bathing his glowing breast in the flush of the morning's splendour, and pouring out his gladness in maddening strains, up there at the gate of day? Think you not that many a poor wretch, waking from uneasy slumbers, with that numbing sense of misery which reminds us that something is impending which, when full consciousness returns, will become a burden too heavy to be borne, has listened to the skylark's matin song with a passionate envy, and cried, Oh! thàt I too had wings like a bird, for then would I fly away and be at rest!

There is something in the clearness, the serenity, the purity of the summer air which is symbolic of the careless rest of the Creation. We watch the bee buzzing from flower to flower, burying himself in the powdery sweetness till he is loaded with his treasure, and then he rises and swims on the shining air until he is lost in the blue distance, floating, humming, in a world which is all sunlight, dewy fragrance, and luscious sweets. And man has that within him which pines for kindred serene delights. "Man is in little all the sphere." The birds and the bees are in his nature, as well as the angels. His soul has a bird-like longing for flight, a bee-like thirst for the honey of Creation. Gladly would he lay down his burden, forget his tasks, and wander in the shining summer air, happy and careless as an insect, free of the burden which grows out of liberty—out of life, immortality, and God.

This rest of Nature, this ceaseless, serene circuit of her life, this joy in mere existence, this happy ignorance of to-morrow and oblivion of yesterday, have a strange fascination for careworn, toil-weary men and women in all ages. It is like the attraction of the clear sea depths in Goethe's exquisite ballad. It has been the inspiration of the world's softest, sweetest poetry, and it breathes a tone of tender music through its noblest and most inspiring hymns. Who can watch the evening clouds sleeping languidly in the golden glory of the sunset, their delicate forms, their opalescent hues, soft islets in the great sea of clear, unfathomable splendour, without breathing for a moment a passionate prayer, as he looks on that world, and then turns to look on this, "*Oh! that I had wings like a dove*," to bear me to those serene, untroubled kingdoms? Oh! that I could bathe my fevered brow in that coolness, and still my throbbing heart in that atmosphere of exquisite and infinite rest

But there is more than this, far more, in this prayer of the Psalmist. There is something far deeper than the sense of a syren power in Nature. David was not dreaming then of that mysterious spell, which draws the life-weary pilgrim from his path, the storm-tossed sailor from his course, the student from his tasks, the workman from his toils, the woman from her household cares and benignant ministries, the warrior from his camps, the statesman from his imperial cares, to lie on flowery shores in the summer sun, fanned by the breezes that have swept the foam crests from the purple sea, and dream, to the music of syren voices, his dream of rest. There are few who have battled hard to make life noble and fruitful, who have not in some moments of luxurious softness mused with the lotoseaters.

> They sat them down upon the yellow sand,
>   Between the sun and moon upon the shore;
> And sweet it was to dream of Fatherland,
>   Of child, and wife, and slave; but evermore
> Most weary seemed the sea, weary the oar,
>   Weary the wandering fields of barren foam.
> Then some one said, "We will return no more;"
>   And all at once they sang, "Our island home
> Is far beyond the wave; we will no longer roam."
>
> . . . . . .
>
> Why are we weighed upon with heaviness,
> And utterly consumed with sharp distress,
> While all things else have rest from weariness?
> All things have rest: why should we toil alone,
>   We only toil, who are the first of things,
> And make perpetual moan,
> Still from one sorrow to another thrown:
>   Nor ever fold our wings,
>   And cease from wanderings
> Nor steep our brows in slumber's holy balm;
>   Nor hearken what the inner spirit sings,
> "There is no joy but calm!"
>   Why should we only toil; the roof and crown of things?

We have had enough of action, and of motion we,
Roll'd to starboard, roll'd to larboard, when the surge was seething free,
Where the wallowing monster spouted his foam-fountains in the sea.
Let us swear an oath, and keep it with an equal mind,
In the hollow Lotos-land to live and lie reclined
On the hills like Gods together, careless of mankind.

.   .   .   .   .   .

Surely, surely, slumber is more sweet than toil, the shore
Than labour in the deep mid-ocean, wind and wave and oar ;
Oh rest ye, brother mariners, we will not wander more.

But David was not thinking of sunny islands and syren voices, which the mariner lashed to the mast maddens to hear as he drifts by. No, far loftier thoughts occupied him, far nobler, manlier cares. These words express the momentary life-weariness of a man, the whole aim and effort of whose life had been to rise to fellowship with God. It was not a sweet intoxication of the senses which stole over him, and breathed forth this touching plaint. It was wrung from him by the sternest realities of life, by brave struggles to fulfil his kingly duty, in spite of the oppositions and malignities of the enemies of *his* throne and of God's, of the desertion of false friends, and the calumnies of those to whom he had laid bare the innermost secrets of his heart.

There was a great dead-weight of ignorance, brutality, stupidity, which had to be lifted, before he could even begin to make such order in his realm, as the man after God's own heart must passionately desire to establish ; and there were moments when the weight pressed with crushing force. It was the patriot, the king, the seer, the prophet, the man whose life was laid on the altar of ministry to mankind—through whose soul there breathed a strain of sympathy with Him who made it His meat and His drink to do the will of Him that sent Him, and to finish His work—who found the burden of life, for a moment, too heavy, the strain too long, and sighed, "*O! that I had wings like a dove, for then would I fly away and be at rest.*"

There are many forms of high and noble work, which in moments of strain and weariness might wring this moan even from the most faithful and courageous lips. For it is a truth, a profound truth, that God constantly associates a high capacity for service with a keen sensibility to suffering, and nurses on bread of affliction and water of affliction, mingled with such joys as the angels taste, the men and the women whom He is training for high service, in the general assembly and church of the Firstborn which is gathering there. We will regard this sentence from various points of view; and in surveying them some of the deepest springs of human sadness will be disclosed.

I. It is the cry of the faithful soul overpressed by temptation.

Overpressed, I say. Behind all the temptation there is the assurance, "*There is no temptation hath taken you, but such as is common to man; but God is faithful who will not suffer you to be tempted above that ye are able, but will with the temptation also make a way of escape that ye may be able to bear it.*"

But it is hard to recall it when the pressure is sore; when the soul, self-distrustful, self-condemning, has to face the deadliest form of temptation—the temptation to think that faith is a dream of a fevered imagination; that spiritual truth is a kind of spectre of the Brocken, the shadow of our own thought on the mists that envelope us; and that Christ is the arch-spectre, the magnified image of self.

The dreadest of all temptations, is that which shakes our grasp of the Hand which alone can strengthen and save. And it is always in the background of life. So beset are we by tempters, that we are ready sometimes to say, A cunning devil rather than a merciful Father, must have ordered these conditions of my life. We are so organised that we cannot but be beset. It is not an accident, it is an inevitable condition of such a nature as ours, in such a world as this. Tempters around, tempters within; tempters lying hid in every thing of beauty we look upon—yea in every touch of sympathy, every joy of love. Is there one moment, life-long, when we are free from them? Why, they beset us even in our dreams. It makes life one long, hard, weary struggle; and we may never hope for release from it but in death.

It was an aged man, a veteran soldier of Christ, who said, "*So run I, not as uncertainly, so fight I, not as one that beateth the air; but I keep under my body and bring it into subjection, lest that by any means, when I have preached the*

Gospel to others I myself should be a castaway." We find constantly that the scenes and the interests from which we have had the keenest expectations of pleasure, have turned into temptations; even our purest and holiest offices, our most self-sacrificing efforts, have led us into the gravest moral perils, from which we have with difficulty escaped. Faithful, high-minded men and women, with profound faith in man's great call and destiny, have yet been so overborne, so crushed down by the sense of the omnipresence of the tempter, that they have fled in wild fear from home, friends, and country, from every occupation and every delight, to bury themselves in the recesses of gloomy forests or savage wildernesses; they have cut themselves off from all human fellowship, treated man as a foe and woman as a fiend, to find in the end the lonely desert as thronged by tempters as the crowded city, and their own hearts as seductive as the softest syren that ever wooed the careless mariner to wreck.

And think you that this spirit, which through the whole Middle Age drove men and women in throngs into the desert, that they might escape from this dread world of temptation, is dead in human hearts? Is life easier than of old? Is the burden lighter? Is the tempter chained? Myriads of myriads of weary combatants, worn out by the battle, are revolving the question still, which made in old time monks and nuns; the sadder perhaps in that they see that there is no way out by that path from the ceaseless strife. "*Oh that I had wings like a dove! Then would I fly away and be at rest; then would I wander far off, and remain in the wilderness"*; there I might at least unarm for the moment; I might lie ungirt by the cool waters under the rustling palms of some Elim, till summoned by the stern behest to face new perils and new toils.

II. It is the sigh of the heart, weary of the strain of spiritual aspiration and effort.

There is rest, surely, from the dread of temptation and the pressure of the burden, in Him who said, "*Cast thy burden on the Lord, and He shall sustain thee.*" "*He shall never suffer the righteous to be moved.*" It is profoundly true, it is the one secret of rest. But those who have felt the strain of high spiritual endeavour, know that there is nothing at times so exhausting to the mere natural strength of mind and heart, as the effort to rise into a serener region, and to hide all our tears and cares in the bosom of the Infinite tenderness and love.

It may be that you have felt the pain so keenly that you have fairly abandoned the effort. Your foot no longer presses the threshold of that higher world, where it was once frequent and familiar. You have begun to think that these higher things are somewhat shadowy and dreamlike. Perhaps you are settling down on substantial comforts, as, on the whole, the most satisfying, or at any rate the least troublesome, good of life. And yet once you had " open vision." The hope of realizing your aspirations one day, was as the daily bread of your spirit. Now you have fallen back again into sensual slumber, beaten, not by the temptations, the cares, the toils, of life, but by the pain of spiritual effort ; the aching of the wings that beat the air of the upper heaven.

But those who have not been conquered by the pain, and who are minded at whatever cost to endure, know moments, and many, when they sigh wearily for a life that demands less effort, for a Pisgah which it costs less pain to climb. We pine for a state in which the quickening flood shall flow round us as the sunlight, in which we shall inhale new life at every inspiration; where the pain and the strain would be to stoop and not to soar. "*Oh that I had wings like a dove!*" There must be some world where purity, honesty, truth, righteousness, and charity are native; where it costs no pain to cherish them; where the heavenly life finds the bread of its nourishment ever ready to its hand; where the light of the face of God chases all dark shadows, and fills the celestial air with the glow which is the breath of life. There is such a world, and one day death will bear me to it. But "*oh that I had wings like a dove,*" that I might visit it, if but for a moment, and bathe my strained and weary soul in its seas of rest!

III. It is the cry of a man who is forced to be spectator of a dread conflict.

There is war on earth and in heaven, and there is something appalling in the shock of forces, of which man is the centre. When the soul tries to measure it, it faints under the effort. The prophets are not the only men who, when they had vision of it, fell down and were as dead men. I have already told the story of the most prophetic man whom we have among us, who when he was bidden by a light, gay, optimist philosopher to look up at the stars, found it "a sair sight." You smile, perhaps, at the conceit, and can afford to smile. Life has not unveiled to you yet its deeper mysteries; nothing, as yet, seems too hard for your young strength, too high for the clasp of your daring and vigorous hand.

The range of this conflict and its issues escape you; for the present you are amply content to live on in this goodly world, where there is beauty enough to gladden you, and where you can shut your eyes on all that saddens. But whole peoples, and the millions, the hundreds of millions of the disciples of the Oriental religions, agree with our sad philosopher—it is a sair, sair sight. The whole universe is full of the cries of battle; groans of wounded and dying burden the air. The conflict is fought out with desperate vehemence. Is there any nook in the worlds within our ken where evil and good are not in death-wrestle; where the advantage won by the good to-day is not balanced, as far as we can *see*, by the gain of the evil to-morrow; and where free beings are not driven to take part in the conflict, and to add their share to the stress and the strain of the universal life?

The whole Creation is groaning and travailing, and who knows what is being born? Who can look on with composure to endless battle, endless misery, waste, and sin? And yet where is the sign of the end of it, here or anywhere? Who has not asked himself madly, in moments when the eye of faith has been dim, and Christ has seemed far away, which is the conquering power? Where is the beginning of the victory? "*Oh that I had wings like a dove!*" I would fly beyond the dust and the din, the moans, the wounds, the tears. There must be some realm in this fair universe which the destroyer's foot has never trampled; where the flowers bloom fair and fear no spoiler's hand. "*O that I had wings like a dove*," and I would forth and find it, and turn my back for ever on this fierce battle-field, where men, angels, devils, are wrestling, writhing, in desperate conflict, where Heaven and hell are agonizing for the prize of an immortal soul.

IV. But man is not only a spectator of the conflict. He is bound to be the servant of the Divine Kingdom, and in sympathy with the Lord of the Kingdom to bear all the burden of it on his heart. "*Oh that my head were waters,*" cried one such, "*and mine eyes a fountain of tears, that I might weep day and night for the slain of the daughter of my people. Oh! that I had in the wilderness a lodging-place of wayfaring men, that I might leave my people, and go from them . . . they bend their tongues like their bows, for lies, but they are not valiant for the truth upon the earth, for they proceed from evil to evil, and they know not Me, saith the Lord.*"

"*Who hath believed our report,*" cried another, "*and to whom hath the arm of the Lord been revealed? For He shall grow up before Him as a* tender plant, and as a root out of a dry ground; He hath no form nor comeliness, and when we shall see Him there is no beauty that we should desire Him."

Such cries were wrung from God's most faithful servants, when they saw the force of the flood of iniquity which was sweeping against the Kingdom, and failed for the moment to see the Spirit of the Lord lifting up the standard against it. Just as God seems to suffer temptations to multiply, He suffers to accumulate difficulties of faith. Man must be made upon a very deep and far-reaching plan, with a large, a boundless future; for very high moral qualities are needed to solve successfully his problem of life. Is there one earnest servant of God in any generation, who has not bemoaned, almost hopelessly, the overmastering flood of evil which sweeps through the world? It is like the toil of Sisyphus, or of the daughters of Danaüs, this effort of the Christian life to help and to bless mankind. "*Oh that I might now die!*" one of the bravest of God's workmen cried. "*I, even I, alone am left.*" The battle is a lost battle, evil masters the good; let me die and escape the shame. "*Oh that I had wings like a dove!*" that I might be loosed from this weary task, and cease to be bound to think and to care for thankless, senseless men.

But who can help thought and care when he sees sin reigning unto death everywhere around him, and men burying themselves in base, sensual, soul-destroying pleasures, reckless of God, of judgment, and of eternity? Here, in the very centre of

Christian civilisation, vice riots, selfishness reigns; the poor live by millions in such squalor that the life of the veriest savage hardly shows darker, while crime organises its armies, and pitches its permanent camp defiantly in our midst. Who can help caring when he sees this abounding misery, and humanity, as he thinks in his sadder moods, sinking deeper and deeper into the pit? And yet there is a terrible temptation to indifference, through the magnitude and complexity of the problem, the impossibility of reaching the root of the evil, and the obduracy and gracelessness of those on whom we have spent the most earnest and constant toil. We will give it up, we cry. We will give up caring, give up giving, give up helping; more harm than good seems to grow out of our efforts; we will fold our hands and let it go as it may. Nay, had Christ folded His hands and let it go—how then? Up! faint heart, the Lord has need of thee; *that* King's government at any rate must be carried on.

V. We believe in progress; we believe in the golden pictures of the prophets; we believe in the reign of the Lord Jesus over all hearts, in all worlds. Yes, we believe; yet there are moments when the heart faints at the vision of all the storm and strife, the tears and the blood, beyond which lies the fulfilment of our hope and the Lord's. We believe with the poet in—

> The God who ever lives and loves,
> One God, one law, one element,
> And one far off Divine event,
> To which the whole Creation moves.

But eyes grow weary with expectation. "*Where is the promise of His coming?*" "*Why do His chariot wheels so long delay?*" We may well urge the question as we survey the present and forecast the future —the stormy ocean, rock-bound, wreck-strewn, which lies between humanity and the haven of rest. The soul shudders at the seas of blood and anguish through which seems to lie the onward path. God leads men on, God leads us on. But through what struggle, loss, and wreck! "*Some on boards, some on broken pieces of the ship, they all escaped safe to land.*" Is it to be thus with life, thus with humanity? we cry in our despondent, faithless moods. Revolution after revolution; war after war; each bloodier and more destructive than the former; while peaceful arts and industries seem to find their highest function in gorging the eagles of slaughter.

What is the master-stroke of our vaunted and glorious science? Is it not the perfecting of the art of mowing down in the fields of battle whole armies of men? The instruments of slaughter in their cruel, delicate beauty, make us shiver at the thought that they are men, brother men, husbands, brothers, fathers, centres of tender thought and passion, who are to be mown down by that iron hail. Is not the uppermost thought in Europe at this moment armament; preparations for war, on a scale which will cast the desolations of "the scourge of God" into the shade? And is not the strongest hope of the philanthropist built on the fact, that war is becoming so fearfully costly that it must starve itself before long. Pity is nothing, charity is nothing, Christ is nothing. No, wars must go on until money fails. Great God, is it ever to be thus? Is this Thy law of progress; or does the devil triumph still in a world which Thy tears and Thy blood have redeemed? "*Oh that I had wings like a dove,*" that I might soar beyond the smoke of the battle, the wail of the wounded, the shriek of the dying, as they lie beneath these mighty chariot wheels that go crushing on. Oh! for a vision of the realms where the skies are stainless, where the fields are fed by the dews of heaven, and not by this bloody rain; where progress is as the growth of flowers, exhaling fragrance, filling the air with the music of its motion and the murmur of its joy.

"*Oh that I had wings like a dove!*" Is there no answer to the cry, in that wonderful picture which heralded the advent of the Comforter to the world? "*Now when all the people were baptized, it came to pass that Jesus also being baptized, and praying, the heaven was opened, and the Holy Ghost descended in a bodily shape, like a dove upon Him, and a voice came from heaven, which said, Thou art My beloved Son: in Thee I am well pleased.*"—Luke iii. 21, 22. A dove-like, brooding glory descended, not to bear us away to some far-off wilderness, but to bring to us here, in the strain and the stress of the conflict, the softness, the sweetness, the serenity of the sphere to which we long to soar. That was God's answer to the cry. "*The comfort of the Holy Ghost.*"

To comfort a man, is to make him strong by stand-

ing by him. This is our strength to bear, to hope—
the Lord is with us. All that we can *see* may be dark
enough and sad enough; the Holy Ghost would lift
us to share the hope and the joy of Christ. We must
climb, we must soar on the wings of faith, and command the horizon of a wider world. There is light
all round, light above. As we rise we see that the
darkness is of the earth, of the moment, the daylight
is eternal. We must stand with Christ. "*For the
joy set before Him, He endured the cross, and despised
the shame.*" In the strength of that joy He bears the
burden of the world, He upbears it with strong, conquering, redeeming hand. He sees gleams of light
upon it which are hidden from our feeble vision; He
sees an end beyond it, whose glorious beauty fills the
whole sphere with splendour and joy. If we share
the sadness of Christ, we must share His gladness;
and believe that every day, every moment, Calvary
is bearing, not here only, but in the universe, im-
measurably blessed and glorious fruit.

Here is our stay, here is our inspiration, when we
long for wings to bear us to the realms where rest is
untroubled, and the sunlight is eternal. God standing by us, "*God with us,*" here in the strain and the
darkness; lifting the burden of the care for our own
future and the world's, which else would crush us, and
laying it on His own Almighty heart.

XV.

FAINT, YET PURSUING.

"*Faint, yet pursuing them.*"—Judges viii. 4.

THE wars of which so much of the Old Testament history is a record, are charged with moral difficulties to the Christian apologist who holds himself bound to maintain that the captains and seers of Israel always interpreted rightly the Divine commandments, and had the explicit warrant of Jehovah for every terrible deed of blood which the narrative declares that they were bidden to do. They furnish a ready and ample storehouse of objection to the unbeliever, who professes to recoil from the records of slaughter and devastation which stain the sacred page; while many a pious student of the Bible, touched by the soft spirit of our modern civilisation, shudders a little as he hurries by these dark passages of his sacred books. That there are dark passages, some of them very dark, may be freely confessed; but perhaps, some shades of the darkness are specially due to the tone of our somewhat sickly and effeminate times. To men who lived in more stormy ages, the difficulties which oppress us hardly presented themselves. It is remarkable that the generation of Englishmen which made the noblest and purest attempt to order the life of a State after the Divine commandment, which is recorded in the world's history, found something in these old books which was in tune with their endeavours and aspirations; something which I think that we, with our modern shivering at the sight of blood, mostly miss.

But these wars of Israel seem to me on the whole, to offer the grandest witness which I find in history, that the "God of heaven" is not as a rule on the side of the "big battalions"; that in fact there is no rule about it as regards bigness, God being always and everywhere on the side of integrity, purity, righteousness, and truth. This assurance has been borne in upon men in all ages by many an impressive lesson. The big battalions at Thermopylæ and Marathon, at Granson, Morat, and the great Armada fight, were shattered against the rock of superior moral manhood, the freeman's resolution to defend all that makes a freeman's life worth the living, or, losing it, to die. But this seems to me to be the one constant, emphatic testimony of Jewish military history, from the day when Abraham with his three hundred chased the Mesopotamian kings, to the last triumph of the nation under the glorious conduct of Judas Maccabæus.

It was freedom, truth, patriotism, and the love of God, which constantly shattered the big battalions in those wars. The race was not to the swift, nor the spoil to the strong. Again and again the armies of the powerful states around them, broke against the rock of Jewish heroism, and were scattered like foam. It was but a little place, that land of promise; and yet, so long as their faith was firm, that small but disciplined and gallant nation held their mountain citadel secure against every foe. The great Nile plain on the one hand, the great Mesopotamian plain on the other, nursed vast herds of men, who suffered themselves to be driven like herds, at the will of the despots who claimed the right to lord it over the world. The brute mass and force of these huge empires hung like a perpetual menace around Jerusalem. But the Jews sang their glorious Psalms, which must have rolled grandly through the field of battle, and while they believed in them they held their freedom against the world. The whole history of their wars, alike of their victories and their reverses, seems to me charged with the assertion, that it is in the might of God's hand, and in the purpose of God's heart, to make the masters of the big battalions understand, that there is that which in the long run conquers more surely and reigns more mightily than brute mass and force—Righteousness and Truth.

I am not saying that the discernment of this in the providential conduct of human affairs, is at all times easy; nor dare we say that the method of the Divine hand, is at all times square with our measures of righteousness and truth. "God's ways are not as our ways, and God's thoughts are not as our thoughts." They proceed upon deeper and truer insight, and aim, by far-reaching methods, at far-off results. To comprehend God's ways we must simply know all things, and command the horizon of eternity.

It is just impossible for us to interpret, with even plausible truth, *all* the ways of God in the guidance and government of men, by any rules which we can formulate. "*Clouds and darkness are round about Him.*" The entire key to His plans is not entrusted to us. As we know Him more perfectly we understand better His dispensations. But enough shines out, not from His word only, but from history, patent to every believing eye, to justify our confidence that "*justice and judgment are the habitation of His throne.*" There is a stream of things without question, outside of us, "not ourselves," which "makes for righteousness," and which sustains and bears onward right-doers. These Jews, when their eye was clear and their faith was firm, struck in with its current, and it bore them again and again, in spite of enormous disparities of force, to victory. The apostle of the light and sweetness of intellectual culture, knows nothing more about this stream or tendency than that it is "not ourselves." We think that we have ample warrant for believing, that it is the pressure of the hand of the living God.

And I am free to confess, that it seems specially hard to discern the working of this law in the days in which we live, and under the conditions of our modern life. The tendency of our times is to vast aggregations, and to high organisation in all the departments of public life. All things run naturally into the monster form, and the complaint is universal that the free play of the individual life is oppressed and hampered. Trades, professions, communities, nations, are organised after the fashion of a highly-disciplined army, in which one thought, one purpose, commands and sways the whole. American political life might be considered fairly to be the highest development of liberty as we moderns understand it ; but in reality, the action of political parties in the United States, is about the most mechanical movement of men to be met with in our world. A few wire-pullers have absolute power to control the whole.

And the vast empires which are formed or are forming around us, the great masses of men which statesmen can place in the field, the elaborately scientific character of modern warfare, and the fell sweep of the arms of precision which are now employed, seem more than ever to throw the power into the hands of those who wield the largest military force, whose armies are the most highly trained, and whose weapons kill at the longest range. War is becoming as scientific as a game of chess ; and science professes to exclude moral elements from her calculations, except as they take shape in material force. Right and wrong have no common measures with the figures of her arithmetic. The power which has the largest area to draw from, arms and skill being equal, will infallibly, according to her prophets, win the day.

For myself, I confess to a certain sadness in watching this tendency to agglomeration and to elaborate organisation everywhere. But I should be much sadder about it, if I did not also see everywhere strong tendencies to disruption. There is a rising spirit in the masses, the advancing spirit I think, the spirit which will be master soon, which regards jealously the tendency to form great unities, and believes that smaller areas are more favourable to a high social development, and to the fair unfolding of man's nobler life. There is a spirit abroad which seems little disposed to rest, until these vast aggregations are resolved into their constituent elements, whereby, in compacter and more limited communities, the individual man may find freer play and larger room.

It is well worthy of our remembrance in these days, that most of the noblest human works, the true heir-looms of humanity, have come forth from free, limited and compact communities, such as the Jewish tribes, the Greek and Italian cities, and the England of Elizabeth. Perhaps the way in which the "power which makes for righteousness" is working in our day, may be by the disintegration of these vast structures which man builds so proudly, and on which they write Babel—confusion—on high; whereby there may grow more room and freedom for the unfolding of man's spiritual life. There is manifestly something in the universe, blessed be God, which counterworks this tendency to excessive mechanical organisation in society: something which will not suffer man to make himself over wholly to the laws which rule so absolutely in one sphere of his life; which breaks up his organisation, which throws out of gear his machinery, and reveals to him, often with terrible emphasis, that man, as well as God, is a spirit, and that in the spiritual only, in that which affords free play to individual will and purpose, can man work and rest.

It was the simplicity and freedom of the life of this little Jewish community—which was kept small by set purpose, the disruption of the nation being ultimately from God (II. Chron. xi. 4)—which made its history so rich in instruction to the world. It is a mine of political truth, which we have yet fully to explore. The stage of Jewish history is occupied to a large extent by typical men; men who loom grandly in the early twilight of civilisation as the heads of the great human orders—the classes into which humanity naturally distributes itself, whose struggles and concerts have made all the stir and progress of society. They seem to sit there, like Jabal in his tent-door on Giotto's glorious tower in Florence, looking out over yet untrodden ages of the pilgrimage of our race. These men, who are furnishing us with a text, are doctrinal for all time. "*Faint, yet pursuing*," describes for all ages the attitude and the action of all the bravest, noblest, most heroic, most victorious soldiers and workmen of the world.

Remember how these men came to be there.

Gideon was the typical man among them, the *eminent* man; but they were all cast in the same mould. Like Gideon's brethren were they, " *Each one resembled the children of a king.*" Gideon was a man who believed profoundly in the vocation and in the destiny of his race. As he saw it groaning and writhing in its iron bondage, his heart was torn by distracting doubt of the goodness and the righteousness of the Divine ways. When the angel appeared to him, the first question which rose to his lips was, "*Oh, my Lord, if the Lord be with us, why then is all this befallen us, and where be all His miracles which our fathers told us of?*" His doubt was to be solved by duty. It is a noble and effectual method—try it, my friend, and light will soon be shining on your path. The sword of the Lord and of Gideon was put into his hands, and as his grip on it tightened, a great hope began to swell and surge in his weary despairing heart. A large host gathered at his summons; but this was to be the Lord's victory; visibly a deliverance dropped from heaven. So the Lord would have him try the people—their temper, their purpose, their devotion to their patriotic work.

He led them, hot and panting, to the edge of a cool stream. Nine thousand seven hundred of his ten thousand men, flung themselves on their knees, and drank deep draughts till their thirst was quenched. Three hundred men alone were of finer temper, and had no knee for the satisfactions of sense at a moment like that. They could eat and drink like the rest when there was no higher work on hand—I dare say more heartily, such heroes have mostly strong appetites—but then, with those wasted fields and violated homes behind them, with the host of Midian lying in the valley, a prey delivered into their hands, and with the trumpet of God ringing in their ears, they had no time, no heart, for kneeling. A drop lapped from the hand sufficed for the moment; and then, " Up and on; the sword of the Lord and of Gideon is bare." Do you wonder that the kneelers were sent back- in shame to finish their draught at their leisure? Do you wonder at the word from heaven, " By the three hundred men that lapped will I save you"? Do you wonder that "faint, yet pursuing," was written of them, when their long day's work was nobly done?

And now what is all this to us? How do these dim, old world records touch our lives?

I. Know, brethren beloved, your election of God.

Gideon was not more directly called to high service in God's kingdom than are you. At the root of all true success in life—I mean by that, the fulfilment of the high ends for the sake of which life was given, and in which alone it can rejoice—lies the conviction, I am called of God *to live*; I am called of God to "take arms against the sea" of evils and of troubles which is surging around me, to make head against it, and to compel it to bear me upward and onward in my heavenward way.

I daresay that you may be sighing sadly enough, like Gideon, Oh! my Lord, if the Lord be with me, why have all these things befallen me? Why have I fallen into bondage; why am I dragged hither and thither by passions which I cannot master; why am I plunged into the pit by lusts which I cannot tame?

I, a called soldier and servant of Christ! Why, I seem to be the sport of every tempter; I seem to fall easily in with the drift of every current; the things that I would not, I do, constantly; one half of my life is spent in feeble indecisive struggling, one half in bitter, but impotent, regrets! Why is the nature so strong; why is the world so seductive; why is the beauty of the flesh so fair; why are the gauds of earth so glittering; why is my weak, vain, easily bedazzled heart, so ready to fall down on its knees to drink of the river, that glides and gurgles so sweetly at my feet? Why is the tempter so close and God so far? Why is not the strength more sufficient for these things, the battle easier for God's soldier, the victory more near and sure?

Oh! my Lord, if the Lord be with me, why all this? And, for answer, the sword of the Lord is put into your hands. "*Wherefore take unto you the whole armour of God, that ye may be able to withstand in the evil day, and having done all, to stand. Stand, therefore, having your loins girt about with truth, and having on the breastplate of righteousness; and your feet shod with the preparation of the gospel of peace; above all, taking the shield of faith, wherewith ye shall be able to quench all the fiery darts of the wicked; and take the helmet of salvation, and the sword of the Spirit, which is the Word of God.*"— Eph. vi. 13-17.

But first you must understand that you are a called soldier. "*I know thee by name, and thou hast found grace in my sight.*" Lay hold on that and be strong: yea, be strong. Ah! you say, how may I dare to realise it—

> I, a child of vain aspirings,
> Futile will, and broken faith,
> Fierce regrets and frenzied strivings,
> Pressed by peril, pain, and death?

I seem but as a mote dancing in the sunbeam, moved, like my fellow motes, by unseen currents; there is so little of purpose, of resolution, of will, in any high sense, in my life. I am but an undistinguished unit in the vast human aggregate; nothing depends on me in life's great battle; it matters little where and how I stand; it matters less where and how I fall!

One thing you must believe, or the despair will be master. God so loved *me*, that He gave His only begotten Son that *I*, through Him, might not perish but have everlasting life. This is the fundamental fact of your being, this is the Gospel of God to your soul. Believe this, lay hold on it, grapple your soul to it; and then, like Gideon, "take unto you the whole armour of God," and fight. Fight under the inspiration of Gideon's history. Your victory, too, is to be a victory of faith. It is to be God's victory, not *for* you simply, but *in* you and *by* you. Believe that there is a force within and behind you, bearing you up and bearing you on with resistless pressure, and making your final conquest as sure as the sweep of the tide or the path of a star. Let the touch of the sword-hilt as you arm for the battle, stir your courage to attempt great enterprises. Soldiers are as their captain. They will follow where he leads, and attempt whatever his voice assures them can be done. World, flesh, and devil will go down before you, if you catch the inspiration of your great Captain's triumph. "*Be of good cheer,*" He cries, "*I have overcome the world.*" "*This is the victory that overcometh the world, even your faith.*"

II. "Faint, yet pursuing," describes the frequent attitude and experience of the Christian combatant, even in the most faithful soldiers of the Cross. In a world whose Redeemer became the Man of Sorrows, it is not given, to even His bravest followers, to pass with assured and joyous step to victory. Faint, for "*without are fightings and within are fears,*" for the best of us. And the feeling never quite vanishes, even when faith is strongest and boldest, that we are terribly over-matched. "*If the righteous scarcely be saved,*" finds a sad expositor sometimes in the experience of the most righteous life.

There is an easily besetting notion which ensnares most of us, and sets us from the first fundamentally wrong, in our estimate of what we are to expect in the Christian life. We have an idea that the Divine light shining on things ought to dissipate all shadows, and reveal to us all which pertains to life and godliness, free from disfiguring mist and from confusion, so clear that we can understand them at a glance. We have a vague notion that the Divine strength entering into a man, ought to make all things easy to him; all endurance, all achievement, all victory. With God's strength within us, what can resist us or rob us of success? And then, when the darkness falls round us perhaps more densely, when new and perhaps graver perplexities afflict us, when we find our strength fail at the critical moment, and again, and again, and again we are worsted by the tempter, we are prone to interpret it as a sign that we are deluding ourselves about our vocation, that our evidences have mocked us, and that we are still the slaves of our dreaded and well-nigh almighty foe.

But it is strange that in all the other departments of life we are always prepared to believe, that what is worth most will be likely to cost most; that a high aim implies a long endurance; that great achievements are the fruit of great patience; that strain and pain, and weariness, are inevitable, if we would make the highest use of our powers. We find it in no wise wonderful if the great ones of the world, the men and women who have created the most precious heirlooms of our race, were oft-times faint, weary, and ready to die under the stress of their mighty travail. Did Dante never faint, and fall as dead, ere he had wrought his glorious work to such divine completeness; or Shakespeare as he travailed in birth of Hamlet, or Bacon when he was creating a new organ of knowledge, or Newton when he spelt out the thoughts of God in the structure of Creation, or Alfred when he bore, like Moses, the burden of the destiny of his nation, or Turner when he unveiled the splendour which lies hidden from common eyes, behind the familiar costume of the world?

It would not startle us to find that such men were often faint, and weary even unto death of the travail of their spirits; ready to cry with Elijah, Let me now die; the work is too great for me; I am at the end of my power, unbind me, good Master, and let me go free! But in matters to which all this is but as ancillary as culture is to life, we are prone to take the first shock, the first strain, the first feeling that we have touched the limit of our power, as the sign that the Lord has forsaken us, if, indeed, He ever stood with us; and that "*Let us eat and drink, for to-morrow we die,*" expresses about the loftiest law of life which we may ever hope to fulfil.

But do thou, therefore, prepare thyself to endure hardness, good soldier of Jesus Christ. The strain of the powers is an essential part of God's education of the spirit. The inner weakness of which it becomes conscious, and the higher strength which comes into it in the strain, are the most precious of all your experiences. This is the experience which will bear the richest fruit through eternity. Faint we must be. There is always the sense that the enterprise is too great for us, the race too hard, the battle too stern and long. And it is too great, too hard, too long, and God means us to feel it, that we may rise to the true strength and dignity of our manhood, by wedding our weakness and emptiness to the Divine strength and fulness, and may thus be "filled with all the fulness of God" through eternity.

Do not be afraid then of the faintness, if only the will to pursue endures. It must come, in such a nature as yours, in such a world as this. The flesh so lusty, the world so gay, the broad path so easy, so bright with the hue and the breath of flowers; intellect so bent on clouding the vision of the spirit and confusing its intuitions, the heavenly voices so hard to catch, lying prophets so many, faithful prophets so few. Who can help fainting when he measures all this, and measures himself against it; forgetful, as we are all forgetful in our poorest moments, that we have to set against it, not ourselves, but God? Take the faintness then as an inevitable consequence of the race and the battle under the present conditions of your being; be it your one concern to pursue.

Faint, yet pursuing. What is the state of mind, or rather the condition of spirit, which is here unveiled to us? It is the state of a man who has embraced a calling, who has set himself to a course, from which there can be no withdrawal. His choice is absolute and final. Here stand I, I can do no other, God help me! If I must die, I must die here! It is the attitude of a man who finds that his whole being is bound up with his aim and purpose; that to forsake it, is simply to forsake his life. Those men with Gideon *must* work deliverance from Midian. Life, if that failed, would become intolerable, so they must fight on until they won the day or died.

And the Christian is the man who *must* find deliverance from evil, from the elements of his own nature, and the elements of the world, which debase and destroy the spiritual part of him, and would make life in the end a thing dreary and terrible, even for the brutes. He must find the way out of the present pain, distress and anguish, through the higher gate which leads out to the sunlight, not through the lower gate which leads out to the pit. How many of my readers are trying this way out from life's travail, with sullen fierce pertinacity. But you know whither it leads. The gloom, the stench of the pit sometimes envelope you ; nay, there have been moments when its flames have flashed out, hot and scorching, across your face. Beware lest the faintness end in a swoon, from which you will awaken there!

But there are those close by you, in your home, in your office, in your daily tasks, who are as faint as you, who are full of the sense of the sadness of life to the high-souled and earnest, the strain of the task to those who count it blessed to endure, who fainting, cry, "*Lord, I believe, but help Thou mine unbelief.*" This hope I cannot resign, this purpose I cannot forsake, this struggle to rise out of my dead self to higher things, I cannot abandon. I am weak, faint, weary, sometimes I feel as if I were dying, but if I die, I will die here. Here at Thy feet ; here by Thy cross ; here where every pain is purifying, where suffering is salvation, here, Lord, give me strength to keep, and to look on, to look up, if strength fails me to pursue. " Faint, yet pursuing " to the last.

Yes! and the hour comes of a yet more deadly faintness, when heart and flesh shall fail, and all, to the dim, tearful, wasted eyes, shall seem vanishing in the awful silence and darkness of death. I suppose that moments will come when all will seem to be vanishing. God, Christ, heaven, the harvest of the pain of life, all vanishing in the darkness that settles around the parting soul. But then the instinct, the habit which we have trained by noble and constant effort, of holding on though faint, of pursuing though weary and ready to die, shall assert its mastery. Through even the faintness of death the soul shall hold on to its purpose, pursue its prize, stretch forth and clasp its Christ. "Faint, yet pursuing," shall be the last word that is said of it, as, when the deathly pallor steals over the war-worn face, the eye flashes once more, the cheek kindles, the head is lifted, and the stiffening lips ring out a triumphant strain:

> *Faint* as I am I take the prey,
>   Hell, earth, and sin with ease overcome;
> I leap for joy, pursue my way,
>   And as a bounding hart fly home,
> Through all eternity to prove
> Thy nature and Thy name is love.

XVI.
THE VICTORY OF LIFE.

" I am He which liveth and was dead, and behold I am alive for evermore."—Rev. i. 18.

THE Apocalypse completes and crowns the Revelation of God. It is not one of the weakest of the arguments for the authority of this book, that without it the fabric of Scripture would be manifestly unfinished. I speak advisedly of the fabric of Scripture. To some it may appear to be a collection of scattered Divine utterances, spoken by the lips of all sorts of men, under all sorts of circumstances, and at all sorts of times; gathered up at random into one book, to be a repertory of doctrine, consolation, guidance and warning, for all sorts of men in all ages of the world. And regarded from this point of view, its manifoldness—the infinitely varied experiences of which it is the utterance and to which it addresses itself—renders the Bible a very marvellous book. In its breadth of human sympathy, its interest for man under all conditions, in all countries, in all ages, it stands forth as incomparably the foremost book in the world.

But to me, I confess, the most conspicuous as well

as the grandest feature of the Book is its unity. It is the thought of one Mind which is uttering itself through manifold free and independent organs; and the unity of that Mind is manifest; through all the rich varieties of modulation the one key-note is never lost. The Divine plan of the Kingdom of Heaven, the Kingdom of a redeemed humanity, which it needed a higher than a human imagination to conceive, rules the whole revelation. From the first chapter of the Book of Genesis, which records what was done "*in the beginning*," to the last chapter of the Apocalypse, which pictures what shall be done in the end, this idea of the Divine Kingdom is manifestly before the mind, not of the writers, but of Him by whom the writers were moved. They comprehend it with more or less of clearness, though at the best but partially. It was much if they had a clear understanding of that part of the plan, the execution of which was trusted to their hands. But I cannot read any book of the Bible, without seeming to see the image of an idea hovering, spirit-like, behind the particular scope and purpose of the book, whether it be History, Prophecy, Psalm, Gospel, Epistle, or Apocalypse. And it is this "idea" which accounts for all the deepest things shadowed forth, rather than contained, in the words of the individual writer, the whole range of which he could but dimly discern; while it links on each part to the whole, which, complex as it is, is perhaps the completest unity to be met with in the higher literature of the world.

It is not mere fancy which attributes something

The Victory of Life. 307

like inspiration to the poet. The world's chief singers have in some sort enquired diligently, what the spirit which was working within them did signify; there seemed to be some higher power acting upon them, and they felt reverently that there was more in their words than they could fully master, which the growing experience of the ages would reveal to mankind. And so these great ones who wrote our Bible, knew that there was more in the words which the Spirit within them moved them to utter, than they could grasp with their understandings; a thought, a plan of God, which in its wholeness eternity only can disclose. No complete plan of the Divine operation in Redemption, could have been before the minds of the various writers of the Bible, even the most masterly, such as Moses, Isaiah, St. John and St. Paul. And yet the Bible as a whole reveals a complete plan, and is the way-book of the pilgrimage of the great human host—of man, fallen in Adam and dead, quickened in Christ and raised—from the Eden of his infancy to the Heaven of his matured, disciplined and victorious powers.

Of that plan it is impossible, to me at least, to doubt, that this book of the Apocalypse is an essential feature. It is like the brow of the human form, circled with the crown. The central picture is crowned humanity; the exile of Eden, through Redemption, the crowned comrade of the Eternal King. It seems to me as if the Scripture could not fitly close its oracle without an Apocalypse. Remember, it began from heaven. "*In the beginning*," from heaven was dropped the first golden link of the chain of history. The Scripture would not have been complete unless the last link also had been visibly taken up into heaven. From heaven and to heaven is the way of humanity, through the depths of pain and of death. That could have been no waybook of our pilgrimage which left us in those depths, even with a promise of deliverance. Man must see into heaven, and catch the vision there of his glorified estate, or the darkness of his house of bondage would bury his hope for ever.

Without the Apocalypse, and that realising hold of the things of the eternal state which it offers to the redeemed, man's comfort and joy of the Scripture would have been as imperfect, as Redemption would have been without the resurrection of the Lord. What the ascension of the risen Saviour is to Redemption, the Apocalypse is to the Scripture. It lifts it into the world of the resurrection, where the risen Man reigns for ever. It unveils to us the wonders and glories of the state which has sorrow, sin, and death behind it, instead of before it. We hear the hymns, we join in the praises, we see the very forms of those who have emerged for ever from this chaos of confusion, of darkness, and of sorrow, in which we are struggling; and in which it seems to us, when the eye of faith grows dim, that our hope and the hope of humanity must be lost. But we see them there, in their shining jubilant ranks, around Him who "*liveth and was dead, and behold He is alive for evermore, and hath the keys of Hell and of Death,*" and hope is saved.

The Apocalypse unveils to us the life of those who have crossed the river, and have set their conquering feet upon the eternal shore. There is no promise so full of consolation, there is no prophecy so inspiring to hope, as this vision of the life of the blessed ones who can sing, "*Worthy is the Lamb that was slain.*" "*Blessing, and honour, and glory, and power, be unto Him that sitteth on the throne, and to the Lamb for ever and ever.*" It is the life which they are living there which we look upon, and the light of it falls with a solemn, mysterious lustre on the dark sea across which we urge our way. The waves which plash and moan around us are crested with an unearthly brightness. The wail of our struggle is crossed and lifted into a hymn by a strain of glorious triumphant music, which falls on the trembling air from the height of the upper world. The light which shines, and the music which sings through the Apocalypse, are the very glow of the heavenly joy, and the inspiration of the heavenly hope. While the central figure of the whole, the Being around whom the lustre glows, the music floats, and the blessed ones throng, is "*the Lamb that was slain,*" whose word, whose self-affirmation, is the sentence of our text, "*I am He that liveth and was dead, and behold I am alive for evermore. Amen, and have the keys of Hell and of Death.*"

I. The broad assertion of the text is, the victory of life.

The living One, He by whom and in whom all things live, has died, and is alive again, and liveth for evermore, Death and Hell lying conquered at His feet. In other words, Life and Death, that which quickens in the universe and that which destroys, have met, shut up to the decisive conflict, and Life has proved itself the stronger. Death seemed to win the triumph for the moment; Life won the victory for eternity. It is the assertion of the eternally superior power of the Life. Henceforth and for ever light is stronger than darkness, truth than lies, God than sin. And the assurance rests visibly—to the eye of faith—on an actual and decisive trial. It is not the region of ideas, but of fact, which is here disclosed. It is not an imagined, expected, promised, or prophesied, but an actual and palpable victory, to the end that "we might have strong consolation, and a good hope through grace." It is in truth the turning-point in the history of man, and in the destiny of the universe. When Death and Life wrestled in the God-Man, and Life trod Death in the dust, the problem which had hung like a menacing shadow over the destinies of all living things, and had buried the world till that hour in a darkness which might be felt, was solved for ever. Death, the insulting spoiler, was stripped of his spoils and slain.

And who, but for Christ, would dare to prophesy that victory? Who, looking into his own heart, his own life, the experience of humanity, or the condition of the world, would venture to affirm that Life was the stronger, and that the dark shadow on the universe was waning before the kindling day. "*Sin reigneth unto death,*" is the wail of humanity, is the wail of life. Our forefathers believed that the night was the stronger power; the womb out of which all things were born, and to which all things would return. Life seemed to them to be a hopeless failure. Loss, pain, regret, fear, anguish, these seemed to them to be the leading threads in the woof of a human experience. Sickness, decay, death, to them seemed to round the whole. States seemed to be hopelessly prone to corruption, rulers to tyranny, children to perverseness, friends to treachery, riches to flight, honour to stain. The battle seemed to them doomed from the first to issue in the triumph of the dark powers; against whom with stern resolution they struggled, and whose yoke they wrestled hard to shake off, but with no hope of ultimate victory.

The Prometheus, the Laocoon, the Hamlet—and Hamlet is profoundly Teutonic, and expressive of the native genius of our race—present to us the picture of human destiny, if we turn away from the Gospel with its Apocalypse. Man struggling heroically, but struggling hopelessly. The eagle of the almighty tyrant preying upon his vitals; the serpents of fate coiling tighter and tighter about his limbs; the native hue of resolution sicklied o'er by the pale cast of thought; "I dare not" waiting ever on "I would"; the face of the heroic combatant set in stern defiance, but settling slowly into utter, agonising despair.

Life seems very terrible to all the nobler peoples who are unblessed by an Apocalypse; and are there not seasons when even the revelation of life and immortality fails to dissipate its terror for us? Know you not moments when a feeling of blank despair about yourself, about your dear ones, about your people, about the world, settles darkly over the spirit? " Progress !" you say ; " I see little sign of it. I remember my bright youth; would to God that I could now recover the freshness, the purity, the hope, the spring, the sense of an unseen sympathy, which then lit my life and made it a joyous thing to be! And where is the dignity, the purity, the loftiness, of the life of the men of old time, the time of great struggles and great achievements, of heroes, apostles, confessors, martyrs, and saints ? What has the world to show in place of the ancient heroism ? Express trains, electric telegraphs, and calicoes at sixpence a yard, go but a little way towards making life noble and beautiful ; and a progress of which these are the chief exponents, may quite possibly be a progress towards a nearer fellowship with the brutes."

Progress is a noble word, a beautiful word. But it is wonderful how some of the purest and keenest searchers for the signs of it, are driven well-nigh mad in all ages, and notably in our own, in their endeavours to discover them. Trace the tone of sadness which breathes through St. Paul's later epistles, and through the writings of St. John. It may help us to understand better the undertone of something like despair, which lends such pathetic power to the writings of men like Mr. Carlyle and Mr. Ruskin in our day. Paul the aged compared what the Church had grown to, with the heavenly beauty of the life of that little company at Jerusalem ; it was like the wilderness to Eden. Progress! The first thing which the Church did was to fall. Read St. Paul's letters to Timothy, and St. John's letters to the Churches, and see what the Church had progressed to. I believe that the progress would just have driven them mad, as it has so many noble thinkers and workers, but for the clear vision of Him "*who liveth and was dead, and is alive for evermore.*"

Faith saved those noble hearts from utter wreck. They could see little that gladdened them in the present, or cheered them in the future, but by faith they shared the vision of Christ and foresaw His final and glorious victory. They understood by faith that God had not wasted such priceless treasure, or staked the future of His kingdom on an experiment, which the devil with all his arts would be able to frustrate. They knew that the victory of Christ was prophetic, and that every enemy of His benign and glorious reign must lie, one day, where death lay, prostrate beneath the Redeemer's feet. And their hope through Christ was unconquerable. May ours be as victorious! Against all the despondency, the despair, into which the reign of sin in us, in our friends, in our country, and in the world, may plunge us, let us set up the standard of Him who "*was dead and is alive again, and who liveth for evermore.*"

Let us consider—

II. The special form which this assertion assumes. It met, and was intended to meet, two grievous forms of error, which in the apostolic age were threatening the truth from quite opposite sides. If they were simply errors of the early Church, we might leave them there among the lumber of the past; but they run through the whole course of Christian history, and rise up in full vigour to affront us at the present day. The Death, the Life; one or the other, men think, must be unreal. He was simply man if He died; THE LIFE could not die. If He was the Life, the essential Eternal Life, His death could have been but a phantom, a mere drama of suffering, full of pathetic power to the spectators, but still with no reality behind. The great biography must be, they thought, either the life of a human martyr, or a drama of sorrow and of death enacted by a God. But John felt that the whole power of the Gospel narrative lay in its solid reality. To him the things which he recorded concerning Christ, were just the clearest and most substantial facts in the history of the world; while men were in fearful peril of substituting for them their theories of Divine things.

How far are we from the heart of this danger now? John saw the apostacy looming in the distance, for apostacy it is, from fact to fancy, from life to theory about life, from Christ to the " Idea of the Divine." He knew that the time was at hand when the Church would be rent by questions of idle or dark philosophies; while the living man Christ Jesus would appear dimly and yet more dimly through the haze. And I believe that he wrote the Apocalypse, that he might keep before the eye of the world the form of a living Saviour, the Man who once lived on earth and died, and who was living, to die no more, in heaven. The solid fact of the Gospel, is the substance of the revelation of the Apocalypse. The form of the living Christ, carrying on the work of this world, is the first figure that we meet with in the opening chapter; and the word of His living lips prolongs its echo to the close. The real life, the real death, the real victory of life through death—this is the Apocalypse. The intense reality of the struggle of the power of life with the principle and power of death, in the experience of the man Christ Jesus; the final effort of the power of death to slay the Prince of Life and to hold Him dead; and the absolute and eternal overthrow of all that, sprung from sin, was making waste the world—these are the great realities which are here unveiled.

To those who were persuaded that the resurrection was a myth—and we can see how deeply even in St. Paul's days this heresy had tainted the Church —the Apocalypse presents the familiar form in the glory of the resurrection. "The Lamb that was slain" appears, wearing the signs of the Cross and Passion, in the midst of the Throne, before which the heads of all created orders, through all the spheres, bent low in prostrate adoration. To those who believed that this glorious and blessed Being had only played at dying, it unveils the mystery of Calvary; it reveals the Cross and Passion and the precious blood, as the theme of the most intense meditation to celestial spirits, the subject-matter of their most blest communion, and the burden of their most exulting and universal songs. It is as though the beloved disciple had said, the fact of Calvary shall never be buried under man's theories of Redemption; the life of the God-Man in heaven shall be unveiled, and shall become part of the life of the race which He has redeemed. Death shall be no barrier, no veil. The world behind the veil shall become as tangibly, visibly real as the world of our daily tasks. The risen God-Man shall dwell among His brethren, shall meet them in their daily paths, and mix with them in their daily toils. He who liveth and was dead, and is alive for evermore, shall appear in their midst; He shall join Himself to them, as once to the two who journeyed to Emmaus. He shall walk with them, talk with them, strive with them, suffer with them, rejoice with them; and shall make them understand that His interest and hope and theirs are for ever one.

Musing thus, his heart was open to the full tide of inspiration. The Apocalypse took shape and grew to completeness under his hands.

"*He that liveth.*" The Author and the Giver of life, He in whom all that lives lives, all that moves moves, all that is has its being, in human form mastered the experience of death. What was the problem which the fatal exercise of freedom proposed for Divine solution? It was this. Shall the life of God perish in all beings whom He has made free? Shall all in the universe that has power to separate itself from His life, die? Shall His reign be perfect only over dumb, dead matter? Shall the stars, the storms, the dews, the flowers, the lights, the shadows, alone obey His will ? Shall He rule supreme in the world of matter, while living hearts, and wills, and voices defy Him, and break away from His sphere ? Shall the morning smile of Creation flash up from the dewy spray and the gleaming meadow, while every eye that has in it the speculation of an intelligent spirit turns from Him, and every voice which utters the decisions of a free will declares, Depart from me, I desire not the knowledge of Thy ways ?

This was the aim of evil. Death is the separation of that which lives in God from the Life that is in God. And evil aims at the separation of the whole sphere of free intelligence from God, and the reign of Death over all that was made in the likeness of God in this world. Nor did the aim appear hopeless. The freeborn sons had yielded to the tempter. Through all the sphere of intelligent being sin wrought mightily unto Death. Very terrible was the aspect of the great world before the face of Him who had made it so blessed. Wrong, misery, cursing, everywhere. The earth full of violence, and the ear of Heaven vexed with the moans of pain or the frantic outbursts of despair.

And He who was the Life entered into the very heart of it. He did not look down upon it, He entered into it; and where the darkness was densest, where the pain was sharpest, where the despair was most dire, the Life entered to try to the last conclusion the question, Shall the reigning power in this universe, eternally, be Life or Death ? Is there power in God to conquer that death which is desolating His dominion? Is there a way of restoring free beings, whom evil has taught to hate Him, to the sphere of His love? And the answer is here : "*Forasmuch then as the children are partakers of flesh and blood, He also Himself likewise took part of the same, that through death He might destroy him that had the power of death, that is the devil; and deliver them who through fear of death were all their lifetime subject to bondage. . . . . For this purpose was the Son of God manifested that he might destroy the works of the Devil.*" He was manifested by Death and by Life. Life bowing itself to Death, Life rising out of Death and triumphing over Death for ever.

Our fathers *were* right in their thought about the night. They were right in their dream of the twilight of the gods, but they failed to see the morning that was beyond it. The living One *was* to die. The Author and Giver of life *was* to pass under the dominion of death. For the moment deep darkness settled over all. There was darkness over the whole land, perhaps over other worlds than this. The Prince of Life slain on Calvary ; the Prince of Darkness master of the hour ; Hell triumphant, Heaven defeated, its King captive, condemned, and slain. And thus the Son of God destroyed the works of the Devil. The victim was the conqueror. Life, bursting from the prison of Death, rent in sunder its bars for ever. He proclaimed the eternal victory of Life, and drew the captives of Death with Him, redeemed, to His celestial sphere. Destroying Death by dying, He destroyed the centre and core of its power. The weakest, most unarmed and submissive of beings, delivered Himself into the hand of the destroyer. The Life which was in Him was the one power which He did not part with. The shattering of the prison-house of death by that simple power, began that triumphant work of Redemption which has placed Death and Hell as conquered captives at His feet, and has raised their victims to sit by Him on His eternal throne.

And He liveth for evermore, and evermore must conquer. The future of the universe is the future of Life ; sin and death are scattered as dark shadows before the waxing day. It is life's glorious, everlasting triumph. "*I am He which liveth and was dead, and behold I am alive for evermore, and have the keys of Hell and of Death.*" Let not your heart be troubled ; ye believe in God, believe also in Him. Believe in the Life. Believe in the victory of Calvary. Believe in the King who has led captivity captive, and has given the gift of Redemption to the world. Death shall not have dominion over you. He who was dead is alive, and liveth for evermore, to conquer death in you, in the world, in the great universe, and to subdue finally all things unto Himself. Hard as it may be to hope, heavy as may be the pressure of evil on you and on the world, the worst pressure has been met and broken. The Lord has overcome the world. Masterful as the world may seem, its strength is broken, it can have the mastery no more. Every age the triumph of Life extends its train ; the circle of light widens ; the Kingdom of Heaven grows. It may be hard to trace it amid the confusions of time; we see it through the Apocalypse amid the serenities of eternity.

We, too, can stand by the seer and see "*a new heaven and a new earth, for the first heaven and the first earth were passed away, and there was no more sea. And I, John, saw the holy City, New Jerusalem, coming down from God, out of heaven, prepared as a bride adorned for her husband. And I heard a great voice out of heaven saying, Behold the tabernacle of God is with men, and He will dwell with them, and they shall be His people, and God Himself shall be with them, and be their God. And God shall wipe away all tears from their eyes; and there shall be no more death, neither sorrow, nor crying, neither shall there be any more pain, for the former things are passed away.*" Round us, too, the strain of that mighty music floats, "*I heard as it were the voice of a great multitude, and as the voice of many waters, and as the voice of mighty thunderings, saying, Alleluia, for the Lord God omnipotent reigneth. Let us be glad and rejoice, and give honour to Him; for the marriage of the Lamb is come, and His wife hath made herself ready. And to her it was granted that she should be arrayed in fine linen, clean and white; for the fine linen is the righteousness of saints. And He said unto me, Write, Blessed are they which are called to the marriage supper of the Lamb.*" Yea, blessed are they, for they rest from their travail, and their works follow them to the sphere of Light and Life on high.

XVII.

THE KEYS OF HELL AND OF DEATH.

"And have the keys of Hell and of Death."—Rev. i. 18.

THIS verse announces and celebrates, as we have seen, the triumph of Life; Death's dominion shattered by the Resurrection, the crown stripped from his brow, his throne prostrate in the dust. The word of the Gospel is not "man shall rise," but "man has risen." The dead is alive again, and liveth for evermore. The triumph of Life is complete; the ages but swell its train. Life has entered the realm of death, has bowed to its yoke and burst it for ever. The great problem of the universe is solved. It is settled now and settled for ever, that the future is to be the realm of Life, and that Death is doomed to die. Till that act of Resurrection Death triumphed. Human and angelic worlds trembled at his aspect, and shuddered under his pall. Freedom, that glorious divine thing, without which the reign of God in His universe had been but half divine, had simply filled the prison-house: angels, men, led in dark captivity; Death reigning in insolent triumph over all. Very terrible to the eye of Him who made all so beautiful, so blessed, was the aspect of the world. Not one child of the race whom He made in His likeness, to be kings of this wealthy and splendid Creation, true to His allegiance! "*All gone astray;*" "*all become filthy;*" "*none doing righteousness, no not one.*"

One deluge had swept over the earth and cleansed its pollution; and a new founder of the race stepped forth into a new world. Again Death won the easy mastery. Again every free-born child of man, as his first act of freedom, refused the Lord of life, and chose the lord of death to be his king. And the tyranny became terrible, the darkness utter. To the eye of the understanding, perhaps to the eye of dark watchers behind the veil, the dream of our Norse forefathers seemed to be slowly fulfilling itself: the twilight of the gods, the bright friends and helpers of man, seemed to be deepening into the eternal night. A shaft of glorious light flashed through that night at the Resurrection, and streams of living splendour have been flowing down, from that hour of Life's triumph until now. Death was conquered, destroyed, in the very shrine of his power! The living one "became dead," with a purpose and for an end. He *became* dead, He "accomplished" a decease at Jerusalem; the Life by its inherent might raised Him up again, and lifted Him to a throne at the right hand of God. Life rising out of death, spoiled the realm of Death for ever. The prison is rent, the bars are broken, the veil is parted. Henceforth Death can reign over none, but those who will to die.

The world of Jesus and the Resurrection is now the true homeland of man's spirit. "*Ye then, risen with Christ, seek the things which are above, where Christ sitteth at the right hand of God.*" The Life of Christ, which is in you by faith, is that Life over which Death was powerless, and is powerless for ever. That Life which is its fountain is perpetually triumphing over Death, and showing openly the spoils. It is a triumph which He has won for, and will complete in, you. Believe in the victory and win it. "*This is the victory that overcometh the world, even your faith;*"—your faith in Him who has overcome. Doubt the power of the Life, and Death becomes your tyrant. Cry, "*Lord, I believe,*" and Death becomes the shadow of a shade. This is the grand lesson of the Apocalypse. It is not the promise, the prophecy, but the *vision* of the triumph which it unveils. The Lord of Life asserting His mastery over Hell and Death, and leading on the triumphal progress; till in the new Jerusalem sorrow, sighing, sin, and death shall be memories of vanished things to the living universe for ever and for ever.

I. There is the deepest meaning in the word, "I became dead," which conveys the exact force of the original.

It implies the act of a will, an effort made, a work done, for an end. There was no abstract necessity that the blessed One should become the Man of Sorrows; that the living One should taste the bitterness of death. The necessity lay, not in the Creator's duty to the creature, but in the Father's love to the child. We can conceive of the Lord of Life and of Light abiding serene in the celestial spheres, blessed in His own blessedness, and leaving a sinful world to stagger on in its blindness, and to bury itself at last in the gloom of the everlasting night. We can conceive that the doom of Sodom, of Pompeii, might have overtaken the whole world which lay in the wicked one ; and that one stern and righteous stroke of judgment might have ended the dark experiment of freedom for ever.

But a Father's heart had to be satisfied, while a righteous government had to be upheld. Hence, a new, and we may call it a divine necessity, arose, whose root lies in that which the moral instinct of man recognises as most godlike in God. "*It became Him of whom are all things and by whom are all things, in bringing many sons to glory, to make the Captain of their salvation perfect through suffering.*" And thus the living One "*became dead.*" "*It pleased the Father that in Him should all fulness dwell.*" He was first-born of life, it pleased the Father that He should become the firstborn of death, that in all things He might have the pre-eminence. First in honour, first in power, first in glory, the Lord's elect one, the Firstborn, He should be first too in strain, in sorrow, in wounds and in death. No being in the universe should be doomed to pass through an experience which the Lord of the universe shrank from sharing ; or be compelled to drink a cup of bitterness, of which the most Blessed had not already drained the dregs.

You observe that I use the words doomed and

compelled. Much of our suffering here is inevitable. We are born into a world of sin and of suffering. The condition of our life is struggle, and sharp pain cannot in anywise be escaped. God does not ask the consent of our will to such a life as that to which we are born. He breathes the breath of life into our nostrils according to His will, and at His pleasure He reclaims it. But much of our experience of sorrow *is* our own work; much of our misery we make for ourselves, by our conscious, lustful, guilty sin. This we must bear alone. There is no necessity for this experience. The anguish of remorse, the horror of despair, are not the things which it became Him to know, when He would become perfect as the Captain of salvation through suffering.

And yet there is an awful, and to us unfathomable sense in which, through the intensity of His sympathy with the race which He came to redeem, nay, rather through the perfectness of His participation of their life, the sinless One did know it. A moment of dreadful God-forsaken darkness passed over His spirit, and the knowledge entered into Him of what a soul accursed from God might endure. But in all the common human experience the Son of Man was to win His pre-eminence by suffering. "*Himself took our infirmities, and bare our sicknesses,*" that all fulness, fulness of knowledge, of sympathy, of power to help and to save, might dwell in Him, and flow forth to all our need.

And He "became dead." It was part of that plan. "*Therefore doth My Father love Me, because I lay down My life that I might take it again. No man taketh it from Me, but I lay it down of Myself. I have power to lay it down, and I have power to take it again. This commandment have I received of My Father."* He entered of His own free will, with no armament but Life, the realm of Death, and by living, demonstrated Death to be powerless. In the might of the Life He arose triumphant, Death and Hell led captive in His train ; and now He holds the keys of their prison-house and bears off all their spoils. Age by age the great company of the ransomed, an ever widening train, comes home with songs ; " *Unto Him that hath loved us, and washed us from our sins in His own blood, and hath made us kings and priests unto God; to Him be glory and dominion for ever and ever. Amen.*"

II. "*Amen; and have the keys of Hell and of Death.*"

Hell —Hades, the invisible world to which death is the portal—all that has to do with death, and the beyond.

The word "keys" of course signifies mastery. To give over the key of a house, is to give possession of the house. To hold the keys of a prison, is to hold the destiny of the captives who are bound in its chains. The word expresses absolute mastery; the power of a Lord to do with *things* what He will.

The commentators on this passage seem to dwell mainly on the idea of release : power to unbind, to throw open the prison doors, and to let the captives go free. It is no doubt a very important feature in the suggestions of the text; power to loose, to ransom, to save. But I doubt much whether it is the chief suggestion. Power of entrance seems to be quite as important a feature of the matter as power of exit; so also power of discipline, power of control, power of ordering and ruling—everything in fact which a complete mastery involves. The Lord has won, not a victory only, but a supremacy. He has not only conquered Death, He has made him subject, and uses him now with royal right as the instrument of His benignant will.

In illustrating this point let me ask you to consider :—

1. The Lord's entrance into the realm of Death and Hell, as the first act of mastery, whereby He has absolutely subjected them to Himself.

I think that David had a clear vision of what is implied in the power of the keys, when he sang, "*Yea, though I walk through the valley of the shadow of death, I will fear no evil; for Thou art with me, Thy rod and Thy staff they comfort me. Surely goodness and mercy shall follow me all the days of my life, and I will dwell in the house of the Lord for ever.*" The Lord's entrance there lit up the darkness of Hades, and turned the prison-house into a home. He entered, and all heaven entered with Him. It was just the conquest for men of this dark domain, and its annexation to the kingdom of God in our world. Death and Hades had become terrible through transgression. Sin had created a realm into which the sunlight had no entrance, whose very existence, as it were, was a defiance of God. The Lord entered it and reclaimed its allegiance. He said, "There shall be no part of the universe whence light, and life, and love are by right excluded. I bear them with Me into the shadow of death; the shadow lifts, vanishes; it is all in the sunlight and for evermore." I see how far this principle reaches. How far did Christ's heart-clasp reach when he said, as the supreme moment of anguish drew near, "*And I if I be lifted up from the earth will draw all men unto Me.*"

God has entered the darkness. He who is "God of God, Light of Light, very God of very God," has entered it to die; to pass within the veil is but to follow Him. To them of old time, in their darker moments when vision was clouded, it seemed like being parted from Him. "God is here in the sunlight. This is the living world which God frequents; here I am near to Him; I shall lose Him if I pass into the shades." The ancients found it hard to shake off the impression that the shadow of death was the shadow of evil. Life to them was the continent of light, while all round a great ocean of darkness spread, which was the domain of the grisly king.

This imagination tinctures all their writings. They shrank from death because they dreaded the dark power, into whose domain they believed that it would usher them. Hezekiah's lamentation is the strongest expression of this dread which we meet with in Scripture; indeed, I know not anything in literature so steeped in this sadness, unless it be some of the Hindoo hymns. "*I said in the cutting off of my days I shall go to the gates of the grave : I am deprived of the residue of my years. I said, I shall not see the Lord, even the Lord, in the land of the living ; I shall behold man no more with the inhabitants of the world." " Mine age is departed, and is removed from me as a shepherd's tent ; I have cut off like a weaver my life ; He will cut me off with pining sickness : from day even unto night wilt Thou make an end of me. I reckoned till morning that, as a lion, so will He break all my bones : from day even to night wilt Thou make an end of me. Like a crane, or a swallow, so did I chatter ; I did mourn as a dove : mine eyes fail with looking upwards : O Lord, I am oppressed ; undertake for me. What shall I say ? He hath both spoken unto me, and Himself hath done it ; I shall go softly all my years in the bitterness of my soul."*—Isaiah xxxviii. 10–15.

Even David in his gloomier moments was touched with it. "*Lord, make me to know mine end, and the measure of my days, what it is ; that I may know how frail I am. Behold Thou hast made my days as an handbreadth, and mine age is as nothing before Thee : verily man at his best estate is altogether vanity. . . . O, spare me, that I may recover strength before I go hence and be no more."*—Psalms xxxix. 4, 5, 13. The book of Ecclesiastes too is deeply tinctured with this gloomy view of the unseen world. Indeed, it seems gloomy all round to the writer of that book. "Vanitas vanitatum ; omnia vanitas," is the epitaph of that preacher, on life and on hope. But David surely, of all the Old Testament seers, had the clearest vision of the truth. There are passages of literally triumphant exultation, which burst from him when he is considering the mercies of his God, the faithfulness of his almighty, eternal Friend. "*But God shall redeem my soul from the power of the grave, for He shall redeem me.*" "*As for me I shall behold Thy face in righteousness, I shall be satisfied, when I awake, with Thy likeness.*" "*Therefore my heart is glad, and my glory rejoiceth; my flesh also shall rest in hope. For Thou wilt not leave my soul in hell, neither wilt Thou suffer thine Holy One to see corruption. Thou wilt show me the path of life; in Thy presence is fulness of joy, at Thy right hand there are pleasures for evermore.*"

Of this, the Lord's entrance to that realm is the prophecy, nay, the earnest. He entered because we must enter; and where man must go, the God-Man passes at the head of the race. He entered that we might enter boldly, and assure ourselves that wherever the God-Man goes on before us, there is for us not a prison-house but a home.

It is impossible for us to imagine the immense revolution in man's notions about death, which sprang from the death of his Divine Lord. He brought the whole realm, by one act, out of darkness into daylight. Men could entertain no terror of that which had no terror for Him. The fact that he "became dead," consecrated death as a temple, and the grave as its shrine. The sense of a beloved presence is

The Keys of Hell and of Death. 331

always and everywhere the dissipation of dread. There is nothing terrible to those who feel themselves clasped in the arms of love.

Realise the passionate devotion of the first disciples to their Saviour—a passion which found the rack as a bed of roses if they might but glorify Him by defying its pain; and then imagine the victory over death which the vision of that beloved form passing through its portals won for them. Dread it! they pined for it, they strained towards it, that they might more swiftly join their ascended Christ; and the glow of their hope passed forth into the world. There was a vague sense that a great crisis had come, that a great though unseen revolution had been accomplished, winning new truth, freedom, and power for men, in those who had hardly heard of the message of the Gospel. The joy, the triumph of the apostolic Church was infectious. The moment that the Lord had entered the gate of Death as a master, a new sense of power as against Death and Hell, lodged itself in the world's sad heart.

2. Having the keys implies control, the power of discipline. He who has the keys has the control of the inmates, to rule and to train them at his will.

Granted that it is a prison-house, that this is the point of view from which the men of old time were fain to regard it, how much of its external character still remains! Have *we* quite shaken off its terror? Could *we* smile, would our eye light up with a flash of triumph, if we felt at this moment Death's cold barb above our hearts? The flesh, and something more than the flesh, shudders in the presence of the angel, though we know his angelic mission. Death is too deeply related to our sin, and Hell is too dread a reality to conscious guilt, for us easily to shake off their spells.

Just as that passionate love, that abounding joy in a complete redemption, which marked the apostolic age, dies down, the terror of death returns on us again. And in any wise death remains. Christ hath abolished death, says the apostle in his absolute way—the apostle, or some apostolic man who was the mouthpiece of his thoughts. And to him death was abolished, "*Willing rather to be exiled from the body, and to be at home with the Lord.*" To faith, wherever it is pure and strong, death is abolished. I heard of one of God's holy ones the other day who had lost one greatly revered and beloved. "Do not wonder if I am not able to grieve," she said, "I feel so near." Death abolished. "*Life and immortality brought to light by the Gospel.*"

But faith is not always strong. The two worlds do not always seem so near. Death as a physical experience, death as a moral experience, remains still a shadow over our house of life. The Lord who has the key, retains it, not as a terror to torment but as a means of discipline. All the associations and influences of death, once so fearful, He retains, and He wields them with a loving hand for the culture and education of our souls. As a place of torment it is for ever abolished. "*The sting of death is sin.*"

When He "*put away sin by the sacrifice of Himself,*" He swallowed up death in victory. Guilt is at the root of that gnawing anguish which makes Hades into Hell, and—save for those who *will* have it, who *will* have death rather than life, cursing rather than blessing, hell rather than heaven—the pains of hell are loosed from humanity for ever.

When the Lord revealed a reconciled Father, He banished the imagination of an eternal torture chamber from the world. Men have restored it, and wielded it with tremendous power, to the profit of the priest and to the detriment of the Gospel. There must be dark horrors in the future for the haters of their own souls, for the lovers of the gates of death ; but the end must be correction, and not vengeance, if the keys of Death and Hell are in the hand of Him who died to save.

The Gospel, which proclaims forgiveness to the sinner, restoration to the prodigal child, scatters the shadow which hangs about the future. No fearful looking for of judgment and fiery indignation, can torment a soul which has looked into the face of God in Christ, and has read the meaning which is there. "*O Death, where is thy sting? O Grave, where is thy victory?*" The Lord has the key of the prison, in which the self-tormented and despairing victims of evil lie groaning. He has unbarred it, and sent them forth from chains and darkness to heaven's glad sunlight, and to the freedom of the sons whom the Son makes free indeed. "*If, when we were enemies, we were reconciled to God by the death of His Son, much more being reconciled we shall be saved by His life."*

And further, all that is dark and sad about Death and Hades, the Lord holds under the control of His loving hand. It becomes an instrument for the nurture and training of our spirits; it lends even a solemn consecration to this earthly life, as it lets fall upon it the lustre of the heavenly world. The keys are in His hand. That implies the control of all the influences which Death and Hades can wield over our spirits. In other words, it is His influence. The natural shuddering at death, takes its place among the benign influences which are educating us. The long pain and struggle in dying which we watch with profound sadness, has a loving meaning and ministry to the dear one who suffers it. It is adding the last touch to the training; it is perfecting the patience; it is laying up holy memories which will make the soul richer and gladder in eternity.

I am often called to see, how the higher graces of the nature get trained to a beautiful perfection by the suffering of death. Never forget that the mind which moved the Lord to become obedient unto death, that the Father's house might again be filled with the sons, brought all the powers of the world to come under His hand. It changed Death from a terror to an angel, and Hades from a realm of pallid shivering ghosts to a sunlit home. We can gaze now on the dreaded form with unruffled serenity. We can pass by the terrible gates with a song; for we know that *" neither death, nor life, nor angels, nor principalities, nor powers, nor things present, nor things to come, nor height, nor depth, nor any other creature, shall be able to separate us from the love of God, which is in Christ Jesus our Lord.*"

3. He holds the keys of deliverance—the exit, the way out, the way through death to heaven.

The key of the entrance, as we have seen, is in His hand. He has entered the shadow of death and dispelled the darkness. He holds, too, the key of its influence. What power it has over human spirits is now His power. He uses it as an instrument of loving discipline, and trains us by it for the world where death shall be no more for ever. But the grand theme of the Apocalypse, is the world behind the veil which He has lifted, and whose life, whose constant interests, fears, cares, hopes, and joys, it reveals. He holds the key as the Lord of the Resurrection. Death is the access, not to a realm of shadow, but to a glorious, transfigured world. In truth it is the synonym of emancipation.

Life is death and death is life, to him who believes. "*Ye are dead, and your life is hid with Christ in God,*" is the witness of St. Paul. This life, to those who have seen with the eye of faith the risen Lord, who believe in His Apocalypse of heaven, becomes a daily dying, and death the birth-throe of the true, immortal life. *This* is the world of shadow, it is death which hides from us the sunlight. On this side the river, the wilderness; there, the peaceful and blessed homes whose sunlight is the unveiled face of God. The struggle of the quickened spirit with the flesh which cumbers it, and with the world which holds it to the dust, is the daily dying, which death completes and resurrection crowns. He who holds the keys, has opened the farther as well as the nearer side of the prison-house. He has left it but a passage, flooded with the light of the celestial world.

We can little appreciate what this Apocalypse of the world of the Resurrection has done for mankind —the vision of the slain victim of Calvary, risen, and reigning on the throne. I believe that nothing so helped the Church, and through the Church the world, to grasp the truth of the Resurrection, and all that has sprung from it, as these wondrous visions. We, too, like the three on the mount of transfiguration, are "*eye-witnesses of His majesty.*" And we know, by the surest sense, that we did not follow cunningly devised fables, when we believed in the risen Jesus, and learned that death was but an inner gate of heaven. The unseen, even though peopled by shapes of terror, has always exercised a strange fascination on mankind. There has been no rest for man in this straitly bounded life. There has been an impulse and a yearning towards the mystery.

> The desire of the moth for the star ;
> Of the day for the morrow ;
> The worship of something afar
> From the sphere of our sorrow.

Man knows by sure instinct that the secret of his

being, the key to his life, is there. The Gospel has made that yearning intense. Death has grown beautiful as a bride to earth's elect spirits. It is the way out into the free universe, the great congress of the first-born; the way to liberty, bliss, glory.

To die in Christ, believing in the life, rejoicing in the life, and in its inevitable triumph; hating the sin which is the anguish of death, and the terror of hell; praying "more light, more life," with dying lips; cleaving, with the strong prevailing grasp of a man who knows that if he loosens his hold he dies, to the Hand which has rent the prison-house, and has brought the captives forth,—to die thus is to enter into life. A moment's spasm, a choking sob, and then the free, broad universe for ever. The shadow of death behind us; pain, weakness, anguish—the straitness of a soul too large for its frame, its work, and its world—become but half forgotten memories, lost at length in the joy which is fed for ever from the fountain of His life, "*who was dead, and behold He is alive for evermore, and hath the keys of Hell and of Death.*"

XVIII.
THE RESURRECTION OF MAN.

"*But now is Christ risen from the dead, and become the first-fruits of them that slept. For since by man came death, by man came also the resurrection of the dead.*"—I. Cor. xv. 20-21.

For man, death has a significance unknown in all the inferior regions of the Creation. The creatures play under its shadow; man alone shrinks and shudders. Death is an unknown factor in the careless life of the Creation; it is a ruling factor, perhaps *the* ruling factor in the natural life of man. There is little need to hand the skeleton round at our banquets: it haunts the secret chamber of every heart. It closes every vista; it rounds every pleasure; it casts a chilling shadow over life's sunniest passages; it lends a passionate sadness to passionate love. All the philosophies have spent their strength in trying to rob it of its terror, and to banish it to the background; in vain, it evades them, and plants itself in the foreground of every life.

Man, standing on the summit level of Creation, occupying the highest stage of development to which the creature has attained, finds himself consciously face to face with a new and terrible experience, which strikes a great shuddering dread into his heart of hearts.

Eve, when she hung over the blood-flecked brow of Abel, might well have prayed for the merciful stroke of annihilation, had she forecast all the bitter anguish of which death was destined to be the fountain, and let slip the promise of the overthrow of death, by Him who should be at once the seed of the woman and her Lord.

With new power, there comes to man in the unfolding of his life a new terror, and the terror seems to be the master. As matter of fact, man finds that life is not worth the living without the hope of immortality. From the shadow, which for the thoughtful, the cultured, the loving, that is for those in whom the higher development is most conspicuous, death casts over life, there is absolutely no escape. *Omnes eodem cogimur;* and to the natural man the way is dark and sad. We are made more dependent in a sense, we are more finely strung, more capable of tender devotion and clinging love, than the creatures; and we live and love under the shadow of the fear that at any moment, in a moment, all our dearest treasures may be scattered, and all our pleasant things laid waste.

That God-like faculty in man, as we cannot but call it, which looks before and after, which peers into the future, and must peer, finds everywhere the shadow of death stretched round its horizon, baffling its penetration, and mocking its efforts to search out the unknown. Is the shadow impenetrable? Is there nothing beyond? In that case the summit of creature development is simply a summit of agony;

the creature attains to the height of its perfection only to recoil before a grisly shape of terror, and to upbraid the force, be it what it may, which has made the universe the theatre of this dark tragedy—on which may the curtain of the everlasting night fall soon!

The Scripture says, that the Father, who has led and watched over the development of the creature, places man, the glory of the Creation, before this awful mystery, and makes him know all its awfulness, that he may stir up faith to deliver him from the terror, and to open to him through the darkness the vision of a larger, freer, more glorious life. Accept this revelation and the shadow vanishes; life lies warm and radiant in the full light of the eternal sun. But if death be the bound rounding man's little life, and ending the development of his being for ever, the universe would become simply an Aceldama; the blood-drops that bead, not the Redeemer's brow only, but the brow of the Creation, are wasted: it is not a Redemption which they prophesy, but a dark struggle against a ruthless Fate.

And man, in any case, cannot but struggle and agonise for victory over the terror. A mother, as she watches the death pallor steal up over the face of her darling, but yesterday so gay and glad, cannot but moan and madden, if she has no vision to lighten her spirit, as she sees her one priceless treasure rifled, and the very casket that held it a mass of rottenness that she must bury out of her sight. And each generation sees, with a heart-ache which lies

The Resurrection of Man. 341

near the root of the sadness of the world, genius full of passionate energy, and charged with glorious gifts for men, struck down in its young prime; parents with households hanging on their efforts, bread, and things more precious even than bread, depending on their constant toil, dropping in a moment and bequeathing to the nurslings of their tenderest care a hard struggle to the end of their days; lovers, whose very life is in each other, sundered at a stroke by the ruthless destroyer, and one torn heart left widowed, to drag its burden through lonely, weary, hopeless years; statesmen, on whose skill and knowledge the conduct of their country through a perilous crisis is hanging, with the destinies of unborn millions in charge, dropping at the helm in the supreme moment of danger, and leaving the vessel so richly freighted all adrift.

These are the shocks by which death keeps its hold on our anxieties and terrors, and conquers a place in the human imagination, and a space on the theatre of life, altogether disproportioned to the scale of our existence; unless it be the passage to a larger, more perfect, more blessed stage of development, where the anomalies of this lower sphere will find their solution, its broken promises their fulfilment, its blighted hopes their fruition, in the "Fatherland" which we seek, and which awaits us on high. Then we can understand perfectly, why the God who made us, and who means to bless us, should so compel our imagination to haunt this gloomy threshold; and should rule life so largely through the shadow which He dissipates for the creatures, while He keeps it sternly before the sight of mankind. But otherwise black night is settling over all.

And this "fear of death" is but part of a yet deeper experience of humanity, which belongs to man alone of all the creatures, and marks him out as a being whose nature has relation with a higher sphere. There is in man a consciousness of inborn corruption which fills him, when he comes to understand the conditions of his life, with a terror of himself. This sense of corruption is closely connected with his constitution as an embodied spirit; so closely indeed that heathen peoples, unguided and unsustained by Revelation, find themselves constantly pressed to the conclusion, that this material body is the origin and seat of the evil which corrupts and destroys the man.

We find then this condition of things established in the sphere of man's experience. This body, so fearfully and wonderfully made, that it is manifestly the masterpiece of the Creation, is so open on all sides to solicitations and temptations, the yielding to which consciously defiles and degrades man's nature, that he is constantly, in all countries, in all ages, and under all possible varieties of culture, driven to hate this incomparable organ of his spirit, to curse it as the source of his misery,[1] to torment and

---

[1] Persius, certainly one of the purest and loftiest of the Roman writers, has this phrase, " This accursed flesh."

to macerate it, and systematically to reduce its strength and to wear out its life, as the only means of deliverance within his reach from otherwise intolerable ills. There is nothing darker and sadder in the history of humanity, than the pain and wasting which this glorious structure has had to endure, at the hands of the zealots of the spiritual; the contempt and shame which have fallen on this wondrous masterpiece of the Creator; and the fierceness with which men have cursed their very existence because of it, and have branded it as the devil's own instrument for the defilement and the torment of mankind.

Here is a new and remarkable experience, which is altogether peculiar to man. And if death be the final term of the individual existence, it is as terrible as it is strange. The body of man, as we have already insisted, must be regarded as the very highest possible form of organisation; it is the form in which all the strivings and tentative efforts which make up the history of the creature, find their perfect attainment; and in which the fruit of the universal groaning and travailing appears. Consider what endless stages of development through unknown eras, have been suffered by the creature with sore strain and pain—for the pain is everywhere conspicuous, however it may be compensated by the grandeur of the result— till on the last and highest stage, by a supreme effort as it were, the human form emerges, and stands visibly at the head of the whole. It contains embedded in its structure clear traces of all the stages through which, by long and agonising[1] process, it has been perfected; it furnishes, we are assured by deep thinkers and students of Nature, the key to the whole order of the material Creation in its organisation, and "is in little all the sphere"; and yet we find it tenanted by a spirit—by something, at any rate, within it, which takes cognisance of it as an instrument, and claims and uses the power to handle it at will—which finds it a terrible source of corruption, of agencies and influences which tend to the degradation and desolation of life.

The man finds himself bound, in pursuing the ends which have now come within the range of his sight as a man, to resist its impulses, to refuse indulgence to its importunate cravings, and to rule its passions with an iron hand. But he finds in the end, after long struggle, that the body is his master. Failing miserably in his effort to tame and to rule it, as man striving in his own strength alone must fail, he is driven in the end to give free rein to sensual desire, rushing thereby headlong to destruction; or if he be of the nobler sort, to turn on it with blind fury and beat it into inanition, moaning the while, "*O miserable man that I am, who shall deliver me from the body of this death?*"

Now if this be the end of things, if this be the outcome of the development of the creature, confusion is the name of the order of the universe, and

---

[1] I use this word in the sense which indicates the measure of the struggle and effort, rather than of the pain.

it reigns supreme in the highest product of Creation —the man who seems made to rule it as its king.

And all the deepest instincts of man's nature, and his noblest philosophies, tell him about the "temple of his body." He is sure that so goodly a tabernacle was meant to be a temple, on whose altar sacred incense should be ever burning; that the body was made and designated to be the handmaid of the spirit, the pure and perfect organ of its expression, the holy and beautiful shrine of its life. It was the Lord who spake of the temple of his body. The temple is originally the portion of space cut off by the rod of the augur for observation, that is for sacred use. And though, in this particular form, the word and the thing are of Roman or rather of Etruscan origin, while our Lord's language and conception belonged to oriental life, yet in every language the word which represents a temple suggests the same idea—something cut off, walled round, or otherwise set apart as reserved for religious uses. This term represents man's highest idea of the relation of spirit and body; and this alone fulfils the promise of Creation, and presents the body as the supreme type of form, and the instrument of life's noblest and most perfect work.

Yet everywhere in the present, instead of the concord, dark signs of discord and struggle appear. All the higher men, those in whom we may fairly look to discover the meaning and purpose of the human, reveal themselves in history as struggling hard to master and to rule the body, and to unite the powers, bodily and spiritual, into one harmonious choir of faculties, the organ of the utterance and the activity of the life. But none realize, though they may touch the concord, while all groan over the discord, which awaits yet the harmonising hand. Paul was an old man, and a veteran in this war when he wrote, "*I therefore so run, not as uncertainly; so fight I, not as one that beateth the air. But I keep under my body, and bring it into subjection; lest that by any means, when I have preached to others, I myself should be a castaway.*"—I. Cor. ix. 26, 27. He was near the end and not the beginning of a long and glorious career, but the perfect concord escaped him still. To me it is imperative to believe—since I cannot accept chaos as the home-land of my being, and the great Anarch as my God—that the discord here, over which the highest and completest men still groan, is but the first step of the development of a concord, which shall fulfil the promise and give fruit to the travail of Creation—a concord whose priest and minister is Death.

In man, too, we see in its full development the faculty of accumulating and digesting experience. That which in the animal passes into the organisation and becomes capable of physical transmission, in man is gathered up consciously by the reason, and becomes a light for the guidance of his individual life. Man observes, considers, compares, and concludes, by means of the material furnished by his daily doings and sufferings; and he is able to build firmly on the results of past experiences the edifice of the future, whereby, through clear stages of progress, life advances to the fulfilment of its idea. Each generation builds on the ground which the last cast up, and made firm above the level of its predecessor; and there is a similar process in every life.

It is with very sore toil and pain that man harvests and garners this experience. "Experience," says Mr. Carlyle with grim humour, "is the best master, but asks terribly high wages." The store which is garnered is the true measure of his wealth; and of his worth—for in this region wealth is worth, and the "good" man is really the rich one—to himself, to the world, and to the Lord. It is this faculty which makes him a being capable of civilisation[1] and progress; and it seems to open to him a boundless field of development, if he may but win the mastery of death. The experience, too, grows richer and weightier, and the worth of the man richer and weightier with it, as age furrows his brow and palsies his physical powers. Just when his glorious faculty is in fullest form, when his wisdom is most mature, and his moral strength most developed, that physical structure, which is the base of his operation and the organ of his influence, wastes and withers away. There is an outer man decaying, and an inner man of wisdom and strength renewed day by day.

[1] There are curious facts which seem to indicate what might be called a dull kind of civilisation in the animal sphere. The ants, for instance, have got to the slaveholding stage, we are told by those familiar with their habits. But can anyone permit himself to believe that some day they will rise to the higher level, and pass an act of emancipation?

It may be said that flesh and spirit just decay together, and that second childhood and fatuity are the destiny of the man in his wholeness. But how constantly do we see after a season of apparent fatuity, the spirit in a moment flashing forth, not in the full splendour of its power only, but with a new splendour, which seems caught from a sphere into whose field it is passing! What is the meaning of the impression which we meet with among all peoples, that the soul of man grows prophetic as it nears the physical boundary of life? It implies anything rather than a belief that body and soul are crumbling together into dust; and it all points to the conclusion, that these divergent tendencies of the component elements of man's nature, prophesy convergence and concordance in another sphere.

We see, or rather we appear to see, waste enough in the Creation, and wreck enough. That is, we see what would be waste and wreck, but that the material is straightway wrought up to higher use. But if this life be all, what awful waste and wreck are here! Powers trained, acquisitions gathered, with almost infinite pain and toil, losing their organ of utterance and influence, just when they become of supreme worth to mankind. It may be answered, perhaps, that the power and wisdom pass into the hearts of disciples, and so carry on their mission of guiding and blessing our race. Ah! how little of every great nature is able to reveal itself; how small a part of every great life is able to give itself to mankind! "*It is expedient for you that I go*

The Resurrection of Man. 349

away," said the greatest. "*I have many things to say to you, but ye cannot bear them now.*" They heard those things, we hear them and live by them, from the world of the Resurrection. The risen Saviour unveiled the meaning of His life of ministry to man. And there is always an interior wealth in every great and greatly disciplined nature, which is the most precious treasure in this universe. And it is this, I am told, the harvest of toils and struggles which might touch the sympathies of the angels, that Death grasps and scatters in the dust.

This form of man's development, the inner growth, the outer decay, is God's great prophecy of resurrection. The powers thus trained and perfected, find their trained and perfected organ in the body of the resurrection in the eternal world. If death is but transformation, we can comprehend perfectly the weakness and faintness of the outer, while the inner man grows rich and strong. The very pain and weakness are the last perfecting touches of the discipline, and have the directest relation to the great future of which death is the harbinger. But if the death ends the development,
> Forsake all hope, all ye who enter here,

is the sentence which must be written over the gate of this life, and not over the gate of hell.

I confess, that I attach less importance than seems to be generally attached to the argument, which is so constantly urged in proof of the immortality of man's spirit, that the inequalities here are too dire and the wrongs too largely unredressed, to consist with the rule of a perfectly wise and righteous Lord of the Creation, unless the balance is to be adjusted and the wrongs righted, on high. I suspect that even here the balance hangs much more evenly than most of us dream. " Happiness of an approving conscience!" says Herr Teufelsdröckh in a sardonic mood; "did not Saul of Tarsus confess himself the chief of sinners, while Nero of Rome, jocund in spirit, spent much of his time in fiddling?" No doubt there was not much room for what goes by the name of happiness in the life of the Apostle Paul. But understand that it was well with Paul, and ill with Nero, through the whole piece. The God who searches the hearts, ordains and sees a fairer distribution of moral awards in this life than our dull apprehension can discover; and those who choose to stand with the Pauls, and not with the Neros, even here have their reward.

But the measure in which the blessedness of these nobler spirits, mixed itself with ideas and influences which belong to the sphere of the spiritual and eternal, the measure in which they fortified themselves by its strength and inspired themselves by its hopes, is a mighty argument for immortality. It is not that they looked to the eternal future to compensate them for present pains and denials; but that without the atmosphere of that eternal state they could not live. Life meant more to men like Moses and Paul than a claim for compensation. They were both willing to be "blotted out of the book of life," if the great ends which Christ had taught them to pursue might be the better gained. But the atmosphere of that world was as needful to their spirits, as the air of this world to their blood. They proved its existence by living in it. Nero lived in his own world and made miserable shipwreck. Paul lived and lives in the world of the Resurrection.

More full of force is the argument from the untimely loss of beings of the richest endowment, and the largest capacity of service to mankind. The brilliant dawnings that are clouded before noon, the splendid promise that is constantly spoilt and wasted before our eyes, the hopes that are born but for frustration, the purposes that are formed but to perish, would lend a profound pathetic sadness to the life of Nature's masterpiece, but for our faith that the God of Nature guards these buds of promise through death's winter, and plants them where they will bloom in the sunlight of a celestial spring, and bear rich fruit unto life eternal.

Nor must we pass from this part of the subject without a glance at the opposite end of the scale. To me the thought would be tormenting, could I believe that the great mass of the struggling and suffering poor have no heritage but death. To a terribly large proportion of them life is a stern, ceaseless struggle, carried on in dens, and under conditions, to which cultured households would shrink from exposing their brutes. May God keep me from ever opening my heart to the dark philosophy, which would teach me that they are destined to be swept out in throngs to destruction, without having had the faintest chance of discovering, what might grow to them by the fair unfolding and culture of their powers!

Thus much, and it is but a hint of what might be said, on the antecedent likelihood of resurrection. It lies in the path, in the just and therefore inevitable order, of development. The next thing to this life of man, the thing with which it travails, which must be born out of all its strain and groaning, is the life of the risen man, in the state which the Scripture describes as eternal.

But we rise into another sphere, a sphere blessed be God, of clear certainty and full assurance, when we read out, "*But now is Christ risen from the dead, and become the first-fruits of them that slept. For since by man came death, by man came also the resurrection of the dead. For as in Adam all die, even so in Christ shall all be made alive.*"—I. Cor. xv. 20-2. "*Blessed be the God and Father of our Lord Jesus Christ, which according to His abundant mercy hath begotten us again unto a lively hope by the resurrection of Jesus Christ from the dead.*"—I. Peter i. 3. The gospel of the Resurrection is, Man has risen, not, Man must rise. A man—no, *the* Man, the Being in human form, in whom the nature and the destiny of man are revealed with a divine completeness—has died on earth after the manner of mortals, and has visibly resumed His human form under higher and more spiritual conditions; has maintained for a time His human intercourse with His disciples and friends, and has borne that human form, visibly, beyond the material boundaries of our world.

This is the clear, explicit, and constant testimony of Scripture; on this the preaching of the apostles rested : this was the power by which, in the language of their enemies, they overturned the world. And this is the miracle of miracles. It establishes at once the claim of Christianity to be considered a supernatural revelation. As a keen sceptic said, we have only to prove the Resurrection, it carries all the rest. While at the same time, it fixes the true home of man's spirit, the sphere of the full unfolding of his powers, and of his perfect and final development, in the spiritual and eternal world.

The evidence of the Resurrection as a historical fact, is thus calmly and clearly summarized by the apostle : "*For I delivered unto you first of all that which I also received, how that Christ died for our sins according to the Scriptures; and that He was buried, and that He rose again the third day according to the Scriptures; and that He was seen of Cephas, then of the twelve: after that He was seen of above five hundred brethren at once; of whom the greater part remain unto this present, but some are fallen asleep. After that He was seen of James; then of all the apostles. And last of all He was seen of me also, as of one born out of due time. For I am the least of the apostles, that am not meet to be called an apostle, because I persecuted the Church of God. But by the grace of God I am what I am; and His grace which was bestowed on me was not in vain; but I laboured more abundantly than they all; yet not I, but the grace of God which was with me. Therefore whether it were I or they, so we preach, and so ye believed."*—I. Cor. xv. 3-11.

I am not about to argue the question of the sufficiency of this evidence. There are treatises devoted to it, in which what may be said on both sides is amply set forth. But there is one point on which I will dwell for a moment, as it seems not to have its full force assigned to it, in many of the arguments on the Resurrection which I have read. One would think that the reappearance of the man Christ Jesus in our world after His unquestionable death on the cross, was one of those simple, definite facts, which admitted of the clearest verification in the days when it is said to have occurred. It was a matter about which there was little room for hallucination. The evidence must be simple, and direct, one way or the other. But it is averred that there was ample room for deception and mystification. The disciples would gladly catch, we are told, at the notion of a resurrection which the apostles propounded, and would become their unconscious accomplices in palming the deception or delusion on the world.

From this point of view the statement of Paul that the risen Lord appeared to five hundred brethren at once, published during the lifetime of most of them, is peculiarly valuable. Still it is said that we have the testimony of devoted or interested witnesses only. The Sanhedrim must have taken some means to satisfy themselves of the truth or falsehood of the story; had we the results of those enquiries and the views of the enemies of the Gospel, at the time when the event was recent and the facts could be fairly tested, it would make the evidence more complete. Is not this exactly what we have furnished to us, substantially though not formally, by the evidence of Paul? He was certainly at Jerusalem while the Church was in its infancy, and when the whole country was ringing with the tale. He was neither an interested nor a devoted adherent of the risen Saviour, but a most determined enemy of the doctrine. He was a man of the highest consideration and influence[1] in the ranks of the persecutors of the infant Church. He was endowed, too, with the keenest intelligence and the clearest insight, and would be likely for his own purposes to make the fullest enquiries as to the truth of the fact that was alleged.

Everything that the Pharisees knew about it, he knew; everything that could be said against it by Jewish Rulers, he would be perfectly familiar with. In his disputations—surely he was among those of Cilicia who disputed with Stephen—he would carefully furnish himself with every argument, which could tell against a sect which he hated and was determined to destroy; and yet he was the man who devoted his whole being to the proclamation of

[1] It seems clear that the apostle continued to be regarded and treated as a person of position and influence, by the Roman officials and others, throughout his career.

this doctrine, and who more than any other man, or all other men, in his generation, made it triumphant in the world. We have in the adhesion of Saul of Tarsus, the testimony of the most instructed and acute opponent of the truth, that it could not be gainsaid.

The point is this. After his conversion, when his furious blinding prejudice had been conquered, and he had accepted with his whole heart the truth of the narrative, nothing that he had become acquainted with during his Pharisaic frenzy against the Gospel, seems to have troubled his mind for a moment. He knew the whole case of the Pharisees, but in his judgment it was worthless; there was nothing in it which seemed to him to demand a formal confutation; his whole strength was thrown into the correction of misapprehensions and the confutation of heresies on the subject, which began to reveal themselves within the bosom of the Church. The evidence of Paul, which his belief furnishes, is from this point of view worth that of a host.

And the "ermine-robed great world" added its Amen. The truth spread from lip to lip, from house to house, from city to city, from land to land, like flame. Men opened their hearts everywhere to the preachers of the Resurrection. It established itself rapidly as the central truth in the belief of the most acute and cultivated peoples; it reached down to the roots of their life and renewed it; it remade their views of life, of death, of things beyond death, and in a word, of all things. It has borne the wear of the thinking, the suffering, the working, of sixty generations; it has led the progress of the great world's civilisation; it lies near to the heart of all that is purest, strongest, and noblest in Christendom, and it is now rapidly spreading through the earth.

"Yes!" it may be said, "men were only too glad to believe it; the doctrine was too fascinating to fail to win its way. Men easily believe what accords with their aspirations and hopes." But that is just what we find from history that men do not so easily believe. There is a touchstone of truth in the human spirit, which in the long run and on a large scale may be relied on. Men would very gladly believe in the teaching which makes light of sin. But they have never been able to believe in it. What agony, what waste of sacrificial tears and blood, might have been spared, if men could but have believed the easy doctrine that sin is a soft infirmity of the blood, not to be too sternly visited, or a necessary factor of progress out of which experience grows. There have been plenty to preach these doctrines; but pleasant as it would be to man to get rid honestly of this torment of conscience, in no age, in no country, have men been able to bind this gospel to their hearts. What man has believed so eagerly and held so firmly, with all the light of cultivated intelligence and a high social development shining around it, is the truth.

I hold that, looking simply at the history of the apostolic age, it is absolutely certain that some such fact as the Resurrection must at that time have planted itself in the world. There was that entire transformation of man's beliefs, that solidification of the dim vaporous imaginations of the heathen mind about the spiritual, that firm, practical grasp of the realities of the world behind the veil, transferring the centre of gravity of man's life and of the life of society from the visible to the invisible sphere, which the fact of the Resurrection of the Lord Jesus explains, and that fact alone. "*But now is Christ risen from the dead, and become the first-fruits of them that slept. For since by man came death, by man came also the resurrection of the dead.*"

And what is the doctrine?

The image of the butterfly, of which so much is made as suggestive of the Resurrection, is valuable chiefly for its vividness and beauty. Far deeper and truer is the image of the seed, which the apostle developes with great fulness in this wonderful passage, which we read out by our new-made graves, where we realize as we read it our victory over death. The Scripture teaches us, that in this mortal body there is the germ of a purer and more perfect spiritual body; in which the spirit clothes itself and stands up in a world of spiritual beings and things, when this weary, wasted, worn-out form is laid aside in death.

Just as man has now a body which perfectly equips him for intercourse with men and with things in this material sphere, so it is the purpose of his Creator, when his discipline here is ended, to clothe him in a body which will fit him for a more perfect intercourse,

The Resurrection of Man. 359

with the beings and the objects of the world which lies behind the veil of death. And the germ of this spiritual body lies buried in this material frame; death disengages it to fulfil its destiny. The question presses on everyone who meditates on the mystery of life and immortality, "*How are the dead raised up, and with what body do they come?*" The apostle answers: just as the seed cast into the soil, corrupting, rises again and clothes itself afresh after a more perfect and splendid fashion, so "*this corruptible shall put on incorruption, and this mortal shall put on immortality.*"

But when does the sowing take place, and when the resurrection? On this point it seems to me that there has been much popular misunderstanding of the apostle's words. What is the mystery of germination? The seed which we cast into the ground, is really but the envelope or the body of the tiny germ which will grow into the tree. The seed is a mass of matter, which, decaying in the moisture of the ground, furnishes nutriment to the germ, feeds it, and cherishes it, until it can throw out its root-fibres, and seek an independent nourishment for itself. But what is sown is a living thing, not a dead thing. Sow a husk, a dead case, and you may watch for ever for resurrection in vain.

And now where is the analogy? The germ of the spiritual body is sown, surely, in the material body in birth and not at death. The seed which is sown containing the germ is entirely a living thing. It is in this material body—while it is a living body, growing and then decaying, for "*We die daily*"—that the germ of the spiritual body is planted. The decay of the outer man, like the dissolution of the albuminous matter in the seed, is really the nourishment of the spiritual germ, through all the experiences with which it is associated. That germ lies hidden in the flesh of our mortality through what we call life : what we call death completes the process ; the mere husk or shell within which the spiritual body was forming, is put off with painful struggle and buried away with the dead leaves of autumn ; while God giveth the emancipated spirit a body "*as it hath pleased Him*," wherewith to stand up in, and to maintain its relations with the beings and the objects of, the celestial sphere.

It is important to observe that in treating of these deep subjects, the sacred writers, as indeed was inevitable, offer but a partial revelation. There are things which it is not lawful, not possible, for man to utter in the life of that world of spirit ; and the things which are uttered have a vagueness and dimness, which remind us that the conditions of that life are beyond the grasp of our understandings. We know but in part, and can prophesy but in part ; and we must be content to find in our knowledge, inconsistences, difficulties, and apparent contradictions, which we can only harmonise when we see face to face, and know even as also we are known. We can catch and hold firmly some clues which will guide us to a sound knowledge ; but the whole truth which will unite the fragments which we discover, and harmonise the scattered notes that reach us, for the present, escapes us. We see but images of things, dimly and brokenly, as in a mirror far from perfect, but they are images of *things*, the perfect forms of which we shall behold with God.

The apostle knows nothing of disembodied spirits, bloodless, bodiless ghosts, such as the heathen dreamed of as flitting through the shades. "*For we know that if our earthly house of this tabernacle were dissolved, we have in the heavens a building from God, a house not made with hands, eternal. For in this we groan, longing to put on over this our dwelling-place from heaven; seeing that we shall really be found clothed, not naked. For we that are in this tabernacle do groan, being burdened; because we would not be unclothed but clothed upon, that our mortal part may be swallowed up by life.*" II. Cor. v. 1-4. The soul in dying drops this shell, this husk of the body that is to be, and which is done with for ever, and is clothed upon with a form which gives to it freedom of range through the spiritual sphere.

Gleams of the glory of that celestial body have been seen in moments of rapture. Moses and Elias appeared all radiant beside their Lord on the Mount of Transfiguration; and the Lamb that was slain was seen,—a glorious form, wearing still the marks of His human passion,—on the central throne, by the seer of the Apocalypse. And here lies the certainty and the clearness of the Scripture revelation. It hides much about that world and the form of its life which cannot be spoken; but it reveals in the clear sunlight the form of the risen and reigning Christ, as the key to all the mysteries of the spiritual sphere. And there are moments, too, when some gleam of this beautiful and radiant form shines out through the eyes and on the lips of the dying. I think that I have seen it at the last moment—this corruptible putting on incorruption, this mortal putting on immortality.

But the Scriptures speak of a day of resurrection still in the far future. They prophesy a further and final transformation—development still—when the great experiment of freedom shall be ended, and Redemption shall have gathered in all its fruits. The worlds as well as man, all created things in all their spheres, shall burst from their bondage of corruption, and put on the brightness of their final glory. Then man too shall experience his last transfiguration, shall reap the harvest of his discipline, and shall take the place in the great scheme of the living universe which is ordained to him through eternity.

And thus death is abolished. Death, the dark fact of the old Creation, in the order of man's development, becomes the womb of his birth into the new. The terror is abolished by that which lies behind it. Death has vanished, and in the place of Death stands Christ. The dark, sad, inevitable experience, which made the life of heathendom one long moan, through Christ becomes a benign and blessed minister. Instead of rounding the whole series of creature development in anguish and terror, it carries it up and out into a larger, freer, and more glorious world. And thus the order of Creation ascends; it tends ever heavenward to the Creator; issuing from God it completes its vast circuit of development, and returns redeemed and glorified—born into the likeness of Him whom it has learned to know as the Father—to rest in the bosom of His love for ever and for ever. "*O the depth both of the riches of the wisdom and knowledge of God! How unsearchable are His judgments, and His ways past finding out! For who hath known the mind of the Lord? or who hath been His counsellor? Or who hath first given to Him, and it shall be recompensed unto him again? For of Him, and through Him, and to Him, are all things, to whom be glory for ever. Amen.*" Romans xi. 33–36.

XIX.
THE DESTINY OF THE CREATURE.

" The creature itself also shall be delivered from the bondage of corruption into the glorious liberty of the children of God."—
Rom. viii. 21.

THE redemption of man carries in its train the redemption of Nature. There is the picture set before us in the book of Genesis, of something like the fall of Nature, when man by transgression fell. Eden vanished, earth became a wilderness, man became a pilgrim, his life became a march through the hungry, wasteful desert, while his Paradise regained lay awaiting him beyond the river of death. This is the poetic picture of the Scripture; and the study of the conditions of the life of man and of the Creation, sustains the idea which lies behind it, that the sphere which surrounds man, the whole world system which serves as the theatre of his life, is set, so to speak, to the pitch of his spiritual nature. As he has fallen into captivity to evil, it is in bondage to corruption; as he rises through Redemption to regain his lost inheritance, the Creation too is in process of being redeemed.

This means, broadly, that the system of things around man is so ordered, as to be always in tune with his moral condition and necessities. He is here a struggling and suffering creature; the whole Creation groaneth and travaileth in sympathy. Like man it is subject to vanity, it is full of discord, battle, and suffering, not that it may seem the more homelike to man, the transgressor, but that it may help the process by which he is being saved. The day will come when man's redemption shall be complete; when every knee shall bow, and every tongue shall confess that Jesus Christ is Lord; when peace shall reign through righteousness in the wide human commonwealth, and sorrow and sighing shall be banished for ever from the experience of our race. And then shall man find himself face to face with a new, a fairer, a more blessed Creation; a new heaven and a new earth shall be the theatre for "the manifestation of the sons of God."

When Eden vanished, a veil was dropped in some way over the splendour of Creation. Earth seemed hard and bare; its Marahs abundant, its Elims few. Perhaps the veil was truly dropped before man's spirit; the eye that had stooped to lust after vanity became dimmed by its degradation. It had lost the power to behold with open face the glory of its world. The splendour is here all round us as of old, but the eye is weak and dim. There are moments when the beauty seems to flash out on us with Eden-like radiance, prophetic of the vision which shall one day burst upon us when death has couched our sight. Some vision, too, seems granted to the child, before wilful sin has dropped the veil over Nature. The poet, who carries the child's eye and heart into manhood, gathers for us into a focus the rays of the pristine splendour, which are still struggling amidst the gloom of our world.

But there are those to whom these records of Eden, to us full of the profoundest significance, are but a shadowy history. Still the same truth would look out upon us through the idea, that the whole system of things which forms the Creation with which man is in contact, was created as it is, and was ordained to develope itself with sore struggle as it does, with a view to the moral discipline and education of mankind. We have heard the cry of the groaning, we have watched the patient travail of the creature. The records of development through all its stages are records of conflict, struggle for existence, strife for mastery. From the molecules of matter clashing and battling around us with furious vehemence, up through all the ascending stages to the material civilisation of man, there are tears enough, there is blood enough, to tempt us to cry, when we see only part of the plan, It is a sad, sad history; the race is to the swift, and the spoil is to the strong everywhere; the chief virtue of things is to endure. But the Scripture tells us that all this is set in the key of man's sinful life. It is as man is. It has been made thus, because man is a being, born into this world to fall and to be redeemed.

Is this view of the relation of man to Nature, and of Nature to man, just the resurrection in a modern dress of the ancient error which made this earth the centre of the universe, round whose circle were ranged in orderly procession the galaxies of stars ? The discovery of the universe which we owe to the human intellect through the methods of science, has dwarfed utterly man's apparent stature in comparison with the world. In the presence of the masses and the forces which surround us, the words of the Psalmist, " *When I consider the heavens, the work of Thy fingers; the moon and the stars which Thou hast ordained; what is man that Thou art mindful of him? and the son of man that Thou visitest him?*" oppress us with an appalling sense of our insignificance in the scale of the Creation ; while this earth of ours seems but as a mote, an atom, floating undistinguished in the boundless ocean of space.

The tendency of much of our modern scientific discovery, is undoubtedly to the depreciation of man, in comparison with the creatures and the worlds which surround him. A leading, I will not say *the* leading school, rather laughs at the notion that he can be a centre to anything ; and his higher endowments, reason, will, and an immortal spirit, are decried or denied, as giving him altogether too large a figure in relation to his surroundings, his origin and his destiny.

But the Scripture seems to give to us the true measure of the magnitude of our nature, and of the place which we are intended to fill in the scheme of the universe; whereby we are enabled to bear up against the slights of sciolists, and to maintain our faith that the true centre of the vast system of things around us, is Man. The Psalmist recognises the fact of man's glorious pre-eminence, though he finds it hard to account for it in the presence of all these immense and countless worlds. "*Thou hast made him a little lower than the angels, Thou hast crowned him with glory and honour;*" why, how—when we consider what man is, and survey all that is around and above him—who can tell?

The clear, explicit answer of Heaven to the question is the Incarnation. Whatever man may be, however the consciousness of his infirmity and sin may humble him to the dust, however his pain and helplessness may tempt him to cry, "*I am a worm, and no man,*" or to moan in his sinful folly, "*I am as a beast before Thee,*" man has been created on a scale and with a capacity which makes his nature not only a possible, but *the* meet shrine for the inhabitation and manifestation of God. "Man is a fretful, restless atom in the Creation," say the scorners, "about as important as a grain of sand is to a mountain in comparison with the All." Be it so, according to the magnitudes which your micrometers can measure. Heaven's magnitudes have other estimations, and God Himself has given to us His measure of the magnitude of man. To us mass is impressive; it is nothing to the eye of Heaven, nay, less than nothing, if we may judge by the revelations of the microscope. The Creator seems to have lavished on organisms which through millenniums no intelligent human eye has had strength to gaze upon, and which a curious art alone enables us to discover, glories of form and colour which rival, if they do not eclipse, the marvels of all these resplendent worlds.

The world has vast desert spaces that its few oases may be luxuriant; countless shoals of creatures are born and perish that a few may be the better prepared for the service of mankind. The order of God seems to be pyramidal: broad, vast bases of undistinguished creatures, that the contracting stages as they ascend may show finer and compacter types of organisation, and that on the summit, a mere speck in comparison with the quantity of the structure, but a masterpiece in comparison with its quality, man may lift up his face to heaven and to God. We are mass-driven and mass-tormented in these days. Quality is a thing which we seem to have lost the means of finely testing; quantity fills the field. It is the magnitude of operations and of occurrences which gives to them their value to this generation. Christ, with His little tattered troop of disciples round Him, would have impressed us only when He was thronged.

And science, dealing with the awful masses and forces of the universe, presses us with one hand in the same direction. A thing so impalpable and intangible as a Will, a power to choose the right and to refuse the wrong, seems but a weak and shadowy matter compared with the momentum with which these planets are sweeping through space. "Son of man," she seems in one mood to say scornfully, "thou art but as a fly on the axle of the Creation; it moves thee and thy small affairs in its vast revolutions, as careless of thy individual life and of its destinies, as of the dust which it scatters as it flashes through space." But on the other hand science is continually brought more closely face to face with a force, an intangible, impalpable power, which is behind the phenomena of Creation, a spiritual presence which eludes her grasp and defies her analysis, an entity with which Will has close correlations, and which a very able scientific thinker says that we had better call Will through all the scale. Still there is a strong tendency in much of the influential thought of our times, to make man of but small account in the scheme of the Creation; and so we carry our appeal from man's understanding, groping in the darkness, to the witness of Scripture, and the judgment of God.

There is a real need in these days that we should once more take our stand on the Incarnation. "God is in Christ." The Word, who was "with God," who "was God," "became flesh and dwelt among us." The Gospel reveals "Emmanuel," "God with us," not with the angels. Narrow and poor as our nature may seem since we have contracted and defiled it by sin, God could dwell in and become man, as He could not dwell in or become an angel. Neither cherub nor seraph can become like man, continent of God. "*To which of the angels said He at any time, Thou art my son, this day have I begotten thee?*" To which of the angels could it possibly be said? "He counteth His angels as winds, and His ministers as flames of fire," is the description of their nature, and of their rank in the Creation. But man, weak, selfish, sensual as his nature has become by transgression, has thus much at any rate of his pristine dignity left to him among all the orders of the creatures, that he has power to become through Redemption as the son of God. We plant ourselves on solid fact, as well as the materialistic philosophers. We claim for man this position of dignity and power in relation to the Creation, because God was in Christ; because He "*took not on Him the nature of angels, but the seed of Abraham*," because through grace man may "*become partaker of the Divine nature, escaping the corruption that is in the world through lust.*"

It is on the Incarnation then that we rest—as restoring in a still higher form, truly in a transcendent form, the original estate of man in the universe, as the being made in the image of God, in His likeness—as we sustain the affirmation of the Scripture, that man's nature and condition contain the key to the constitution and the condition of his world. Man is as his circumstance is, say an influential school of thinkers, and they support their views by a wonderful parade of one-sided facts gathered with singular diligence and care. "Given," they say, "the conditions of life, the climate, the scenery, the food, the physical influences, and we can construct the race and forecast its history;" just as a great physiologist from a bit of bone will construct the form of an undiscovered bird, which one day will be found and prove that he was right.

Nature is as man is, is the answer of Scripture. Man is a fallen being, fallen through the abuse of his freedom into sin and into straits, and the whole system of things around him has been constructed with a view to his being redeemed. *"For the earnest expectation of the creature waiteth for the manifestation of the sons of God. For the creature was made subject to vanity, not willingly, but by reason of Him who hath subjected the same in hope; because the creature itself also shall be delivered from the bondage of corruption into the glorious liberty of the children of God. For we know that the whole creation groaneth and travaileth in pain together until now. And not only they, but ourselves also, which have the first-fruits of the spirit, even we ourselves groan within ourselves, waiting for the adoption, to wit, the redemption of our body. For we are saved by hope: but hope that is seen, is not hope: for what a man seeth, why doth he yet hope for? But if we hope for that we see not, then do we with patience wait for it. Likewise the Spirit also helpeth our infirmities: for we know not what we should pray for as we ought: but the Spirit itself maketh intercession for us with groanings which cannot be uttered. And He that searcheth the hearts knoweth what is the mind of the Spirit, because He maketh intercession for the saints according to the will of God. And we know that all things work together for good to them that love God, to them who are the called according to His purpose."*—Romans viii. 19–28.

We have seen that the Scripture narrative of the fall presents to us, as parallel with the degradation of humanity, something like a fall in the condition of the world. Eden vanished, and Nature became the hard, stern nurse and monitress of man. Whether you say that a flood swept over the early home of our race, and destroyed the beauty and splendour of the pristine paradise ; or whether you say that it was man who suffered the eclipse, that a film fell before his sin-darkened sight, so that though the splendours were around him the power to behold and to enjoy them was dead, or at any rate numb ; or whether you take a wider view, and say that the whole structure of the world and the whole order of its development were so arranged from the first, as to make it a severe training school for our wanton and prodigal race, the result in any case remains, that this earth is no Paradise for men, but a wilderness, a place of pilgrimage, a school of training, but in no sense a home or a rest.

That sentence on man which unveils, as God only could unveil, the full conditions of his life as a conscious and guilty transgressor, is a sentence on the earth as well as on man. "*Cursed is the ground for thy sake,*" must surely mean, not as a curse to thee, but for thy chastisement, with a view to thy culture, thy training to obedience and faith. "*And unto Adam He said, because thou hast hearkened unto the voice of thy wife, and hast eaten of the tree of which I commanded thee, saying, Thou shalt not eat of it: cursed is the ground for thy sake; in sorrow shalt thou eat of it all the days of thy life: thorns also and thistles shall it bring forth to thee; and thou shalt eat the herb of the field: in the sweat of thy face shalt thou eat bread, till thou return unto the ground; for out of it wast thou taken; for dust thou art, and unto dust shalt thou return.*"—Genesis iii. 17–19.

I am not insisting on the historical truth of this picture, but on the spiritual truth which lies behind it. It manifestly implies a distinct adaptation of the physical conditions of the world of which man became the citizen, to the unfolding of his moral and spiritual nature under the influence of that Redemptive work, the first prophecy of which was, in the very sentence, given to the world. It is evident that earth was intended to be to man through the whole range of his history, what on a minor scale the wilderness became to the Israelites—the place of "wanderings" and of hard, sad straits; with memories of fairer and easier conditions of life behind it, and visions of a Canaan of transcendent beauty and richness beyond. We are justified in regarding that wilderness experience of the chosen race, as the key to the actual condition of man the transgressor in this wilderness world. God has caused this history to be written for our learning. The children of the patriarchs were manifestly set forth as the microcosm, in which we may most profitably study the macrocosm, human society. It is on this principle alone that we can understand the large place which the children of Israel fill in the scheme of Revelation. They stand for all mankind. And we see them under a bright light as it were, with the veils off, that we may study to the best advantage the methods of God in the education of our race.

The Destiny of the Creature. 375

The wilderness into which they were led forth for their training, was literally "the pastures." Not the hard, bare, thirsty, stony tract which we understand by desert, but pastures—wide, sweeping plains of moderately luxuriant verdure, with low rolling hills breaking the monotonous outline, cut by rich, deep valleys at intervals, well wooded and watered;[1] while mountain gorges of glorious beauty, of sublime form and brilliant colour, penetrated everywhere the great chains, whose grand and soaring summits stood sentinel around.[2] The wilderness was hard and bare, no doubt, compared with the lavish, wanton luxuriance of Egypt on the one hand, and the goodly and gracious fertility of Canaan on the other. But on the whole, it was a good place to dwell in for a while, a noble training school for a nation, as their gallant and disciplined bearing when they went up to claim their Canaan revealed;[3] while here and there was an Elim with its springs and palms, where the tired wanderer might rest awhile, and dream his dream of a brighter world.

Not otherwise is earth to all of us, not otherwise is life. This earth has broad, bare tracts of savage desert, hateful both to beast and to man, with rich, sunny, luxuriant regions scattered around the wilder-

---

[1] They have since been denuded; the region is much more like a true desert now.
[2] In striking contrast to the long level lines of rock which flanked the valley of the Nile.
[3] We see what the wilderness training had done for that people, in such passages as Joshua i., and indeed in the whole history which that book records.

ness borders, which are the settled homes of our race. But in the physical order of our earth the wilderness is truly a part, and an essential part, of the fruitful field, and it ministers in wondrous ways to its fertility. The most terrible deserts have noble functions to fulfil when we regard earth as the theatre of history. The great Sahara helps—it is but help, other and yet stronger influences are at work—to lift the line of perpetual ground-frost round the North Cape of Europe, while it runs into quite low latitudes on the coasts of Labrador and Kamtchatka. It is the Arabian desert mainly which makes Syria the garden of the East; while the great Australian desert lends to South-eastern Asia one of the softest and richest climates in the world.

But it is impossible to shut out the fact that on earth desert is predominant. We speak of India and China as teeming hives of human population. The great Asiatic desert would swallow both of them, and be desert still. Look at the vast spaces in Asia, America, Australia, Africa, and even in Europe, where human population is sparse, or altogether wanting, and compare their spaces with those of the fertile nooks that teem with men.

And God has so ordered it, that the habitable regions which afford the fairest facilities to human intercourse—and intercourse means development and civilisation—shall lie in climates which impose the more rigorous conditions, and demand hardy industry from their inhabitants. The infancy of civilisation was nursed around the soft Mediterranean shores, where sunny seas and frequent ports tempted timid sailors to the voyages which scattered the seeds of civilisation abroad. But the north-westward movement of the head-quarters of the civilising forces, into the reasons of which I cannot in this place enter, has gradually transferred the centre of the world's industrial and political activity to hardier regions, and has given the sceptre to the races who have to toil hardest to win from Nature the nourishment of their life.

Work is demanded of man by the very structure of his dwelling-place. "If a man will not work, so neither shall he eat," is written as plainly in the book of nature as in the Bible. But work deepens into toil among the nobler peoples, and new visions of toil are opened to us as man subdues and occupies the waste places of his world. The Elims which gem the earth, the watered gardens such as Lot saw, which might recall fair Paradise, but woo man to wantonness. We constantly see them transformed by his transgression into the truly desert places of Nature. We can see, as we survey them, how Eden was lost to the transgressor. Some of earth's fairest, brightest regions he has made foul and pestilential wastes by sin.

Creation has been made subject to vanity; instability, decay, death, seem to the mere natural man to rule it. It is as though it presented to him everywhere the sad counterpart to the sadness of his heart. Heathen peoples, who have never learned the reason of this subjection to vanity, nor caught the ray of hope which shines on it from the Word of God, inevitably in the end come to find Nature a terror; and as I have more than once pointed out in its various aspects and bearings, their development is crushed through wide regions by the hardness, the sternness, and the sadness of the world. Famines, earthquakes, tornadoes, volcanic and oceanic floods, in the end poison for them the fragrance of roses, smirch the enamelled mantle of Creation, and dim the lustrous beauty of the stars. The wilderness becomes a holy and beautiful vestibule to those who have grasped the promise, and clasped the hope; who know that the main thing which they ought to pray for here is strength to toil and to endure; and who welcome all its benign but purging discipline, because they see in the far distance the gleam of the light of the glorious Canaan in which their toil and pain is to bear blessed fruit. But to men left alone with Nature, the element of terror becomes preponderant. They hear the voice of her groaning, and faint before the vision of the burden and the anguish of the universal life.

There is something which appals us when we fairly try to realise it, in the suffering of the dumb creation under human tyranny. One shudders to think what agony, in the very homes of earth's most polished and developed peoples, the brute creation is doomed daily to endure. It is a sad, sad history—man's dealing with the creatures whom God has delivered bound and helpless into his hand. And then, there is the perpetual wasting, or rather, for there is no waste, what looks like the constant degradation of the structure. Imperceptibly but surely the grandeur and beauty of the forms of Nature are being worn down, and a dull monotony seems to be the only ultimate result. Evolution, by the constant and familiar action of the forces which are always at work around us, is the modern key to the physical history of Creation, excluding crises, convulsions, and catastrophes. But as matter of fact, the forces which are at work are silently effacing the salient features of this earth of ours, and must reduce it in time to a formlessness strangely suggestive of the second childhood, through which that which is mortal in man returns to the dust.

No doubt there are eruptions, elevations, upheavals, some of them volcanic, some of them, as in Scandinavia, Greenland, and South America, secular. But we see nothing at work which can supply a qualitative compensation for the waste. The land gains on the sea, if the sea gains on the land. The quantities may be fairly balanced, but the land-gain is fertile mud, the land-loss is cliff, and rock, and all that makes the picturesque beauty of our dwelling-place. And man sees that there is no stamp of permanence on anything that is around him; that Nature grows old and decays like himself. The two are made in concert, one key-note tunes them both. Together with man, Nature has, not made herself subject, but been made subject to vanity by a higher Will; together with man, Nature shall one day be redeemed.

Just as there seem to lie in the background of

man's thought, vague memories of a state of holier and happier relation with his fellows, of an earlier estate of purity, happiness, and peace, so he seems to be haunted by images of a fairer and brighter world. All that he looks upon in the world around him in its bravest dress moves him more to tears than to songs. It is like the new splendour of the second temple, which made the old men weep when they recalled the glory that was gone for ever. Something fairer, of more perfect form, of more lustrous hue, rises up behind all our visions of the beauty which God has spread round us here. In his Art man strives to pourtray it. Art is said to hold the mirror to Nature, and to reflect her likeness. What Nature? The Nature that is stained and flawed and subjected to vanity, or Nature redeemed, transfigured, glorified? Man's highest Art, as we see in the last works of great masters, loses itself in the impossible. But the things which are impossible with man are possible with God, as shall be seen one day, in a Creation restored.

We traced in a former discourse the groaning and the travail of all things—the struggle for life filling the sphere of the Creation with its battle-cry; and we saw how this struggle prolonged itself with dire result in human history. But we saw too that man has a vision of a fairer order, of which, not strength, but love shall be the centre. As he rises higher in his spiritual development, the strength which strives for mastery is deposed from its supremacy, and the love is exalted which helps, and heals, and saves. And this holier principle is to rule, he believes, through the vast Creation. The Lord, who is Love, proposes to Himself, as the object of His sacrifice, the subduing all things in all worlds into His peace. Man cannot be at rest in a discordant and distracted Creation. That principle which makes blessed and holy order in the sphere of the human, he longs to see working through all the spheres. The world which has fallen to the key of his humiliation and travail, he yearns to see raised again to the level of his redeemed and purified nature. He looks with inexpressible longing to see sorrow and sighing banished from the Creation, as it shall be, the Scripture tells us, when sin is banished from his life.

In the last discourse I considered the principle of embodiment. Man is an embodied spirit. The true germ of a human body is a human soul. The soul contains within itself the principle of its investiture. Like the seed, when the outer envelope perishes it takes to itself a new form and clothes itself afresh. The Bible knows nothing about a state of disembodied spirits; no half-lit, shadowy, shivering world, haunted by pale, regretful forms, is the vision which it presents to us of what lies behind the veil of death. "Not unclothed, but clothed upon," in one bright moment; absent from this body, at home, embodied, with the Lord. The soul having completed the course ordained to it in this scene of its discipline, finds itself clothed upon with a form which exactly fits its moral development, which marks out its condition and stature, and enables it to enter into full relations with the beings and the things that stir its interest and make the charm of its life.

This principle of embodiment, which connects the body directly with the spiritual principle, with the moral mind which makes the man, has its terrible as well as its gracious aspects. There are men living, and this book may come into the hands of such, who are sedulously, however unconsciously, preparing themselves to put on at death the body of a beast. You doubt it? Why, look at them; you may see it already forming within. Watch them; they grow more gross, more prone, literally more brute-like, year by year. What is that but the soul moulding from within the body that is, and shaping here and now the body that is to rise out of its wreck.

This lends an awful significance to the elections of our freedom. We are making, by our daily habits of thought and action, the limbs and organs which are to stand up in death in the eternal world. We may be fitting ourselves to wear at once a form radiant and exulting, strong to roam in freedom through the celestial spaces, and to take in all the bright impressions of the worlds which are hidden from us by the veil of death. Or we may be fitting ourselves to put on a form obscene and loathsome, meet to herd with all the base rout of the Creation, and to crawl in the dust of that loftier sphere. Men, women, understand that you are making now the body of the future; you are making that which is to be the blessed organ and helpmeet, or the torment and curse, of the spirit in eternity. Live like a beast, and you may see in faces that you sometimes meet and shudder to look upon, the likeness to which you are growing. Live like Christ, and the form which He bore through the gate of death is the image of the glorious tabernacle which awaits you, when the death-swoon for the moment is over, and "in your flesh" you shall see God.

And as is the body of the resurrection so is the world. As the Bible knows nothing of a disembodied, so also it knows nothing of a homeless spirit. How much of the purest joy of life springs from our contact and relation with the Creation which surrounds us. The Creation animate and inanimate. Why should we believe that one single source of delight and culture which is open to us here shall be closed by death, if death means resurrection? We know nothing about the immortality of animals. I see no reason for believing it. The personality of the individual is wanting, and it is that which survives the shock of death, and stands up in life in higher worlds. But though the individual may perish, the type may be immortal. And the end of all this groaning and travailing of the animal Creation, to watch which here sometimes fills us with sadness, may be the survival of the nobler forms and those most related to the human, to attend us as the outer fringe of our humanity, in the world which lies, for us, beyond the river of death.

And as the Creation has shared our fall, the Scripture assures us it shall share our resurrection.

We know not where the Immortal are, what splendour their eyes are already beholding, what power is throbbing in the pulses of their twice-born life. Some suppose that they are still around us; that here is the new earth and the new heaven which has already received them to its home and to its rest. This earth may be the home of two humanities; the humanity which is being, and the humanity which has been, redeemed. I know not. Sometimes one feels that the blessed ones are not far away; that their forms still tread unseen the pathways of the world, seeing, knowing, wonders and splendours which at times flash out on us, but in the main are hidden from our sinful sight. But here or there God has worlds into which to bring forth the children of the resurrection, in which Nature shall bask in a light, and shine with a splendour, of which here we see faint images only in our dreams.

But this we know. The lost peace, the lost purity, the lost glory of the Creation, shall one day be restored to us. " This corruptible shall put on incorruption, this mortal creature shall put on immortality." Highly as the faculties of the body and the spirit may be developed, keen as may be their perceptions, intense as may be the delight which they are capable of taking in the sights, the sounds, and the myriad suggestions of an external world, there will always be around us a Creation that is attuned to the keynote of our spirits—capable of yielding to the child of the resurrection the purest satisfactions, while it draws him ever upward to the uncreated fountain of life and benediction, and is the minister which leads him to, not the syren that tempts him from, God. There are worlds awaiting our purified and perfected nature, where all that jars in this corruptible Creation shall be for ever silenced, where the moaning shall be hushed, the struggle shall be ended, and the peace of God, which is the peace of love, shall be established and shall rule for evermore.

And this is the inheritance which some of you are selling for a beast's indulgences; drinking, gambling, rioting, or dawdling through a round of vapid amusements, and despising the citizenship of all these worlds. As the man is, so will be the character of the Creation that surrounds him. The universe has worlds where the most glorious human faculty, perfected by life's tremendous discipline, shall see face to face the things which God hath prepared, at once to satisfy its most passionate longings, and to educate its power for yet higher developments in store. But remember, the universe has, too, lairs for beasts, and sties for swine. " Behold then, ye despisers, and wonder." Wonder at the work which the Lord will do, at the world which He will bring forth from all the wreck and waste of this sin-stricken Creation, and tremble lest the home of your being should be found at last, not in the heights of that blessed celestial sphere, but in its dust.

"*Awake, awake, thou that sleepest, and arise from the dead, and Christ shall give thee life;*" life that shall lift up thy head, a risen man, in a world of such glory as eye hath not seen, ear hath not heard, imagination hath not conceived of here—when the kiss of death hath sealed thy immortality. That life shall still expand and discipline thy regenerate powers, drawing them forth to their full perfection in the last, the great resurrection day. Then the day of the manifestation of the sons of God, and of the whole fruit of life's travail, shall be fully come; the creature shall be delivered from the bondage of corruption into the glorious liberty of the children; and then for man, for nature, "*the sun shall no more go down nor the moon withdraw herself; but the Lord shall be their everlasting light, and the days of their mourning shall be ended.*"

XX.
THE DESTINY OF MAN.

" When I consider Thy heavens, the work of Thy fingers; the moon and the stars, which Thou hast ordained; what is man, that Thou art mindful of him? and the son of man, that Thou visitest him?"—Ps. viii. 3-4.

THIS question is pressed upon us with continually increasing force, by the rapidly widening knowledge of the universe which the human intellect is mastering, by the innumerable worlds which the telescope unveils to us, the secrets of whose constitution the spectroscope enables us in some measure to explore. The heavens which shed their lustre on the Psalmist in the clear Syrian sky, contained at most a few thousand stars, none of which, nay, not even the most glorious of luminaries itself, had he any reason to consider comparable in mass and in importance with our world. Earth to him was the centre of all things, and the lord of earth was man. And yet, so vast and deep were the spaces over which his speculation ranged, so radiant were the orbs which glittered in his sky, that man seemed to shrink into miserable insignificance by comparison, and it was hard to believe that he could be worth the notice and the care of the Creator, in the midst of all these lustrous worlds.

But now the earth itself is as puny and insignificant in comparison with the universe, as man seemed to be to David when weighed against the stars. Man is not a slighter, weaker being, physically, in comparison with the mass of the earth which is his dwelling-place, than is the earth itself, when compared with the vast spaces in which it seems to float as a mote might float in a sunbeam, and with the masses and the motions of these innumerable worlds. The stars which are visible to the naked eye, are the mere outlying sentinels of the numberless hosts which the telescope unveils. The small patch of sky which a great telescope commands as its field of view, is supposed to contain at least as many stars which are invisible to the naked eye, as the whole vault of heaven exhibits to the unaided sight.

Each new power which is added to the telescope, brings into view myriads of new worlds. And far as the armed eye can penetrate, even to stars from which the light, travelling as it does nearly 200,000 miles in a second of time, would be tens or even hundreds of years in reaching us, no bound or hint of a bound to the universe appears. We have not the faintest reason for supposing that those specks of light whose rays tell us, not what they are, or even that they are, at this moment, but what they were hundreds, possibly thousands of years ago, are any nearer than we are to the outer bound of the Creation. The infinitely small and the infinitely great are hardly to be regarded as hyperbolical

The Destiny of Man. 389

terms. Where existence begins no microscope has discovered. Where it ends no telescope has explored.

Sirius, the most lustrous star in our heavens, has been found, by perhaps the most brilliant scientific observation of our times, to be receding from our earth at the rate of some fifteen miles in every second; and yet the distance is so vast, that this rate of recession during, say, two thousand years, would make no difference in its apparent magnitude and brilliancy: it must have appeared to the ancients precisely as it appears to us now. I think that this gives one the most awful impression of the vastness of the spaces and magnitudes with which we are dealing; it makes this earth of ours but a dust-speck whirling in the infinite vortex. Does not Dante Rossetti speak of its "spinning like an angry midge"? And it wrings from us, as the brain faints under these measures and numbers, the cry which George Herbert interprets:

> Oh, rack me not to such a vast extent;
> Those distances belong to Thee:
> The world's too little for Thy tent,
> A grave too big for me.

"*When I consider Thy heavens, the work of Thy fingers, the moon and the stars which Thou hast ordained; what is man, that Thou art mindful of him? and the son of man, that Thou visitest him?*"

The only answer to the question, and the ample answer, is the Incarnation. Be man what he may in point of mass and force, compared with the *things* which surround him, God *has* been mindful of him, God *has* visited him; God has made man's nature His shrine, His organ of manifestation, as He has not manifested Himself, and cannot manifest Himself by all these worlds. The Incarnation enables us to lift up our heads in the face of the overwhelming spaces, masses, and forces which surround us, and to believe that a human spirit, dowered with the knowledge of good and of evil, is more to God, is more precious and more prolific of all that God regards as the end of Creation, than the whole universe of mere material worlds.

But if man may thus, strong in the knowledge of the Incarnation, which alone gives him a firm grasp of his spiritual nature and its relations, lift up his head before the material mass of the Creation, however vast, however boundless it may seem, and may wear his crown in the presence of suns, and moons, and constellations, what shall we say of him in relation to the beings by whom this universe may be peopled, and who may be teeming in all these innumerable spheres? What becomes of man, of his interests, his election, his redemption, if these worlds are all peopled by intelligent beings like man, if each of these suns which shine in the midnight sky has a troop of satellite planets round him, all like our earth, the abode of intelligent life, needing from God the same care, the same nurture, the same love? Does it not weaken the ground of our assurance, that this little mote in the universe has been the scene of such transcendent transactions, when we measure what we might call its claim on God in the scale of millions of inhabited worlds.[1]

This is no new question. As my readers well know, it has been keenly debated, and has been within our times the subject of fierce intellectual controversy, the echoes of which have hardly yet died away. The author of a book called " The Plurality of Worlds " asked boldly, what reason have we for supposing that these worlds are inhabited? and answered, following in the track of Mediæval Christian thinkers, that the weight of such evidence as we can obtain is rather against the opinion that they are inhabited than in its favour. This bold deliverance called forth a storm of opposition. Works were written in abundance to confute the presumptuous philosopher, the most popular of which, if not the most convincing, was Sir David Brewster's " More Worlds than One." It is a controversy which of course it is quite impossible to settle. But it certainly seems a great step towards the negative conclusion, that the only orb which we can survey, or hope to survey, with tolerable accuracy, and on which signs of anything like human habitation might with due pains be discovered, appears to be a wreck; more like the crater of a vast, extinct volcano, than an orderly, beautiful, habitable world.

It is a matter on which we must be content with

---

[1] Twenty millions has been given as a rough estimate of the number of stars within the range of telescopic sight.

such evidence as we can get, and the condition of the moon seems to give no hint of its habitation or habitability by beings organised upon a type so high as man. Further, the physical conditions of the various planets of our solar system, to say the least, look in the same direction. I am not attempting to play the astronomer. I have not the least right to offer an independent opinion on such matters. And theological astronomy, and science generally, I imagine, is rather apt to provoke a smile from the masters of the scientific schools. I only note the result which seems to be now very generally accepted, that the physical conditions of life in the planets, however much they may vary, are such, that beings of a high order, according to our human notions, could not dwell in them, or find in them a fit theatre for the development of any high form of life.

According to our human notions! Yes, it may be answered, but what are those notions worth? It is natural that men should think that their own organisation is the normal rule for the Creation, and that their own is the highest form of life. To the negro, Adam must be black, and the devil must be white; and so we see all things through the medium of our own prejudgments, and think ourselves and our world, being children of vanity, the centre of all the spheres. But it is only the fly on the wheel, after all, we are told, crying, See how we move. Science, we are instructed, rebukes this vain imagination, by revealing to us infinite varieties of types of organisations, and innumerable worlds. And so it is set down to the credit of our intolerable vanity if we suppose that creatures, living under such vastly different conditions from our own, as manifestly obtain in the planets, must belong to a quite inferior grade of life. The only satisfactory answer to this question must rest on the revelation which has been made to us, as to the essential nature and constitution of man. "*And God said, Let us make man in Our image, after Our likeness. So God created man in His own image; in the image of God created He him, male and female created He them.*"

Nor does this truth rest alone on a sentence in a venerable document which is difficult of interpretation, and the value of which as evidence of the primal condition of man is in dispute. It is sustained and emphasised by the Incarnation; while the truth of the Incarnation is sustained by the fact that it alone affords the key to the mystery of man's constitution and life. "*Wherefore seeing the children were partakers of flesh and blood, He also Himself likewise took part of the same.*" "*To as many as received Him to them gave He power to become the sons of God.*" We see, then, that according to the statement of Revelation, and the witness of history, man sustains an altogether peculiar and lofty relation to his Creator. Made in the image of God, he is capable of receiving Him into his nature, nay, he was so made that He might so receive Him, and become partaker himself of a Divine nature through Redemption; he is capable, further, of being transformed into the glorious image of God his Redeemer, and of dwelling as a son in the bosom of His love through eternity.

This is the solid truth of man's being as declared in the Scripture, and that it is the truth is witnessed, as we have seen, by the whole character of his life's experience, and his manifest destiny. We have, then, solid ground to go upon in assuming that the human is the supreme type of form, and that the highest purpose of God in the Creation is wrought out through the life of our race. And if we see that the conditions of life in worlds of which we can obtain some knowledge, are utterly unsuitable for any being in anywise like man, we have some strong ground to rest upon in the conclusion that, in our system, this earth is the only world which is the theatre of any high developments of life.

But how far will this conclusion carry us? Our system! It sounds very vast, very grand. Neptune, the outermost planet of our system, is nearly 3,000,000,000 miles from the sun.[1] But this vast space is but as an handbreadth, compared with the spaces with which we have to deal in the great universe. Dare we carry our speculation further, and believe that these innumerable worlds, where there may be, perhaps we may say must be, splendours of light and colour such as we can but faintly dream of here, are tenantless? Dare we imagine that from

---

[1] I use round numbers, and specify numbers as little as possible. It would be easy of course to parade wondrous strings of numbers, but the kind of effect which they produce is worth very little, and is of very small account in such an argument as this.

all this glorious choir of shining worlds no breath of intelligent praise goes up into the ear of the Creator; that save here, in this little far-off nook of the Creation, the voice of worship and prayer is dumb? There is something in our instincts that shrinks from, may I not say shudders at, the conclusion. We imagine instinctively, and cannot but imagine, that this whole universe was made to be the theatre of a lofty, intelligent, and religious life. And the instinct has the testimony of Scripture to sustain it, and must be in the track of a blessed and glorious truth. *"The creature itself also shall be delivered from the bondage of corruption, into the glorious liberty of the children of God."*

But why should we not believe that the creation of man, was the first step towards the peopling of the universe with beings of this lofty spiritual order; and that the working out of the higher stages of the Divine plan begins now, and in our world? It is quite possible to conceive that man is the commencement of that higher, that spiritual order, with which, as we have seen, the whole Creation has been travailing in birth; and that man is destined, in ways which are hidden from our scrutiny, to take high part in the developments of life in all these worlds. And why should we not believe it? There must be beginning somewhere, why not now and here?

But is it possible to believe that this vast universe is, so to speak, in the first stage of development, and that as regards all the higher interest which man's life lends to earth's history, the Creation is at present a waste? Again we must look to the little that we can see and know, to help us in our vague guesses at the truth about the unseen and unknown. Let us take this earth of ours as an instance of the Divine method in the Creation. Man, however long he has been a denizen of this earth, is at any rate a recent denizen. As the Alps, the Andes, and the Himalayas[1] are the youngest of the mountains; man is the youngest, while he is beyond comparison the noblest, creature in his world. We have no measure of the number of millions of years, during which this earth was a waste as regards the higher developments of life— when it was the habitation of monstrous, obscene forms which haunted its marshes, or of the still earlier and more rudimental creatures that wrought in its primæval waters, building up the rock on which the solid structure that bears us is founded, before the continents were uplifted and the higher life of our globe was born.

Sir W. Thompson and others seem to think it possible to fix some limit, beyond which even the most rudimental forms of life could not exist. A layman like myself is bound to listen with great respect to the judgments of such masters; but still even the reader unlearned in the lore of science can see that the calculation rests on such vague data, and

---

[1] Just as in the development of the chick in the egg, the last thing to be formed is the vertebral column, which binds all the scattered limbs and organs into a unity; so, regarding the earth as in some sort vertebrate in type, the spinal column which holds it all together, and gives it a characteristic form, was the last to appear.

assumes such a uniformity of operation—which seems at the least highly uncertain when the conditions are so different from those which now obtain—that any conclusions founded upon it must be regarded as very far from established; especially as scientific men of equal eminence dispute the validity of the whole argument. But granting that limit, at no matter how many hundreds of millions of years, beyond that limit, there is the unmeasurable period during which the heated vaporous mass was cooling, and settling, and taking shape as a world—as perhaps Saturn is settling now.

Here then is man, a being of a few thousands, or granting the longer limit which some demand, tens of thousands of years, at the utmost; and here is the earth, as many hundreds of millions, multiplied probably by hundreds still, preparing to be his dwelling-place, and to furnish, to the being made in the image of God, the theatre for the development of a spiritual life. The Being who made the world must be a Being of an infinite patience. Verily the day of the Lord is a long day. He waits and works through countless stages of preparation, for high results. The highest products of development are always late of birth, and in number limited. Estimate the mass of common undistinguished humanity, and compare it with the elect few, in whom we are taught to believe that He begins to see of the travail of His soul and to be satisfied. Again, how many of us men and women of the commoner clay, form the base and the lower stages of the pyramid of the human, on the summit of which rise up the lofty few, whose dower is "the hate of hate, the scorn of scorn, the love of love"?

The history of this earth, which lay waste, or rather, let us say, fallow, during unmeasurable eras, slowly developing the theatre of man's brief life, is just parallel to the history of the great universe, if, as is possible, and as we have ventured to suppose, we are commencing here on earth that higher order of spiritual existence, which is destined through the ages to fill all worlds with the voice of worship and the song of praise. We see the beginnings of this higher order upon earth. Time was, and not so long ago, when man was not. Spiritual life, the life of a being dowered with moral freedom, appeared as a new thing in this earth; why not in the great universe, which like the earth through all those eras of eras may still be waiting for its lord?

There seems to be no reason then in the nature or in the analogies of things, why we should not accept the conclusion which has been already suggested. But the vital question after all is, why we should. And our answer to it will depend very largely, on the view which we may take of the relation of Redemption to the higher developments of life. Redemption is the means of the full unveiling of the Divine nature. Never, until a being capable of Redemption, and because of his high capacity for the reception of the life of God worth redeeming at infinite cost, had sinned and suffered, was it known, could it be known, that God is Love. "*Herein is love, not that we loved God, but that He loved us, and sent His Son to be the propitiation for our sins."*

This manifestation of the Divine nature becomes the basis of a new, a loftier, a more fruitful relation between the Creator and the creature man, than could be conceived of apart from Christ's redemptive work. The redeemed man, like the Prodigal brought home, knows the Father more perfectly, and is more perfectly known of the Father, than any creature in the mere condition of nature can either know, or be known and loved. All the vast and various experience which springs out of the knowledge of evil, and the knowledge of the Love which redeems from evil, enriches the sphere of man's life unspeakably. God sustains to man as his Redeemer, and man sustains to God, a unique relation, in which all the fulness of Godhead is manifested on the one hand, and man is filled with all the fulness of God on the other.

The full development of a free and finite moral being, seems to demand such an experience as man has passed through as a sinner; saved, restored, by the all-suffering, all-sacrificing Divine love. This earth of ours has been the theatre of a transaction, and has been the scene of an experience, of infinite significance, such as must stand alone in the history of Creation. Suppose that these worlds are inhabited by beings created after the same type as man, beings who have sinned and suffered as man, are we to suppose an almost infinite series of Incarnations? Surely there is profound meaning in the word "*once offered,"* "*now once in the end of the world hath He appeared, to put away sin by the sacrifice of Himself.*"

There is something in this thought of an endless repetition of redemptive sacrifices from which the mind instinctively shrinks, and which the whole revelation of the unknown things of God in Scripture seems to deny. We are beset by this difficulty. If these myriads of worlds are teeming with inhabitants of a lofty type of development, all needing the same Divine care and love, how can we understand the selection of this little earth of ours to be the scene of such transcendent manifestations of God? It seems to add a heavy difficulty to a Christian's belief, if he is compelled to look upon these galaxies of stars as the homes of beings of kindred nature and experience with himself, and who have precisely the same claims on the Creator, and the same need.

The difficulty has been met by doubting the need. It is said that man may quite probably be the only transgressor in the universe; the only being needing this special provision for his rescue from the ruin of a fall. Then comes in the question which I have already glanced at. Dare we regard Redemption as a special provision; a scheme devised by love to meet what might be regarded as an accidental defect in a universal plan—one world only out of so many myriads falling into sin and straits? I feel no hesitation about the answer. Redemption must be, as I have said, the means of the very loftiest development of which a finite being is capable. It establishes at once between God and its subjects a bond, closer, stronger, dearer, than can possibly exist out of its pale. It must then in the nature of things lie near to the heart of God's plan of universal government; it must be the key to the spiritual order in all the worlds.

The only fair way out of the difficulty seems to me to lie in the idea, that we men stand on the threshold of the higher, the spiritual development of life in this universe; that till now the vast Creation has been groaning and travailing in pain together; slowly wrestling itself so to speak out of chaos into cosmos, slowly taking shape and dress to fit it to be the theatre of the higher unfoldings of life. And now in the end of the world of physical groaning and travail, man appears. His form is the highest product of the energy which has shaped the creature, while there is breathed into him a spirit which relates him directly to God, and to the spiritual sphere. With us begins a new development of being; in man a spiritual order appears; an order destined to fill the universe, and to outlast eternity. And here, on the very threshold of this higher order, the key to its constitution, the instrument of its progress, at once the law and the inspiration of its life, lies a great act of sacrifice; the sacrifice of the only-begotten Son of God, that man, and all that is to grow out of man for the universe and through eternity, might be saved.

To me there is something transcendently beautiful and glorious in the thought, that the whole destined development of spiritual life in the universe rests on the atoning sacrifice of incarnate God; and that this revelation of God's righteousness and of His redeeming love and mercy, is the foundation-stone of a temple wide as the vast Creation, and lasting as the throne of its King. That spiritual order which is to rise in the universe as the crown of the natural order, rests on the incarnation, the sacrifice, and the reign of the eternal Word. The very first step up into that higher life which God has opened to the creature in humanity, is through the gate of sacrifice, which, full of pain as it is and must be here through the weakness and sickness of our nature, in the higher stages of our growth will be the law of the perfect and blessed life, because love will be its inspiration, and love will be its reward.

And this is what is meant by the vision of the Apocalypse; the Lamb that was slain in the midst of the throne, the great high throne of the Creation. The love that suffered and triumphed on Calvary, is to be the ruling spirit henceforth through all the spheres of that new Creation, which is destined to grow out of human travail and anguish. Man, and all that is to come through man, is to learn by the Redemption that was wrought on Calvary, to know the mystery and to live the life of the Divine love, in the blest communions of eternity.

It was the end of a world when the Redeemer suffered; the end of the old world of the corruptible creature; the beginning of a new world of which the God-Man is the founder, and in which the redeemed man, renewed in a yet diviner fashion after the image of Him that created him, is to lead forth the ever-

The Destiny of Man. 403

lasting processions of life. You will not fail to note how through the whole of the New Testament, and most fully in the Apocalypse, the future of the universe is connected with the fruits of the redemption of our race. Sciolists may see in this only the vanity of the human, bent on reducing all things on earth and in heaven to its measure. But the mystery of Incarnation seems to instruct us, that God has laid in our nature the deep foundation of that spiritual order, which is to reign ultimately in all these worlds, and in all that is to grow out of them, through eternity.

I have spoken much, and have asked you to think much, of Redemption. But what lover of mankind is there who does not bear with him a constant sadness, through the thought of the feeble hold that Redemption has upon the world? There seems to be a sad unreality about it all, when we speak of the large scale on which man is created, and the lofty possibilities of his life. And where are the men who are exemplifying it, who reveal in their lives the true scale of their being, and are trying, as the Stoic says, "to hold fellowship with God"? They seem to be scattered here and there like the bright particular stars in the galaxy; but the great multitude around, as far as man's eye can search, care for none of these things, and make light of these mysteries; while to the mass of mankind Redemption is an unknown word.

Now I hold that the one deadly, damning sin under the Gospel dispensation, is the refusal to be redeemed. Whatever original sin may be, it is done away by the atonement; what man is and does by nature is no barrier between the soul and the holy and righteous God. Through the offering of the Lamb of God who taketh away the sin of the world, God declares His reconciliation to man. "*God was in Christ, reconciling the world unto Himself, not imputing their trespasses unto them.*" There is now one deadly sin, the spiritual sin, refusing to be reconciled to God. But the great mass of mankind have never heard even the whisper of His Gospel; men, like us, of the same stuff, the same quality, the same capacity to be saved.

Scientific theorists may class the savage as closer in type to the ape than to the man. Those who have lived among them know better. They have seen the gleam of the human spirit in the eye, they have heard the human heart-beat; they know that these are brethren, dear as themselves to Christ, and capable as themselves of tasting the joys of salvation, and of beholding the glories of the Father's Kingdom in eternity. "*Go ye out into all the world, and preach the gospel to every creature.*" The idea that it is in the purpose of the merciful God who was capable of the sacrifice of Calvary, to doom the great mass of the ignorant heathen to eternal torment, for not believing on Him whose name even they have never heard, is too terrible for any man to advocate publicly in these days; unless he wishes the Gospel which he preaches to wither under the execration of mankind. With the age of feudalism, the wrecks of which are rapidly vanishing, the possibility of man's believing in such a gospel has passed away for ever. But the heathen pass out in countless throngs into the world behind the veil, ignorant of this transcendent fact in the history of the universe, which God has laid as the basis of all the higher developments of life, and in which, as men, they might claim a right to hope to share. What if the doom on them as they pass out into the great universe, is to be taught the Gospel, and to learn the mystery of Redemption in other worlds?

The great aim of the whole culture of men upon this earth, of that great drama of action and of suffering which we name civilisation, seems to be, to develope to a very high pitch of knowledge and of power an elect company, who stand out from the mass around them as the apostles, the teachers, and the leaders of their times. The highly civilised races are but an election, as it were, compared with the great human family; and in the elect races the trained lovers of truth, of righteousness, of God, are but a little band, the sharp apex of the pyramid of life. And yet consider what has been spent to train them; the awful, the infinite cost by which their Lord has made them capable of being His helpers in blessing and saving, all which He yearns to gather to Himself. The full sphere of this glorious ministering faculty, of the mind and the spirit which has caught its inspiration from the sacrifice of the Lord Jesus, cannot lie within the bounds of our mortal sight. What if God is training His chosen ones to be His helpers, His teachers, apostles, saviours, in other spheres? The words of the Master to those who had "followed Him in the regeneration," seem to open to them in the future some such mission as this.

One's heart bleeds, one's soul faints, to think of the innumerable multitude, who, not in heathendom, but here in the heart of Christendom itself, pass life's outer gate without one fair hearing of the message of the Gospel. There must be—simple, absolute justice demands it—some tremendous distinctions in the dealings of the Judge of the whole earth, who is also the Redeemer of all mankind, with the souls that pass before His face for judgment. There are "*few stripes*" for some, the Master declares, "*many stripes*" for others—for me, for you, if with Christ before us, we turn away and will not have Him to be our king. What if the trained servants of the Kingdom here, those who have learned to find their joy in blessing, healing, helping, saving, like Christ, shall find the field of their work widening, as they rise through the mist of death, and are free of the great universe for ever? What if there are worlds waiting for their ministry, where their trained Christ-like faculty may be drawn forth to larger effort, nobler aim, deeper and more blessed sacrifice; till they pass at last, their ministry ended, into the inner circle and nearest to the throne.

I know that there is a dread shadow in the background, which we must look at before we can pass from the contemplation of the destiny of our race.

There is the vision of the abyss, where lost souls, the souls that will not be redeemed, are said to writhe in intolerable anguish; the smoke of whose torment ascendeth for ever, and blots the brightness of the universe through eternity. Eternal sin, eternal suffering, eternal moaning of souls in anguish, eternal blackness of darkness and horror of death! And the merciful Christ looking down upon it all; the Redeemer who wept over the first touch of the agony, and shed His blood in unutterable pain and shame that it might be spared! To a Father's eye, one must think, that cloud which buries the moaning and the writhing of the children, would poison the very bliss of heaven. And yet what fiat can hinder it, while a soul lives that refuses to be reconciled to God ?

It is a vision of horror which makes men shudder, and from which in these days, when the benigner aspects and conditions of power are in the ascendant, there is desperate struggle to escape. Some formulate the theory of the annihilation of the hopelessly impenitent, and hold, that after they have suffered awhile the awful penalty of their transgression, a merciful stroke will dash their sin and their moaning out of the living universe for ever. It seems to me a miserable extrication from a tremendous difficulty. It makes life on a fearful scale an abortive experiment; it robs suffering of its holiest ministries; it degrades our nature from its essential dignity ; it makes light of the mystery of the Incarnation ; it presents God as a vindictive tormenter of souls, and it runs counter to what seem to be the deepest and most far-reaching passages of the Divine word.

Others formulate a theory of universal Redemption; through struggles, anguish and terror, all will be drawn to the Father, all will be brought home at last. In this direction lie, I freely confess, all my beliefs and sympathies, but I can see no way to formulate the theory. It seems to me to deny the inalienable power and prerogative of freedom; nor can I construct a harmony of passages to support it from the word of God. What force of Divine love may be brought to bear before the experiment of freedom has final issue, I know not. What power may lie yet in anguish, to break down the rebel will, and to lay the bruised and humbled captive of mercy at the Saviour's feet, no mortal can explore. But I seem to see the gleam of a great hope in the distance. I cannot understand it; I cannot reconcile this and that, and make complete my little theory of the ways of the unsearchable and eternal God. There lies a meaning in these glorious words deeper than I can fathom, and for which there is no room that I can see in any of our theologies: "*By Him to reconcile all things unto Himself; through Him, whether the things on the earth, or the things in the heavens.*"—Col. i. 20. "*Having made known to us the mystery of His will, according to His good pleasure which He purposed in Himself, that in the dispensation of the fulness of times He might gather up in one all things in the Christ, the things in the heavens, and the things on the earth, in Him."*—Eph. i., 9. 10. And in that yet profounder and more prophetic word of Incarnate God—the vision which He saw on high as He entered the cloud of the last agony, and which nerved Him to endure—with which I gladly close the words which I have endeavoured to speak on the destiny of man : " AND I, IF I BE LIFTED UP FROM THE EARTH, WILL DRAW ALL MEN UNTO ME."

www.ingramcontent.com/pod-product-compliance
Lightning Source LLC
Chambersburg PA
CBHW030549300426
44111CB00009B/913